Popular Mechanics

THE BOY MECHANIC

Popular Mechanics

THE BOY MECHANIC

200 CLASSIC THINGS TO BUILD

HEARST BOOKS

A division of Sterling Publishing Co., Inc.

New York / London

www.sterlingpublishing.com

Library of Congress Cataloging-in-Publication Data
Popular mechanics : the boy mechanic : 275 things for a boy to build.
    p. cm.
  Projects and informative articles taken from Popular mechanics books and magazines spanning the first two decades of the 20th century.
  Includes bibliographical references and index.
  ISBN-13: 978-1-58816-509-1 (alk. paper)
  ISBN-10: 1-58816-509-4 (alk. paper)
  1. Handicraft for boys—Juvenile literature. I. Title: Boy mechanic. II. Popular mechanics (Chicago, Ill. : 1959)
  TT160.P6752 2006
  745.5—dc22

                          2005026661
10 9 8 7 6

Book design by Barbara Balch

Published by Hearst Books
A Division of Sterling Publishing Co., Inc.
387 Park Avenue South, New York, NY 10016

Popular Mechanics and Hearst Books are registered trademarks
of Hearst Communications, Inc.

www.popularmechanics.com

For information about custom editions, special sales, premium and corporate purchases, please contact Sterling Special Sales Department at 800-805-5489 or specialsales@sterlingpub.com.

Distributed in Canada by Sterling Publishing
c/o Canadian Manda Group, 165 Dufferin Street
Toronto, Ontario, Canada M6K 3H6
Distributed in Australia by Capricorn Link (Australia) Pty. Ltd.
P.O. Box 704, Windsor, NSW 2756 Australia

Manufactured in China
Sterling ISBN 13: 978-1-58816-509-1
       ISBN 10: 1-58816-509-4

CONTENTS

FOREWORD

We've come a long way over the last century or so. From humble beginnings, the car has become the SUV and luxury sedan. The first wireless radios have been replaced with transistorized models that have themselves given way to satellite communications and a whole new meaning for the term "wireless." Computers, and technological innovations of all stripes, have far exceeded the wildest dreams of visionaries and even science-fiction writers of the early twentieth century.

But perhaps we lost something along the way. The "good old days" of the early 1900s embodied a truly simpler time, but also a time when self-sufficiency was a highly valued skill. It was a period in history when the measure of a man—and a boy—

was gauged by his working knowledge of general sciences, his proficiency in outdoor skills, and his ability to craft projects in wood and metal. The times called for innovation, and the home mechanics of the period rose to that call, using the rawest of materials, a minimum of technology, and a maximum of ingenuity.

This book captures the spirit of that time. It contains a mother lode of projects and informative articles taken from *Popular Mechanics* books and magazines spanning the first two decades of the twentieth century. In making this book, we changed very little, allowing the style of writing to evoke the tenor of the times. Some of these topics are quaintly dated. Some, such as passages on setting up camp on an outdoors trip, are still useful and applicable even though the attendant fixtures and technology have changed quite a bit. Others, such as a mission-style candlestick or any of a number of handcrafted toys, are right at home in our modern lives. And, of course, there are those topics which are simply too odd, bizarre, or funny to leave out—the sail for a boy's wagon and a mirror for rowing a boat come to mind.

The modern reader must realize that at the time of first publication, available materials and tools were severely limited by today's standards. When tackling any of the projects, feel free to substitute more modern techniques, equipment, and hardware. And it should go without saying—but is important enough to reiterate—use all necessary safety precautions called for in today's workshop.

However, you certainly don't have to get your hands dirty to enjoy this book. The topics and text itself make for entertaining reading and say as much about history as they do about skills and crafting.

So enjoy a trip to the not-so-distant past and bygone pastimes, courtesy of *Popular Mechanics,* then and now.

The Editors
Popular Mechanics

{ CHAPTER 1 }

WORKSHOP TOOLS
and PROJECTS

—

USEFUL TOOLS *for* HOME MECHANICS

— MAKING T-SQUARES —

The making of a single article of any kind presents a distinct problem in itself, but the production of a large number of the same article must be done in a different way, if efficiency and uniformity in the product are desirable qualities. For instance, making a large number of T-squares means the material is not made up in the same manner as for one. A number of these instruments were required and were made as follows, with no other equipment than bench tools and a band saw. The squares were made of mahogany, having both stock and blade edged with maple. The blades were fastened to the stock with five ⅜-in. button-head screws.

The material for the heads and the blades was glued up and finished to the sizes given in A and B. The material was cut to gauge lines on the band saw, the blades being a scant ⅛ in. thick, and the stocks, ⅜ in. Two of each were cut from each prepared piece, first from one side and then from the other. They were then faced off on both sides and two more pieces cut. With careful cutting, six blades and six stocks were made from each piece. This left one side of each piece to be planed after sawing. The holes for the screws were drilled with a small hand drill.

For assembling, a jig was made by nailing a piece of stock, ⅜ in. thick,

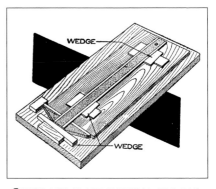

STOCK AND BLADE MATERIAL FOR MAK-
ING THE PARTS, AND THE JIG FOR
ASSEMBLING.

to a straight drawing board. One end of the piece was planed straight and true before it was fastened into place. Stops were provided to locate the stock and hold the blade square with it. Wedges were used to keep both stock and blade against the stops while the screws were inserted. The wedges were not driven with a hammer, but pushed in firmly with the fingers.

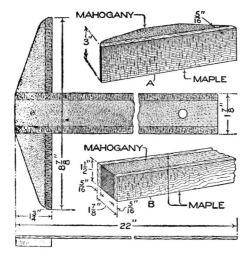

DIMENSIONS FOR A
T-SQUARE OF WHICH
A NUMBER WERE
TO BE MADE IN
DUPLICATE.

— A COMBINATION TOOL —

Combining a square, plumb, and rule, the tool illustrated is well worth the slight time and trouble required in making it. Wood is used for the T-shaped piece, the long edge of which is graduated in inches and fractions, while the angles at the corners are used as squares. The plumb consists of a weighted pendulum made from a piece of clock spring. Brads or pins are inserted at the proper points on the three ends of the device to indicate

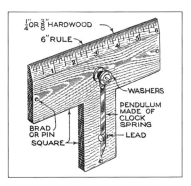

the true plumb line, when using the tool to test the level of a surface.

— HOMEMADE CARPENTER'S VISE —

The sketch shows an easily made, quick-working wood vise that has proven very satisfactory. The usual screw is replaced by an open bar held on one end by a wedge-shaped block, and the excess taken up on the other end by an eccentric lever. The wedge is worked by a string passing through the top of the bench and should be weighted on the other end to facilitate the automatic downward movement. The capacity of the vise, of course, depends on the size and shape of the wedge-shaped block.

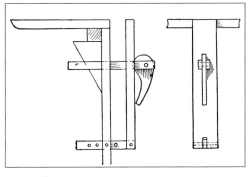

VISE MADE ENTIRELY OF WOOD.

— GROOVE CUTTER FOR WOOD —

Having occasion to cut some grooves in a board and not being properly equipped for such work, I made the tool shown in the sketch. Although rather crude in appearance it will do good work if properly made. It consists of a handle, *A*, shaped to afford a comfortable grip for the hand, and a cutter, *B*, made of a short piece of hacksaw blade, clamped along the left side of the handle by the strip *C*, which is held with screws. A pin, *D*, driven into the handle and allowed to project about ¹⁄₁₆ in., prevents the blade from sliding back under the clamp. For guiding the blade, the arrangement *F* is employed. An extension, *E*, is nailed on the right side of the handle, and holes made near each end for two screws having round heads, such as may be obtained from discarded dry batteries. These screws are for securing the sliding stop *F*, which is a flat piece of hardwood. The wood has slots cut near the end for screws to pass through to provide for adjustment.

In use, the guide *F* is adjusted until it is the desired distance from

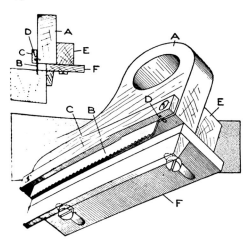

TWO SLOTS ARE MADE WITH THE CUTTER, AND THE STOCK BETWEEN THEM REMOVED WITH A CHISEL.

the cutter and then secured by the screws. The tool is handled like a plane, care being taken not to bear down too hard, because the cutter may bind and cause it to be pulled from the clamp. In cutting a groove, two slots are cut and the stock between them removed with a chisel.

— A Carpenter's Gauge —

The home workshop can be supplied with a carpenter's gauge, without any expense, by the use of a large spool and a round stick of wood. The stick should be dressed to fit the hole in the spool snugly and a small brad driven through one end so that the point will protrude about 1/16 in.

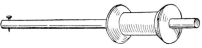

Round stick in a spool.

The adjustment of the gauge is secured by driving the stick in the hole in the direction desired. A better way and one that will make the adjusting easy is to file the point end of a screw eye flat and use it as a set screw through a hole in the side of the spool.

— Block Plane Converted for Use on Circular Work —

Few amateur craftsmen can afford to own a circular plane, yet this tool is decidedly necessary for such round work as tabletops, half-round shelves, segments, and the like. Any ordinary block plane will accomplish such work if equipped as illustrated. A piece of half-round hardwood is cut the width of the plane and attached with countersunk machine screws, as indicated. The block elevates the rear end of the plane, causing it to follow the curve of the work on which it is used.

HARD-WOOD BLOCK

— HOMEMADE CALIPERS —

A good pair of calipers can be easily and quickly made by anyone in the following manner: Procure a piece of spring wire about 15 in. long and bend it as shown in the sketch, allowing the ends to point inward or outward as the style demands. A loop of heavy wire is fastened around the center so that it can be slid back and

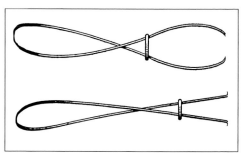

THE SPRING WIRE IS BENT SO THAT THE POINTS TURN IN OR OUT AS DESIRED.

forth along the wire. This serves the purpose of an adjuster.

— A HANDY DRILL GAUGE —

The accompanying sketch shows a simple drill gauge that will be found very handy for amateurs. The gauge consists of a piece of hardwood, ¾ in. thick, with a width and length that will be suitable for the size and number of drills you have on hand. Drill a hole through the wood with each drill you have and place a screw eye in one end to be used as a hanger. When you want to drill a hole for a pipe, bolt, screw, etc., you use the gauge to determine what size drill must be used in drilling the hole.

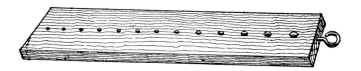

DRILL GAUGE.

THE VERSATILE QUERL *and* OTHER UTENSILS

— A TABLE KNIFE SHARPENER —

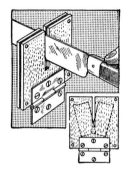

The knife sharpener shown can be easily made of two pieces of thin wood, such as cigar-box covers, about 2 in. wide and 2½ in. long, and two discarded safety-razor blades of the heavier type. Lay the wood pieces together and saw a slot down the center for about 1¾ in. Lay the two razor blades at an angle of about 2 degrees on each side of the slot, as shown, fasten them to one of the boards, and securely attach the other board over them.

To sharpen a knife, run it through the slot two or three times. The sharpener can be fastened with a hinge so that it will swing inside of the drawer or box that the knives are kept in, and it will always be ready for use.

— CLEAN PENCIL SHARPENER —

Pencils may be sharpened without spreading the dust from them by the use of the device shown in the illustration. A piece of emery paper is fixed to one side of the cover of the box. By turning over the cover with a handle after a pencil has been sharpened, the dust may be dropped into the box and removed from time to time.

EMERY PAPER

— NAIL CARRIER MADE OF CANS —

Four ordinary tin cans, fastened to a wooden block as shown in the illustration, make a serviceable and practical carrier for nails, staples, or similar materials used in making repairs on the farm or in the shop. The tops of the cans are cut out carefully and the edges smoothed so as not to injure the hand when removing nails from them. The tops are cut to the shape shown and attached to the block. The handle is provided, making it convenient to carry the

contrivance. If cans made with covers that may be pried off are used, the central block should be extended and the handle nailed directly to it.

— KNIFE, FORK, AND SPOON HOLDER —

This holder is made of a piece of sheet copper of sufficient thickness to support the number of pieces of cutlery used. The piece is notched to admit the different pieces, and its back edge is bent at right angles to provide means of fastening it to a support, a wall, or the back of the kitchen cabinet. It will save space as well as time, because it is much easier to grasp one of the articles when

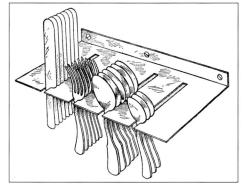

THE HOLDER KEEPS THE CUTLERY IN A POSITION FOR EASY SELECTION AND GRASPING.

wanted than if they are kept in a drawer.

— THE VERSATILE QUERL —

"Querl" is the German name for a kitchen utensil that may be used as an eggbeater, potato masher, or lemon squeezer. For beating an egg in a glass, mixing flour and water, or stirring cocoa or chocolate, it is as good as anything on the market.

This utensil is made of hardwood, preferably ash or maple. A circular piece about 2 in. in diameter is cut from ½ in. stock and shaped like a star as shown in *Fig. 1*, and a ⅜-in. hole bored in the center for a handle. The handle should be at least 12 in. in length and fastened in the star as shown in *Fig. 2*.

In use, the star is placed in the dish containing the material to be beaten or mixed, and the handle is rapidly rolled between the palms off the hands.

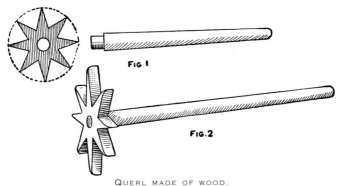

FIG I

FIG.2

QUERL MADE OF WOOD.

— EGGSHELLS AS FLOWERPOTS —

Here is a novel method of caring for small plants until they are ready to be set out in the garden. Holes were bored in the bottom of the till of an old trunk and eggshells fitted into them. Seeds were planted in the shells and names of the varieties were marked on them. The arrangement is compact, and when the plants are ready for planting, the shells may be broken, and the plants set without disturbing the roots.

IN *the* WORKSHOP

— GUIDE FOR CUTTING MORTISES —

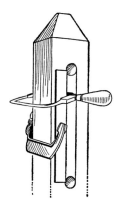

After spending considerable time in cutting one mortise in a piece to make the settee described in *Popular Mechanics* magazine, I devised the plan shown in the sketch, which enabled me to cut all the mortises required in the time that I cut one in the ordinary manner. Two metal plates, one of which is shown in the sketch, having perfectly straight edges, are clamped on the piece with the straight edge on the line of the mortise. A hacksaw is applied through holes bored at the ends and a cut sawed along against the metal edges.

— HOW TO LOCK A TENONED JOINT —

A tenon placed in a blind mortise can be permanently fastened, when putting the joints together, by two wedges driven in the end grain of the wood. In some cases, where the wood to be used is very dry and brittle, it is advisable to dip the tenon in warm water before applying the glue.

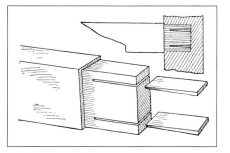

WEDGES IN TENON.

The glue must be applied immediately after the tenon is removed from the water, and then inserted in the mortise. The sketch shows the application of the wedges as the tenon is forced into place.

— Sawhorse with Collapsible Casters —

To save the labor required to carry a sawhorse from one work site to another, a workman equipped it with a set of collapsible casters, as shown in the drawing. The caster axles are inserted through slots in the legs of the sawhorse, and washers and cotter pins are used on the projecting ends to prevent side play. A simple system of wooden toggle levers raises and lowers the casters from the floor. To lower the wheels, when it is desired to move the horse, the handle is pushed inward. To remove them from contact with the floor the handle is given an outward pull.

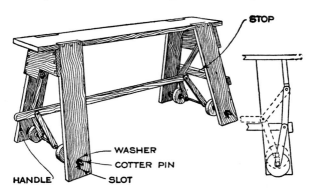

A SAWHORSE EQUIPPED WITH A SET OF CASTERS. BROUGHT TO BEAR AGAINST THE FLOOR BY PRESSURE ON TOGGLE LEVERS, THE CASTERS MAKE CHANGES OF LOCATION EASY.

— Sliding Box Cover Fastener —

While traveling through the country as a watchmaker, I found it quite convenient to keep my small drills, taps, small brooches, etc., in boxes with sliding covers. To keep the contents from spilling or getting mixed in my cases, I used a small fastener as shown in the accompanying illustration. The fastener is made of steel or brass and fastened by means of small screws or tacks on the outside of the box. A hole is drilled on the upper part to receive the pin that is driven into the sliding cover. This pin should not stick out beyond the thickness of the spring, which is bent up at the point so the pin will freely pass under it. The pin can be driven through the cover to prevent it from being pulled entirely out of the box.

— HOLDING WOOD IN A SAWBUCK —

Anyone who has used a sawbuck knows how inconvenient it is to have a stick roll or lift up as the saw blade is pulled back for the next cut. With the supplementary device shown in the sketch, which can be easily attached to the sawbuck, these troubles will be eliminated. It consists of two crosspieces hinged to the back uprights of the sawbuck and a foot-pressure stirrup fastened to their front ends as shown. Spikes are driven through the crosspieces so that their protruding ends will

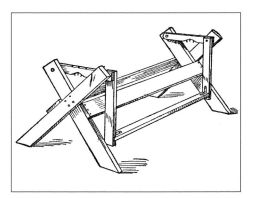

THE HOLDING ATTACHMENT EASILY ADJUSTS ITSELF TO THE STICK OF WOOD PLACED IN THE CROTCH.

gouge into the stick of wood being sawed. The stirrup is easily thrown back for laying a piece of wood in the crotch.

— REMOVABLE DRAWER STOP —

When I least expect it, the small-tool drawers of my tool chest have often dropped out after I had left them partly open. The result was a waste of time in picking up the tools, not to mention the possible injury to them. I made small clips, like those shown in the sketch, fitted to the back of the drawers as in A. When it is desired to remove the clips, the portion that extends

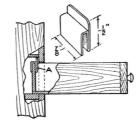

above the drawer may be bent forward. This is necessary only where the space above the drawer is small. The clips may be made large enough to fit drawers of various sizes.

— CUTTING THIN WOODEN DISKS —

Instead of cutting thin wooden disks with a coping saw, making it necessary to smooth off the circumference of the disk, more satisfactory results may be had by

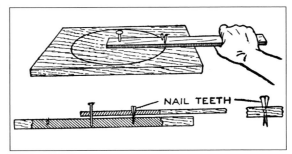

DRAW THE STRIP WITH ITS SAW-TOOTH BRADS AROUND THE CENTER, CUTTING OUT THE DISK.

the following method: Determine the center from which the circumference of the disk is to be struck. Drive a nail through a strip of wood about 1 in. wide and ¼ in. thick, and into the center of the proposed disk. At a point on the strip, so as to strike the circumference of the disk, drive two sharp brads as shown in the sectional view off the sketch. Arrange

them to act as saw teeth by driving them at an angle, with a slight space between the points. By grasping the end of the strip and drawing it carefully around the center a number of times, the disk may be cut cleanly. By cutting from one side nearly through the board, and then finishing the cut from the other, an especially good job results.

The first appliance necessary for the boy's workshop is a work-bench. The average boy who desires to construct his own apparatus can make the bench as described herein. Four pieces of 2- by 4-in. pine are cut 23 in. long for the legs, and a tenon made on each end of them, ½ in. thick, 3½ in. wide, and 1½ in. long, as shown in A and B, *Fig. 1*. The cross-pieces at the top and bottom of the legs are made from the same material and cut 20 in. long. A mortise is made 1¼ in. from each end of these pieces and in the narrow edge of them, as shown at C and D, *Fig. 1*. The corners are then cut sloping from the edge of the leg out and to the middle of the piece, as shown. When each pair of legs is fitted to a pair of cross-pieces they will form the two supports for the bench. These supports are held together and braced with two braces or reconnecting pieces of 2- by 4-in. pine, 24 in. long. The joints are made between the ends of these pieces and the legs by boring a hole through each leg and into the center of each end of the braces to a depth of 4 in., as shown in J, *Fig. 2*. On the backside of the braces bore holes, intersecting the other holes, for a place to insert the

nut of a bolt as shown in HH. Four ⅜- by 6-in. bolts are placed in the holes bored, and the joints are drawn together as shown at J. The ends of the two braces must be sawn off perfectly square to make the supports stand up straight.

In making this part of the bench be sure to have the joints fit closely and to draw the bolts up tight on the stretchers. There is nothing quite so annoying as to have the bench support sway while work is being done on its top. It would be wise to add a cross brace on the backside to prevent any rocking while planing boards, if the bench is to be used for large work.

The main top board M, *Fig. 2*, may be either made from one piece of 2- by 12-in. plank, 3½ ft. long, or made up of 14 strips of maple, ⅞ in. thick by 2 in. wide, and 3½ ft. long, set on edge, each strip glued and screwed to its neighbor. When building up a top like this be careful to put the strips together with the grain running in the same direction so the top may be planed smooth. The back board N is the same length as the main top board M, 8½ in. wide and only ⅞ in. thick, which is fitted into

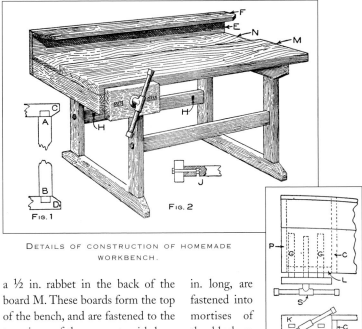

DETAILS OF CONSTRUCTION OF HOMEMADE
WORKBENCH.

a ½ in. rabbet in the back of the board M. These boards form the top of the bench, and are fastened to the top pieces of the supports with long screws. The board E is 10 in. wide and nailed to the back of the bench. On top of this board and at right angles with it is fastened a 2½ in. board, F. These two boards are ⅞ in. thick and 3½ ft. long. Holes are bored or notches are cut in the projecting board, F, to hold tools.

Details of the vise are shown in *Fig. 3,* which is composed of a 2- by 6-in. block 12 in. long, into which is fastened an iron bench screw, S. Two guide rails, GG, ⅞ by 1½ in. and 20 in. long, are fastened into mortises of the block as shown in KK, and they slide in corresponding mortises in a piece of 2- by 4-in. pine bolted to the underside of the main top board as shown in L. The bench screw nut is fastened in the 2- by 4-in. piece, L, between the two mortised holes. This piece, L, is securely nailed to one of the top crosspieces, C, of the supports and to a piece of 2-by 4-in. pine, P, that is bolted to the undersides of the top boards at the end of the bench.

— SAFETY CHOPPING BLOCK —

Chopping of pieces of wood, which must be broken into short lengths, is often dangerous. The chopping block shown in the illustration was designed to overcome this element of danger and it may be used for chopping small kindling wood as well as for breaking up heavier pieces. When the blow is struck on the wood to be broken, the pieces are thrown away from the person chopping. The sketch shows the device in use for the chopping of short pieces of wood, and the heavy portion may be used as

THIS CHOPPING BLOCK MAKES FOR SAFETY IN THAT PIECES CHOPPED ARE THROWN AWAY FROM THE WORKER.

a seat. The smaller sketch shows how the block is built up of 2-in. planks, bolted together.

— HOMEMADE PICTURE-FRAME MITER BOX —

Any person wishing to make a picture frame or to cut down an old one requires a miter box for that purpose so that the molding may be properly held while sawing it, and also for nailing the corners together. I made a miter box, as shown, and found it to be just the thing for this purpose. It is built on a base similar to an overturned box, the saw guides being held on the ends of a piece, constructed as shown in A. Holes are cut in the top, as shown in B, for one of the guides and for the two wedges. Two pieces, C, are fastened with their outer edges at perfect right angles on the top.

The frame parts are clamped

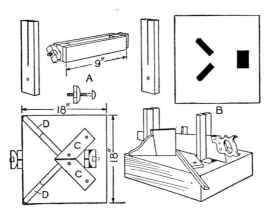

HOMEMADE MITER BOX FOR SAWING FRAME MOLDING AND
TO HOLD THE PARTS FOR FASTENING TOGETHER.

against the pieces on top with the wedges driven in between the frame parts and the brackets DD. After cutting the frame parts they are held tightly in place while fastening them, in any manner desired.

— BOX COVER WITHOUT HINGES —

Two ordinary boxes may be fitted together as one without using hinges if nails or screws are inserted at points along the edges so that they will slip into holes bored at corresponding points in the edges of the other box. The nail heads or screw heads should be filed off or cut off after being placed in position.

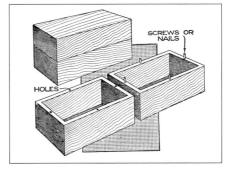

BOX COVER USING PINS INSTEAD OF
HINGES TO KEEP IT IN PLACE.

Under Lock *and* Key

— Simple Lock for Drawer or Chest —

A simple lock for a drawer or chest, which will make it impossible for anyone not in on the secret to open the drawer without resorting to force, can be made in a few minutes.

A piece of stiff wire is bent to the shape shown in the drawing and fastened to the inside of the drawer case with screw eyes. A piece of spring wire is wrapped around a rod to make a compression spring, which is slipped over the staple provided for the stem of the lock. This spring locks the drawer automatically when it is closed. A hook, bent on the upper end of the wire, fits into a slot cut in the underside of the chest top.

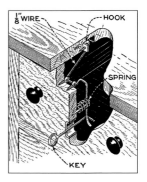

The front of this slot is fitted with a brass wearing plate against which the hook bears. The lock is opened by a bent-wire key, inserted into the keyhole and turned until the bent end comes over the stem end of the lock, which is pulled forward.

— Simple Concealed Locking Device for Cases of Drawers —

A simple method of providing a homemade locking device for a tier of drawers is shown in the sketch. The use of only one keyed lock is necessary, as is common in manufactured cases. This is applicable to new or old cases, where a space of about 1½ in. is available between the back of the drawers and the rear of the case.

The device as detailed consists of a locking bar sliding in guides, screwed or fastened to the back of the case. Attached to the bar are latches one less in number than there are drawers and spaced apart the distance that each drawer top is above the one below. The upper latch is the master feature. The top of this is beveled off, forcing it downward when the top drawer is closed. The locking bar with the other latches also moves down, and the latch fingers engage the backs of the drawers. The connecting bar is operated by a light coil spring set on a shouldered rod at the bottom of the bar, as detailed.

The master latch may be attached at any place on the bar, and should be placed at the bottom drawer for cases too high to be reached handily. To make the device for a small space, a ¼ in. metal rod with metal fingers

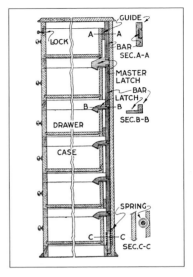

clamped on can be used. Metal striking plates are then put on the back edges of the drawers.

— WOODEN LOCK WITH COMBINATION KEY —

The lock shown in the sketch and detailed drawings is made entirely of wood, and it is nearly impossible to pick or open it without the use of the key. The casing of the lock is 5 by 5 in. and 1 in. thick, of hardwood, oak being suitable for this as well as for the other parts. Three tumblers, a bolt, and a keeper are required. The key is shown inserted, indicating how the tumblers are raised by it. The bolt is slotted and a screw placed through it to prevent it from being moved too far. The lock and keeper are bolted into place on a door with carriage bolts, the heads being placed on the outer side.

The detailed drawing shows the parts, together with the dimensions of each, which must be followed closely. The lock casing is grooved with two grooves extending the

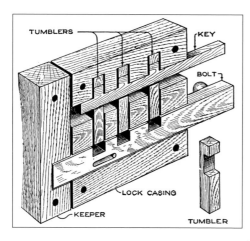

LEFT: THIS LOCK IS MADE ENTIRELY OF WOOD AND CANNOT BE PICKED EASILY.

BELOW: THE DETAILS OF CONSTRUCTION MUST BE OBSERVED CAREFULLY AND THE PARTS MADE ACCURATELY TO ENSURE SATISFACTORY OPERATION.

length of the grain and connected by open mortises, all ½ in. in depth. The spacing of the mortises and the grooves is shown in the views of the casing. Three tumblers, ½ in. square and 2½ in. long, are required. The bolt is ½ by 1 by 8 in., and the key ¼ by ¾ by 5½ in., and notched as shown. All the parts of the lock must be fitted carefully, sandpapered smooth, and oiled to give a finish that will aid in the operation, as well as protect the wood. Aside from its practical use,

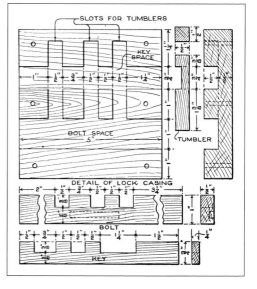

this lock is interesting as a piece of mechanical construction.

— A QUICKLY MADE DOOR LATCH —

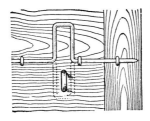

A door latch that is efficient as well as simple may be made by bending a piece of iron rod and pointing one end, as shown in the illustration, then securing it to the door with staples. Or small rods may be bent in the shape of a staple and the ends threaded for nuts. The door is locked by turning the handle in the position shown by the dotted lines and securing it with a padlock.

HOUSEHOLD HELPERS

— A KITCHEN UTENSIL HANGER —

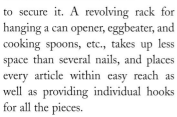

Every cook knows how troublesome it is to have several things hanging on one nail. When one of the articles is wanted it is usually at the back, and the others must be removed to secure it. A revolving rack for hanging a can opener, eggbeater, and cooking spoons, etc., takes up less space than several nails, and places every article within easy reach as well as providing individual hooks for all the pieces.

The rack is easily made of a block of wood 2½ in. in diameter and 1 in. thick, an arm, ¾ in. wide by ¼ in. thick and 6 in. long, and a metal bracket. The arm is fastened to the bracket and the bracket to the wall. A screw is turned through a loose-fitting hole bored in the end of the arm and into the disk. Screw hooks are placed around the edge of the dish as hangers.

— A TROUSER HANGER —

A wood frame, similar to a picture frame, is made up and hinged to the inner side of the closet door with its outer edge hung on two chains. The inside of the frame is fitted with crossbars. After hanging the trousers on the cross-bars, the frame is swung up against the door where it is held with a hook. Several pairs of trousers can be hung on the frame, and when flat against the door it takes up very little space. The trousers are kept flat so that they will hold their crease.

TROUSERS CAN BE EASILY HUNG ON THE CROSSBARS TO KEEP THEIR CREASE.

— AN IRONING-BOARD STAND —

An ordinary iron-ing board is cut square on the large end and a slot cut 1½ in. wide and 4 in. long to admit the angle sup-port. The support is

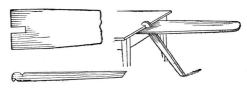

STAND ATTACHED TO TABLE.

placed against the table and the board is pressed down against the outer notch that jams against the table, thus holding the board rigid and in such a position as to give free access for ironing dresses, etc.

— HANDLE FOR A DRINKING GLASS —

Measure the bottom part of the glass and make a band of copper that will neatly fit it. The ends of the copper can be riveted, but if a neat job is desired, flatten or file the copper ends on a slant and braze or solder them together.

Attach to the band an upright copper piece a little longer than the glass is high. To this upright piece rivet or solder a bent piece of copper to form a handle. The glass is set in the band and the upper end of the vertical pieces is bent over the glass edge.

— A HANDY LAUNDRY CABINET —

A cabinet in which all necessary washing materials, such as soap, bluing, soap powder, and the like, may be kept in one place will be appreciated by the laundress. The overall dimensions of the cabinet illustrated are 5 by 12 by 20 in., and the swinging compartment or

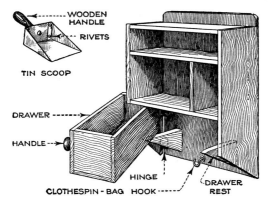

A CABINET FOR THE LAUNDRY, IN WHICH ALL
WASHING MATERIALS ARE KEPT TOGETHER.

drawer, which is used for soap powder or chips, is 4 by 5 by 10 in. If desired, a door can be fitted to cover the upper compartments. A hook is screwed underneath the soap drawer, from which the clothespin bag is hung. A simple scoop for handling the washing powder is easily made from a piece of tin and is kept in the drawer.

— DEVICE FRIGHTENS FLIES AT SCREEN DOOR —

An effective means of frightening flies away from a screen door may be made from a spring curtain rod and cotton duck. Scallops of 8-oz. duck, 6 in. long, are fastened to the pole, on opposite sides, as shown. The ratchet on the end of the pole is arranged so as not to catch. A small cord is wound around the pole and fastened to the screen door. The rod supports are fixed near the top of the door frame.

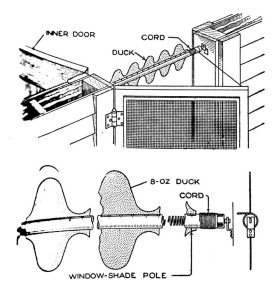

THE SCALLOPED ROLLER REVOLVES RAPIDLY WHEN THE DOOR IS OPENED, FRIGHTENING FLIES.

— Felt Tires for the Rocking Chair —

It is aggravating to the housekeeper when the varnished surface of a floor becomes worn by the rockers of a chair. This annoyance can be prevented and longer life given the floor finish by gluing a strip of felt to the underside of each chair rocker. Liquid glue or linoleum cement can be used for holding the felt strip to the wood. In order to bring the felt into contact with the wood at all points, the method of clamping shown in the drawing

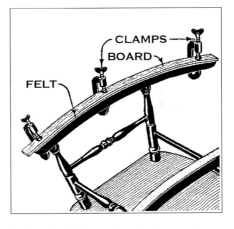

should be used, and the board and clamps allowed to remain overnight.

—Shoe Guard Prevents Soiling and Damage —

Many good shoes have been ruined by acid, oil, paint, whitewash, and other materials, which, had the shoes been suitably protected, would not have injured them. The shoe cover illustrated is made from a piece of rubber, canvas, or other material, cut to shape and fitted with a cuff of the same material, to which the buckles from a pair of old arctics are fastened. A strap fastened to the projecting ears of the

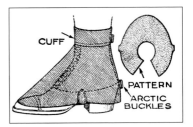

guard passes under the instep like a legging strap. The old buckles are at the back and allow the cover to be slipped on or removed quickly.

— A Hinged Window Box —

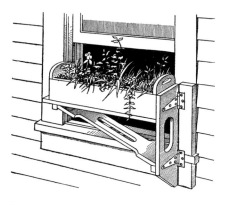

A window box arranged to rest in a hinged bracket on the outside of a window, as shown in the sketch, has advantages over the usual method of fixing the box permanently. The box is separate from the supporting frame and may be removed from it. The frame is attached to the window casing by means of T-hinges and is strongly supported by a bracket. When it is desired to clean the window, the device may be swung around and out of the way. This feature is also desirable when it is raining, for the flowers in the box may be watered conveniently in this way.

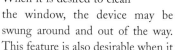

THE FLOWER BOX IS ARRANGED TO SWING AWAY FROM THE WINDOW SO THAT IT WILL NOT BE IN THE WAY.

— Hand-operated Whirling Fan —

The whirling fan illustrated is more convenient than a fan of the ordinary type, and may be made by a boy of only moderate mechanical skill. The materials necessary for its construction are easily available in the home. The sketch at right illustrates the method of operation. The details of construction are shown in the working drawings on the next page.

The wing of the fan is cut from a sheet of bristol board, and is 6 in. long and 5½ in. wide. It is formed by gluing two pieces together, the upper end of the driving shaft being glued into place at the same time. The small sketch at

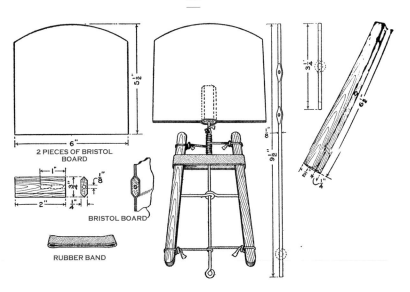

2 PIECES OF BRISTOL BOARD

BRISTOL BOARD

RUBBER BAND

THE WHIRLING FAN IS SUPERIOR TO ONE OF THE ORDINARY VARIETY AND MAY BE MADE AT HOME OF MATERIALS READILY AVAILABLE. THE DETAILS OF CONSTRUCTION ARE SHOWN IN THE SKETCH AND IN THE WORKING DRAWINGS.

the left shows the size and shape of the piece of wood into which the driving shaft is fastened at its upper end.

The driving rod, shown at the right of the larger sketch, is ⅛ in. in diameter and 9½ in. long. The flattened portions near the upper end are drilled to receive the ends of the cords that wind and unwind on the shaft at the top of the handles. A brace of similar wire is fixed near the middle of the handles so that they pivot on its ends when the lower ends of the handles are pressed

together, as shown in the sketch at the right. The handles are of wood, ¼ in. thick, ½ in. wide, and 6½ in. long. Their ends are rounded and slight notches are cut into the corners near the ends to provide for the tying of the cords.

A wide rubber band, slipped over the handles near their upper ends, causes them to close at the top. When the fan is in use this will reverse the rotation of the fan. It is necessary only to squeeze the handles inward, and the reverse action is repeated.

LABOR SAVING DEVICES

— A BELL-RINGING MAILBOX —

The annoyance of watching for the arrival of the mailman was overcome by the fitting of an electrical alarm to the mailbox, as shown in the sketch. A strip of metal, A, was pivoted in the box and weighted on one end. A bell, B, was wired to dry cells in the box below the container for the mail. When the mail

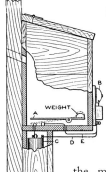

is dropped into the box, the end A is forced down, forming an electrical contact and completing the circuit from the cells C through the wire D and back through the wire E. When the mail is removed, the weight raises the metal strip.

— MOTOR-DRIVEN ENTERTAINER FOR THE BABY —

A contrivance that keeps the baby entertained by the hour, at intervals, and is a big help to a busy mother, was made in a short time. I mounted four wooden arms on a small motor as shown. On the ends of two of the arms, I fixed small pinwheels, one blue and the other yellow. The other arms hold curious-shaped pieces of bright cardboard, one red and the other green. The driving motor is run by one two-volt cell. The revolving colored pinwheels amuse baby in his highchair,

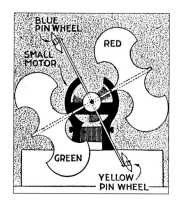

and the device has well repaid the little trouble of making it.

— Device for Suspending Parcels from Overhead Hooks —

To hang small sacks or other articles out of reach overhead, so that they may be easily taken down, I use a double-eye hook that I made of wire. A single piece of wire is used and twisted into two loops, as

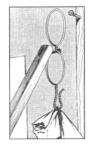

shown, and then formed into a twisted hook. I use a pole with a nail, hooking it into the lower loop to raise the parcel; this leaves the upper loop free to be hooked on the nail above.

— Scraper for Dishes —

Housekeepers will find the scraper shown to be silent and more rapid than a knife for cleaning dishes. It consists of a handle cut from a piece of straight-grained wood, with a kerf sawn in the wide end to a depth of ¾ in., into which a piece of sheet rubber is inserted. The rubber may be cut from an old bicycle-tire casing and is

fastened with two or three brads driven through the handle. The ends of the brads are bent over or riveted. The edge of the rubber should be made straight.

— A Nonrolling Thread Spool —

A spool of thread may be kept from rolling by gluing squares of cardboard to the ends. The squares should be a little larger

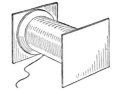

than the spool. This will save many a step and much bending over to pick up the spool. The spool, when it falls, will stop where it landed.

— EMERGENCY LIFTING DEVICE OF ROPE AND LEVER —

When block and tackle, chain hoists, or similar equipment are not at hand, the simple arrangement shown in the sketch is useful for lifting heavy loads. Make the lever A of a piece of 2- by 4-in. timber and cut notches into it for the ropes, as indicated. From a suitable support, B, fix the ropes C and D to the lever A at the proper notches, permitting the ends C-1 and D-1 to be drawn down and fastened to the floor or other support as required in raising the load. Fix the rope E to the load W and suspend it from the lever A at the proper notch by means of a loop, E-1. To raise the load, bear down on the end of the lever when it is in its original position A-1, bringing it to the position A-2. This will bring the lower rope to position E-2. Draw up the slack in rope D, to bring the loop to position D-2, and fasten it. Then lift the lever A from its position A-2, to the position A-3, and draw up the slack in rope C to bring the loop up to position C-2. The lower rope will be brought to position E-3. By repeating this process, the load may be raised gradually. The ropes may, of course, be of various lengths within the range of the support and the operators.

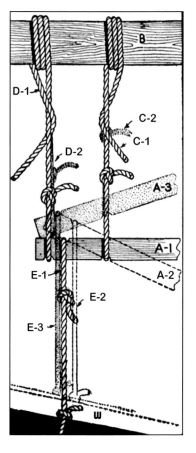

Secret Hiding Places

— Concealing the House Key —

The time-honored custom of concealing the house key under the doormat or in the letter-box when the family has not enough keys to go around is so well known that an unauthorized person seeking to enter the house would look in these places first of all.

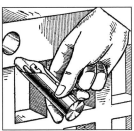

A simple and effective hiding place for the key can be quickly and easily made with the aid of an auger and two pieces of tin. Pick out an obscure section of the porch railing, and in the edge of this bore a ¾-in. hole, about ¼ in. deeper than the length of the key. Make a piece of tin into a cylinder, the same length as the key, so that the latter will slide easily into the hole. At one end of this cylinder solder a 1-in. disk of tin, which will make it appear as in the illustration.

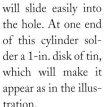

If the key is placed in the cylinder and the latter pushed into the hole until it is flush with the surface, it will scarcely be noticed by anyone not in on the secret. By painting it the same color as the railing it will become still more inconspicuous.

— A Secret Box Lid —

A simple secret box lid, which cannot be opened by anyone who does not know the secret, is made by pivoting the lid near one end by means of two nails driven through the sides of the box into the edges of the cover. A hole is drilled in the middle of the opposite end of the lid to take a spring and a nail from which the point and head have been cut. When the lid is closed, the nail is pushed into a hole drilled in the end of the box, locking it securely. To open the box, it is necessary to push the bolt out of the hole in the box by inserting a heavy pin through a small hole, which leads from the outside to the nail socket, and by pressing down on the short end of the lid. The lid can be given the appearance of being solidly nailed by using shortened nails and some other side may be made to appear as the cover. A shortened nail can be pushed into a small hole leading to the bolt and, when in position, will conceal this perfectly. Some kind of mark should be made on the head of this nail, to distinguish it from the corresponding one on the opposite end.

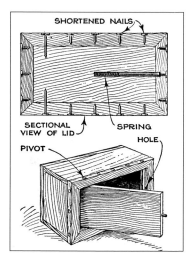

SHORTENED NAILS

SECTIONAL VIEW OF LID

SPRING

HOLE

PIVOT

— A Secret Trinket Case for the Bookshelf —

Practical use as well as the novelty of its construction makes the trinket case shown in the illustration well worth the time and effort necessary to make it. Various kinds of wood—preferably of the better cabinet varieties—are suited to the design shown, like that used in cigar boxes. The size shown is that of a bound volume of a magazine like *Popular Mechanics,* and may be adapted to special needs. The back and the cover slide in grooves, which are not visible when the "book" is closed. This makes it difficult and

interesting for one to discover how the case is opened. The back may be marked and lettered to resemble a bound volume closely. If special secrecy is desired, it may even be covered with leather, in exact duplication of those on a bound set of magazines kept in the bookcase with it.

Make the pieces for the frame of the box first. If possible, make one strip of the proper width—2 in., in this case—and long enough for the two ends and the front. Make another strip 1¾ in. wide and long enough for the partition and false back of the tray.

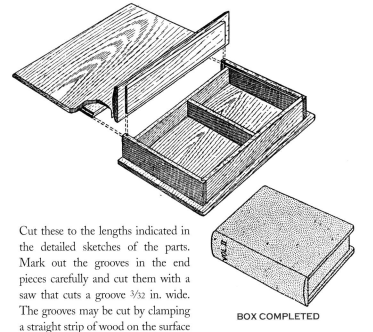

BOX COMPLETED

THIS TRINKET CASE IS A PRACTICAL NOVELTY THAT MAY BE USED AS A SECRET CONTAINER TO BE SET ON THE BOOKSHELF WITH SIMILAR BOUND VOLUMES.

Cut these to the lengths indicated in the detailed sketches of the parts. Mark out the grooves in the end pieces carefully and cut them with a saw that cuts a groove 3/32 in. wide. The grooves may be cut by clamping a straight strip of wood on the surface of the ends the proper distance from the top and sawing cautiously along the strip to the proper depth. The grooves across the grain may be cut similarly, or in a miter box.

Glue the pieces of the frame together, taking care that the corners are square. If necessary, place blocks inside to ensure that the clamping will not disturb the right angles of the box. Shape the bottom and cover pieces nearly to the final size before gluing them; then, if small nicks are made in the edge, they may be removed by a cut of the plane when the case is complete. Glue the sliding pieces to the cover and to the back. This must be done carefully, and it is convenient to drive small brads part way into the second piece from the inner side to prevent the pieces from slipping while being glued. If proper care is taken, only a small amount of glue will be forced out, and this can be removed with a chisel when dry. The edges may be trimmed off to their exact size and the entire construction given a final light sanding. It is then ready for the stain and shellac or other finish. The parts that slide in grooves should not be shellacked or varnished because this is apt to cause them to stick.

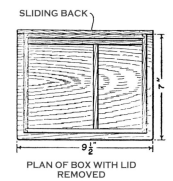

PLAN OF BOX WITH LID
REMOVED

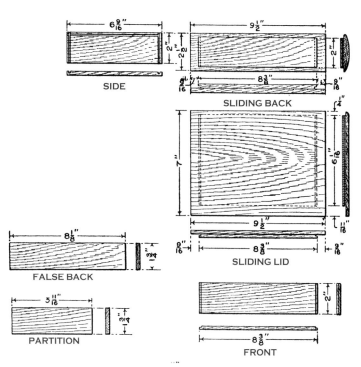

ALTERNATIVE LIVING ARRANGEMENTS

— BIRD HOUSE MADE OF AN OLD STRAW HAT —

A birdhouse of an old straw hat is a practical and easily contrived affair. Cut a hole in the crown of the hat. Then nail the hat against a board of proper size. To protect the hat against the rain, put a roof over it, as shown.

A perch is also provided. Such a birdhouse can be hung against the trunk of a tree, or nailed against a wall. Leaving the hat in its natural straw color, and painting the rest a dark brown, produces a satisfactory effect.

— HOUSES MADE OF POLES —

Being forced to take the open-air treatment to regain health, a person adopted the plan of building a pole house in the woods. The scheme was so successful that it was decided to make a resort grounds to attract crowds during holidays, by which income could be realized for living expenses. All the pavilions, stands, furniture, and amusement devices were constructed of straight poles cut from young-growth timber with the bark remaining on them. Outside of boards for flooring and roofing material, the entire construction of the buildings and fences consisted of poles.

A level spot was selected and a house built having three rooms. The location was in a grove of young timbers, most of them being straight. Thirteen trees were easily found that would make posts 12 ft. long, required of the sides, and two poles 16 ft. long, for the center of the ends, so that they would reach to the ridge.

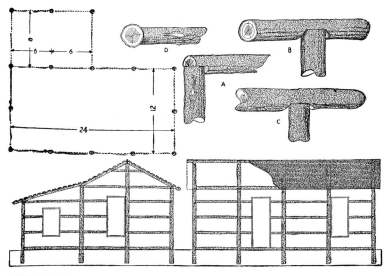

THE FRAME CONSTRUCTION OF THE HOUSE MADE ENTIRELY OF ROUGH POLES,
THE VERTICALS BEING SET IN THE GROUND, PLUMBED, AND SIGHTED
TO MAKE A PERFECT RECTANGLE OF THE DESIRED PROPORTIONS.

The plot was laid out rectangular and marked for the poles, which were set in the ground to a depth of 4 ft., at distances 6 ft. apart. This made the house 8 ft. high at the eaves with a square pitch roof; that is, the ridge was 3 ft. high in the center from the plate surfaces for this width of a house. The rule for finding this height is to take one-quarter of the width of the house for the height in the center from the plate.

The corner poles were carefully located to make the size 12 by 24 ft., with a lean-to 8 by 12 ft., and then plumbed to get them straight vertically. The plates for the sides, consisting of five poles, were selected as straight as possible and their ends and centers hewn down to about one-half their thickness, as shown in A and B, and nailed to the tops of the vertical poles, the connection for the center poles being as shown in C.

The next step was to secure the vertical poles with crosspieces between them, which were used later for supporting the siding. These poles were cut about 6 ft. long, their ends being cut concave to fit the curve of the upright poles, as shown in D. These were spaced evenly, about 2 ft. apart from center to center, on the sides and ends, as shown in the sketch, and toe-nailed in place. The door and window openings were cut in the horizontal poles wherever wanted, and casements set in and nailed. The first row of horizontal poles was placed close to the ground and used both as support for the lower ends of the siding and to nail to the ends of the flooring board, which were fastened in the center to poles laid on stones, or better still, placed on top of short blocks, 5 ft. long, set in the ground. These poles for the floor should be placed not over 2 ft. apart to make the flooring solid.

A lean-to was built by setting three poles at a distance of 8 ft. from one side, beginning at the center and extending to the end of the main building. These poles were about 6 ft. long above the ground. The rafter poles for this part were about 9½ ft. long, notched at both ends for the plates, the ends of the house rafters being sawed off even with the outside of the plate along this edge. The rafter poles for the house were 10 in all, 8 ft. long, and were laid off and cut to fit a ridge made of a board. These poles were notched about 15 in. from their lower ends to fit over the rounding edge of the plate pole and were then placed directly over each vertical wall pole. They were nailed both to the plate and to the ridge, also further strengthened by a brace made of a piece of board or a small pole placed under the ridge and nailed to both rafters. On top of the rafters, boards were placed horizontally spaced about 1 ft. apart, but this is optional because other roofing material can be used. In this instance metal roofing was used and it required fastening only at intervals. To prevent rusting, it was well painted on the underside before laying it and coated on the outside when fastened into place. If a more substantial shelter is wanted, it is best to lay the roof solid with boards, then cover it with the regular prepared roofing material.

Some large trees were selected and felled, then cut into 4-ft. lengths and the bark removed. If desired, the bark can be removed in 4-ft. lengths. The bark was nailed on the outside of the poles, beginning at the bottom in the same manner as laying shingles, to form the siding of the house. If a more substantial house is wanted, boards can be nailed on the poles, then the bark fastened to the boards; also, the interior can be finished in wallboard.

The same general construction is used for the porch, with horizontal poles latticed, as shown, to form the railing. It is very easy to make ornamental parts, such as shown, on the eave of the porch by splitting sticks and nailing them on closely together to make a frieze. Floors are laid on the porch and in the house, and doors hung and window sash fitted in the same manner as in an ordinary house.

A bandstand was constructed on sloping ground and, after setting the poles, the floor horizontals were placed about 2 ft. above the ground on the upper side, and 4 ft. on the

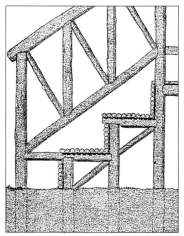

THE STEPS ARE SUPPORTED ON PAIRS OF VERTICAL POLES SET IN THE GROUND TO MAKE DIFFERENT LEVELS

lower side. The poles used were about 18 ft. long. Instead of placing the horizontals 2 ft. apart, the first was placed 1 ft. above the floor, the next at about one-half the distance from the lower one to the plate at the top, and the space between was ornamented with cross poles, as shown. A balcony or bay was constructed at one end, and a fancy roof was made of poles whose ends rested on a curved pole attached to the vertical pieces. Steps were formed of several straight poles, hewn down on their ends to make a level place to rest on horizontal pieces attached to stakes at the ends. A pair of stakes was used at each end of a step, and these were fastened to a slanting piece at the top, their lower ends being set into the ground. The manner of bracing and crossing with horizontals make a rigid form of construction, and if choice poles are selected for the step pieces, they will be comparatively level and of sufficient strength to hold up the entire load put on them. The roof of this building was made for a sunshade only and consisted of boards nailed closely together on the rafters.

An ice-cream parlor was built on the same plan, but without any board floor; the ground, being level, was used instead. There were five vertical poles used for each end with a space left between the two poles at the center, on both sides, for an entrance. This building was covered with prepared roofing so that the items offered for sale could be protected in case of a shower.

A peanut stand was also built without a floor, and to make it with nine sides, nine poles were set in the ground to form a perfect nonagon. The poles were joined at their tops with latticed horizontals. Then a rafter was run from the top of each post to the center, and boards were fitted on each pair of rafters over the V-shaped openings. The boards were then covered with prepared roofing. A railing was formed of horizontals set in notches, cut in the posts, and then ornamented in the same manner as for the other buildings.

Fences were constructed about the grounds, made of pole posts with horizontals on top, hewn down and fitted as the plates for the house. The lower pieces were set in the same as for the house railing. Gates were made of two vertical pieces the height

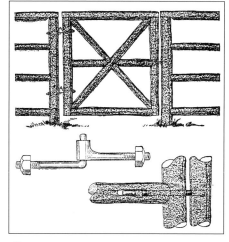

GATE OPENINGS WERE MADE IN THE FENCE WHERE NECESSARY, AND GATES OF POLES HUNG IN THE ORDINARY MANNER.

of the posts, and two horizontals. They were then braced with a piece running from the lower corner at the hinge side to the upper opposite corner, the other cross brace being joined to the sides of the former, whereupon two short horizontals were fitted in the center. A blacksmith formed some hinges of rods and strap iron, as shown, and these were fastened in holes bored in the post and the gate vertical. A latch was made by boring a hole through the gate vertical and into the end of the short piece. Then a slot was cut in the side to receive a pin inserted in a shaft made to fit the

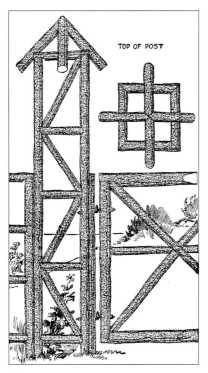

TOP OF POST

built up of four slender poles and were considerably higher than the fence poles. The poles were set in a perfect square, having sides about 18 in. long, and a square top put on by mitering the corners, whereupon four small rafters were fitted on top. The gates were swung on hinges made like those for the small gate.

The swings were among the best and most enjoyed amusement devices on the grounds. Several of these were built, with and without tables. Four poles, about 20 ft. long, were set in the ground at an angle, and each pair of side poles was joined with two horizontals, about 12 ft. long. Spreaders were fastened between the two horizontals to keep the tops of the poles evenly spaced. The distance between the poles will depend on the size of the swing and the number of persons to be seated. Each pair of side poles is further strengthened with crossed poles, as shown. If no table is to be used in the swing, the poles may be set closer together so that the top horizontals will be about 8 ft. long. The platform for the swinging part consists of two poles, each 12 ft. long, which are swung on six vertical poles, each

horizontal hole. A keeper was made in the post by boring a hole to receive the end of the latch.

Large posts were constructed at the entrance to the grounds. On these, double swing gates made up in the same manner as the small one were attached. These large posts were

ALL FURNITURE, TOGETHER WITH THE LARGE LAWN SWINGS, TOOK ON THE GENERAL APPEARANCE OF THE WOODLAND, AND AS THE PIECES WERE MADE UP OF THE SAME MATERIAL AS THE HOUSES, THE COST WAS ONLY THE LABOR AND FEW NAILS.

about 14 ft. long. These poles are attached to the top horizontals with long bolts, or rods, running through both, the bottom being attached in the same manner. Poles are nailed across the platform horizontals at the bottom for a floor, and a table with seats is formed of poles at the ends. The construction is obvious.

A short space between two trees can be made into a seat by fastening two horizontals, one on each tree, with the ends supported by braces. Poles are nailed on the upper surface for a seat.

Other furniture for the house and grounds was made of poles in the manner illustrated. Tables were built for picnickers by setting four or six poles in the ground and making a top of poles or boards. Horizontals were placed across the legs with extending ends on which seats were made for the tables. Chairs and settees were built in the same manner, poles being used for the entire construction.

Have Trunk, Will Travel

— Making One's Own Steamer and Wardrobe Trunks —

The Steamer Trunk

Only ordinary tools such as a hammer, saw, plane, and an old flatiron are needed to build the steamer trunk described in this article. In addition, a glue pot is needed, and a brush or two, for gluing and painting the finished trunk.

There are several kinds of lumber that can be used and in the order of their desirability they are: three-ply veneer, basswood, spruce, and sugar pine. The veneer costs a trifle more, but is lighter and more durable, and if used in conjunction with fiber, it is possible to make a trunk that is

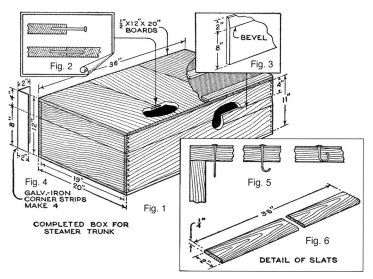

COMPLETED BOX FOR STEAMER TRUNK

A PROFITABLE UNDERTAKING DURING THE LONG WINTER MONTHS IS THAT OF MAKING TRUNKS, IN ANTICIPATION OF NEXT SUMMER'S VACATION.

almost indestructible. If any of these woods is used, secure all ½-in. material, dressed on both sides, and as clear as possible.

In making the steamer trunk, 12-in. material can be used with no waste. A box is made to the dimensions shown in *Fig. 1*. To prevent the top and bottom from warping where the boards are joined, 1½-in. wire nails are driven into the edges of the boards at about 6-in. intervals. Cut off the heads and butt up the next board, as indicated in *Fig. 2;* if desired, these joints can be glued before they are driven together.

After the top and bottom are in place, mark a line on each side 4 in. from the top. Then, starting at a corner, carefully cut through the boards and around the entire box, keeping to the mark, until the box has been sawn into two parts—a lid and a bottom. This method ensures the absolute matching of both parts. The lower part is laid on its side and a line is marked on each side 2 in. below the edge. Another line is marked in the middle of the edge and, using the plane, the outside of the boards is beveled off down to the 2-in. mark, as in *Fig. 3*. Some strips of galvanized iron, as shown in *Fig. 4*,

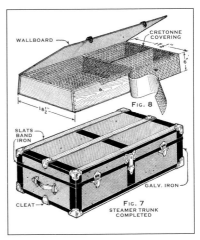

THIS STEAMER TRUNK, WHILE NOT COST-ING NEARLY SO MUCH AS A PURCHASED ARTICLE, WILL BE FOUND QUITE AS STRONG AND SERVICEABLE.

are bent at right angles between two blocks. After bending, they are punched at 1-in. intervals on the edges to take 1-in. clout nails; these nails are easily bent and therefore the punching is necessary. A quarter of an inch from the edge is about the distance to place the holes, which should be punched without raising any burrs.

What is known in the theatrical profession as "scenic linen" is used for covering the trunk, and about 2 yards of this will be needed. This material can usually be obtained from any stage carpenter or scenic artist at little or no expense. Even if bought new, the cost is small. A 14-in. strip, the length of the piece, is cut off. A pot of glue is mixed and the outside of the box is given a light coat; this may be thin, as it is intended only to fill up the pores of the wood. When this has dried, apply a thicker coat as smoothly as possible. While the glue is still hot, lay on the linen and smooth it with a rubbing motion. After the sides have been covered, the top and bottom pieces can be cut and glued on in the same manner; these should be cut ½ in. smaller than the surface they are to cover.

The galvanized iron corners are now nailed in place, the method of clinching the nails being clearly illustrated in *Fig. 5*. The nail is driven through the wood, the point curved with a pair of round-nose pliers, then, holding the old flatiron against the head, the curved point is driven into the wood and clinched by a sharp hammer blow. A strip of galvanized iron about ½ in. wide is nailed on each edge of the box, and strips about 2 in. wide across the center of each side and at the ends of the top and bottom, the nails being clinched as described. The black bands in *Fig. 7* show the location of these strips.

Eighteen running feet of oak, or hickory, cut and formed to the dimensions shown in *Fig. 6,* are needed for the slats, which take up a great deal of the wear a trunk is subjected to. Six 3-ft. slats are cut and fastened with clout nails to the top and bottom of the trunk, 6 in. apart. As the wood is too hard to prevent the entrance of the nails without bending them or splitting the wood, it is necessary to drill a hole wherever a nail is to be inserted. A light strip of band iron is run around the whole trunk at the point where top and bottom join; this iron is applied in the manner described for the sheet-iron corners, the nails being inserted every 6 in. Next place a pair of 6-in. strap hinges on one side; three hinges are better, and even four may be used. The following hardware, which can be obtained from almost any hardware store, is required: Two strong trunk clasps, four slat cleats, eight corner irons, a pair of trunk handles, and a good trunk lock.

The inside of the trunk is lined with a suitable pattern of cretonne, or similar material, which is applied with ordinary flour-and-water paste. Two ¾-in. strips of wood, 1 by 19 in., are screwed to the inside of the trunk, one in each end of the lower part, and 2 in. from the edge, to support the tray.

The tray is made of material as light as can be obtained: ½ in. for the ends, and ¼ in. for the sides. The top and bottom are made of wallboard, about ¼ in. thick. The tray is built to the dimensions shown in *Fig. 8,* and is made narrower at the top so as to give the lid freedom in closing. After the tray is finished and partitions added as desired, the lid is attached with a piece of muslin, which is glued to the tray and acts as a hinge. The tray is then covered with material similar to that with which the trunk is lined. Small straps and buttons are fastened to the lid and tray, respectively, to keep the lid from opening.

The Wardrobe Trunk

For the benefit of those who prefer a wardrobe trunk instead of the steamer trunk, this article describes and illustrates its construction and dimensions.

Covering a trunk with fiber increases the cost of construction but little, while adding immeasurably to its life. However, a little extra work is required to apply it. Either with or without fiber, the box is built in a similar manner to the steamer trunk, the cut in this case being made in the exact center of the box, which is 24 in. deep. The other operations, such as bracing the corners, etc., are the same with the exception that when using fiber, galvanized iron angle pieces are not used on the edges. In their stead, fiber or rawhide, already pressed into shape, is used; 1½ in. angle fiber or rawhide can be obtained from manufacturers of fiber or rawhide and, in many instances, from electrical supply houses. Holes must be drilled in the fiber or rawhide to take the nails, as both are tough. With such a trunk, no wooden slats are necessary, but when the sheet fiber is used, it is riveted down with round-head nails to the wooden base, after lines dividing the surface into 4-in. squares have been drawn on each side of the trunk. The nails are placed along these lines, as shown in *Fig. 9.* In addition to using angle fiber on the corners, all the outside edges are similarly protected. The angle fiber is applied after the sheet fiber has been riveted in place to cover the exposed edges. Metal corners are used on this style of trunk as in the steamer trunk, as an additional protection, the standard practice among baggage handlers being to roll a trunk on its corners. The fiber covering, however, should not be applied until the interior accessories of the trunk have been installed, as it is necessary to fasten some of them through the wood.

Of the interior arrangement of the wardrobe trunk, little need be said, as the taste and needs of individuals will differ. The clothes rack that supports the hangers is made by fastening two tripods—or crowfoots, such as those used in the installation of electric-lighting fixtures—to the inside of the trunk. These fittings can be obtained in various sizes, and should preferably be threaded to take a ⅜-in. pipe or rod. Stove bolts are used to attach them to the trunk before the fiber or canvas covering is applied. The bolt heads are countersunk to prevent a bulge on the outside. The projecting arms, which carry the clothes hangers, are made of ⅜-in. iron rod. Two 8-in. lengths of rod are required for each arm. One

end of the arm is threaded to screw into the fitting and the two sections of rod are joined by a knuckle, as illustrated in *Fig. 10*. The outer end of each arm has a hole drilled through it, and a small ball-head pin, taken from a pair of hinges, is inserted to prevent the hangers from slipping off.

The clothes hangers are best made of three-ply veneer, cut to the form

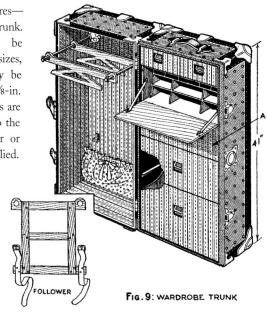

FOLLOWER

FIG. 9: WARDROBE TRUNK

THIS ILLUSTRATION SHOWS A FIBER-COVERED TRUNK, THE INTERIOR ARRANGEMENT OF WHICH MAY BE ALTERED TO SUIT INDIVIDUAL REQUIREMENTS.

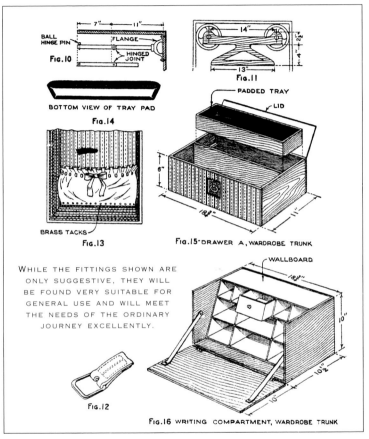

FIG. 10

BALL HINGE PIN — FLANGE — HINGED JOINT

7" — 11"

FIG. 11

14" — 13"

BOTTOM VIEW OF TRAY PAD

FIG. 14

BRASS TACKS —

FIG. 13

PADDED TRAY — LID

FIG. 15—DRAWER A, WARDROBE TRUNK

WHILE THE FITTINGS SHOWN ARE ONLY SUGGESTIVE, THEY WILL BE FOUND VERY SUITABLE FOR GENERAL USE AND WILL MEET THE NEEDS OF THE ORDINARY JOURNEY EXCELLENTLY.

FIG. 12

WALLBOARD

FIG. 16 WRITING COMPARTMENT, WARDROBE TRUNK

and dimension shown in *Fig. 11*. The veneer will not crack or warp as readily as straight-grained wood. About nine hangers will be needed, and these can all be sawn out at one time, if a band saw is available.

To hold the clothes securely in place, the follower, shown in *Fig. 9*, is placed on the arms after all the hangers have been put in position. Two straps are riveted to the bottom of this follower, and pass through buckles that are attached to the back of the trunk. The tongues are removed from the buckles, *Fig. 12,* so that the straps can slide through them and be pulled up tight before the trunk is closed.

The drawers are supported by strips of ½-in. angle iron, riveted to the trunk before the covering is applied. The bottom of one section is equipped with a shoe or laundry bag made of the same material as the lining of the trunk. The bag is hemmed all around and, being considerably fuller than the width of the box, it is gathered at the top and provided with a drawstring or an elastic band, as shown in *Fig. 13,* which keeps the shoes or linen in place.

The top drawer may be fitted with a padded compartment for jewelry or other valuables. The padding is best done by cutting snug-fitting pieces of heavy cardboard, corresponding in size to the sides, ends, and bottom of the compartment. Cotton batting is first laid on the cardboard to the required depth, after which it is covered with muslin, which is glued to the underside of the cardboard, as in *Fig. 14.* A piece of dark-colored velvet or similar material is next applied over the muslin and glued in the same manner. The padded compartment is placed at the rear of the drawer, as shown in *Fig. 15,* so as not to attract attention when the drawer is opened or the trunk left unlocked. Each drawer is fitted with a suitable handle or drawer pull for convenience in opening.

Fig. 16 illustrates the desk compartment, which may be added if desired, although the space it occupies may be devoted to the storage of clothing or other belongings.

When the trunk is packed, the pins in the ends of the horizontal arms supporting the clothes hangers are removed, and the follower is put in place. This is pulled up tightly, the straps buckled, the pins replaced, and the arms turned inward, thus holding all the clothing firmly in place.

The canvas-covered trunk described in Part I is painted before the applications of the slats and metal fittings, with a priming coat of white metal primer. A little lampblack is added to give this coat a grayish tint. The entire outside of the trunk is given a coat of this priming, which is then allowed to dry for at least 24 hours. The body coat, which is usually dark brown or dark olive green, is applied after the priming coat has dried. This paint can be bought ready prepared, but it is best to apply it in the flat and afterward give it a coat of varnish. The flat color is known as color ground in Japan, or gold size; it is thinned down with turpentine to which a few drops of raw linseed oil have been added as a binder. A very neat job can be made by painting the canvas brown or green, and then painting the galvanized iron or fiber fittings black, leaving the brass corners, locks, and clips bright. No paint is placed on the wood slats, which are given two coats of orange shellac. The entire trunk is then given a coat of the best varnish.

If a fiber-coated trunk is to be painted, the priming coat is unnecessary, the color coat being applied directly to the fiber and finished as described above.

— TRUNK BOOKCASE FOR CONVENIENT SHIPMENT —

Mechanics, engineers, and other persons are sometimes engaged in work that keeps them at the same locality only a few months. Those who desire to carry with them a small library will find the trunk bookcase, as shown, convenient. It may be shipped as a trunk and used as a bookcase in one's hotel or dwelling. Articles other than books may be packed in it. The outside dimensions when closed are 31 by

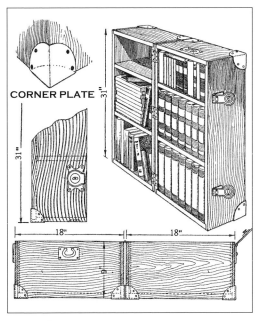

A SMALL LIBRARY MAY BE SHIPPED HANDILY IN THIS BOOKCASE.

18 by 18 in., providing for three shelves. It may be made of ¾-in. pine or whitewood, and stained, or covered with impregnated canvas. The outer corners are reinforced with metal corner plates and suitable hardware is provided.

— THREE-CASTER TRUCK FOR MOVING CRATES AND FURNITURE —

A convenient truck for handling heavy objects, especially in the home where commercial devices for this purpose are not available, is shown in the illustration. It consists of a frame built up of three 1¼- by 2- by 14-in. strips, fixed to a disk, ⅞ by 12 in. in size. Revolving casters are mounted under the ends of the arms, giving great freedom of movement in transporting loads. The three-caster arrangement is better than the use of four casters, because it accommodates itself to irregularities in the floor.

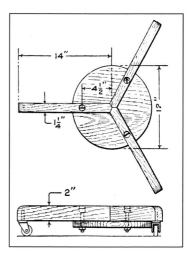

{ CHAPTER 2 }

HANDCRAFTED FURNITURE

—

BOOK IT

— A BOOK HOLDER —

Books having a flexible back are difficult to hold in an upright position when copying from them. A makeshift combination of paperweights and other books is often used, but with unsatisfactory results.

The book holder shown in the sketch will hold such books securely, allow the pages to be turned easily, and conceal the smallest possible portion of each page.

The holder can be cut out of a box corner and fitted with two screw eyes,

FIG.1

FIG.2

which have the part shown by the dotted lines at A *(Fig. 1)* removed. The length of the backboard determines the slope for the book rest.

— COMBINATION BOOKCASE AND WRITING DESK —

In planning a writing desk, much convenience can be added by providing it with a bookcase in which may be stored those reference works most frequently used.

The material required, figuring exact size, is as follows:

- *2 sides,* ⅞ by 16½ by 67 in.
- *1 bottom shelf,* ⅞ by 12 by 32¼ in.
- *1 bottom shelf,* ⅞ by 12 by 32¼ in.
- *1 top shelf,* ⅞ by 9¼ by 32¼ in.
- *1 back,* ⅜ by 40 by 31 in., made of pieces of convenient widths
- *1 desk board,* ⅞ by 16⅛ by 30 in.
- *1 lower bookcase shelf,* ⅞ by 9⅛ by 30 in.
- *1 middle bookcase shelf,* ⅞ by 8⅜ by 30 in.
- *1 desk cover,* ⅞ by 15½ by 30 in.
- *1 upper back rail,* ⅞ by 5 by 30 in.

Bookcase Doors
- 4 stiles, ¾ by 1¼ by 19 in.
- 4 rails, ¾ by 1¼ by 13½ in.
- 2 mullions, ¼ by 1 by 17 ½ in.
- 2 mullions, ¼ by 1 by 13½ in.
- 1 pigeonhole stock, ⅜ by 7 by 72 in.

Main Drawers
- 1 front, ¾ by 4 by 30 in.
- 2 sides, ⅜ by 4 by 15½ in.
- 1 back, ⅜ by 3¼ by 29½ in.
- 1 bottom, ⅜ by 15¼ by 29½ in.
- 2 drawer slides, ⅞ by 1½ by 15 in.
- 1 lower rail, ⅞ by 1½ by 30 in.
- 1 molding strip, ¼ by ⅜ by 120 in.

As the main sides are of considerable width, it would be best to make them of two pieces glued together. In order to obtain a strong and neat joint, have this done by an experienced joiner or in the mill. The back edges should be carefully planed and rabbeted ⅜-in. deep by ½-in. wide for the ⅜-in. thick back. The bottom or foot piece of the sides should be squared up with the back edges, or the completed desk is liable to be winding or warped. The bottom and top shelves or main cross braces should be marked and cut out and, to be in harmony with the shape of the sides, the lower-shelf tenons are made wider than those on the upper shelf. The top shelf should be rabbeted ½ in. deep by ⅜ in. wide, to fit the back boards that are nailed to it. The

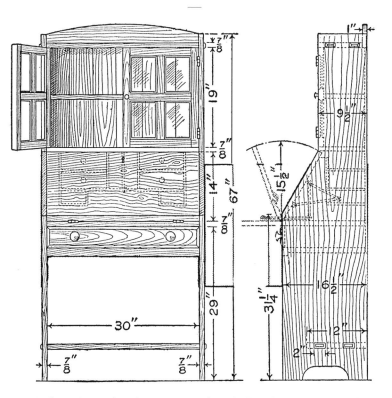

required mortises in the sidepieces are marked from the corresponding tenons of the shelves, and can then be cut out with a chisel. When finished, the four parts constituting the frame should be assembled, and may be held together with blind screws or dowel pins, passed through the tenons.

The desk board and two library shelves should then be fitted and fastened in place with blind screws through the sides, or with cleats from the inside. For a neat, finished appearance, the back boards should be carefully joined, exposing no cracks and fastened with nails driven into the various shelves. The upper rail, resting on the bookcase, and the lower rail, forming part of the drawer support, can then be fitted and secured to the sides with blind screws, either from the outside or diagonally through the

COMBINED BOOKCASE AND WRITING DESK WHICH CAN BE MADE UP IN GOLDEN OAK, MISSION, OR MAHOGANIZED BIRCH AND WILL COMPLEMENT OTHER FURNITURE OF LIKE CONSTRUCTION.

rails from the inside. Drawer slides are fitted in place flush with the top edge of the lower rail and fastened to the sides with screws.

In making the drawer, the usual construction should be followed. The front piece should be rabbeted near its lower edge to fit the drawer bottom and notched ½ in. at each end to fit the sides. The bottom and end pieces fit into grooves cut in the sides. Suitable drawer pulls or knobs should be provided.

For the doors of the bookcase, the best construction would be to tenon the rails into the stiles about ½ in. The glass panel fits in a notch, ½ in. deep and ¼ in. wide, cut around the inside edge of the door. It is held in position with molding strips. In order to give the door an appearance of being divided into four parts, mullions or cross strips are fitted with the rails and stiles, and fastened to them with brads. The doors are attached with butt hinges.

In making the desk door, a specially selected board should be used because the finished appearance of the desk will greatly depend on this. The ends and sides should be perfectly squared, and the lower or hinge end cut beveled corresponding to the edge of the desk board. Butt hinges are used to secure it in position and hinged brackets or chains are provided to support it when open. When closed, it rests against a strip fastened to the lower side of the bottom bookcase shelf.

In arranging the pigeonholes have the inside boards rest on the desk board so the entire arrangement of the drawers and shelves may be withdrawn easily.

When thoroughly sanded and finished to taste, a serviceable, handy, and attractive piece of furniture is obtained.

— BOOKRACK —

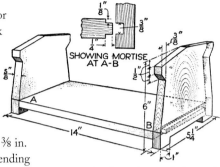

SHOWING MORTISE AT A-B

The material necessary for the illustrated bookrack is as follows: 2 end pieces, ⅝ by 5¼ by 6 in.; 1 shelf, ⅝ by 5¼ by 13 in.

The shelf is cut rectangular, 5¼ in. wide by 14½ in. long. Its two ends should then be provided with tenons ⅜ in. thick by 4¼ in. wide, and extending out ¼ in.

The end pieces, after being cut to the given dimensions, are marked off and cut out for mortises to fit the shelf tenons. In assembling the parts, they are glued in place and clamped with hand screws until the glue has set. Any of the good Mission stains, properly applied, will give a finished appearance to the bookrack.

— A FOLDING BOOKRACK —

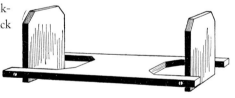

THE ENDS OF THE RACK TURN DOWN, MAKING A STRAIGHT BOARD.

Having need of a bookrack that I could pack away in my trunk and still have room for my clothes, I made one as follows: I procured a piece of pine, ⅝ in. thick by 6 in. wide by 18 in. long, and laid out the plan on one side. Holes were drilled in the edges, ¾ in. from the ends, to receive 1½ in. round-head brass screws. The design for the ends was sawn out with a scroll saw and the edges smoothed up with fine sandpaper, whereupon the surfaces were stained and given a coat of wax. The screws were put in place to make the ends turn on them as on a bearing. In use the ends were turned up.

— A Homemade Book Holder —

A piece of board and four finishing nails furnished me with the necessary materials to construct a book-holding apparatus when in a hurry. Each nail, being driven through the board, could be turned to release and pulled out far enough to accommodate a thicker book. In fact the device was adjustable.

NAILS

NAILS DRIVEN IN A BOARD AND BENT IN THE SHAPE OF SCREW HOOKS TO HOLD A BOOK.

— Easily Constructed Wall Shelves —

All that is necessary to make and support the simple set of wall shelves, shown in the illustration, is lumber for the shelves, four screw eyes, four screw hooks, sufficient picture-frame wire to form the braces and supports, and wood screws for attaching the wire. On the topside of the upper shelf are fastened the four screw eyes, two near the wall edge and the others near the outer edge. To support the upper shelf four screw hooks are used; two placed in the wall and spaced to match the set of screw eyes nearest the

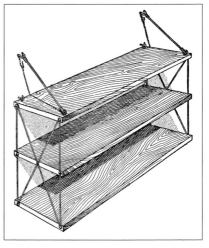

SHELVES FOR BOOKS SUPPORTED WITH PICTURE-FRAME WIRE TO THE WALL.

wall, the others being placed above the first and connected to the outer set of screw eyes with the wire, thereby forming strong inclined supports. The remaining shelves can be hung to suit by the supporting wires, which can be fastened with screws to the end of each shelf.

Seating *and* Storage

— Hall Seat with Storage Compartment —

The illustration represents a simple design for an easily made and substantial hall seat, provided with a compartment for odds and ends. It is advisable to make it of wood to matching its surroundings. The following material is necessary:

- *2 ends, ⅞ by 14 by 28 in.*
- *2 rails, ⅞ by 6 by 38 in.*
- *1 seat board, ⅞ by 14 by 36¼ in.*
- *1 bottom board, ⅞ by 12¼ by 36¼ in.*
- *2 seat cleats, ⅞ by ⅞ by 12¼ in.*
- *2 bottom cleats, ⅞ by ⅞ by 11½ in.*

The two ends, A, are marked to

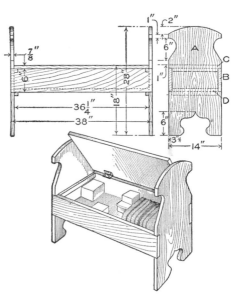

DETAILS SHOWING THE CONSTRUCTION OF A HALL SEAT TO BE MADE IN MISSION STYLE.

the same outline and cut with a coping or scroll saw. If a fine-toothed saw is used, the edges of the boards can be easily smoothed with sandpaper. Otherwise a file is necessary to remove the coarse saw traces. The rails B are cut to size and squared up at the ends, after which they can be placed at the proper places on the ends A, which may then be marked for the notches to receive the rails. In fastening the rails to the end pieces, 2-in. round-head screws can be used. The seat C is attached to the back rail by 2-in. butt hinges. To prevent the seat from sagging in the middle, it is supported on each side by cleats screwed to the end pieces A. If the seat is liable to warp it can be held straight by two cleats screwed underneath. The bottom board D may be held in place by means of screws through the rails, or by resting on cleats screwed to the end pieces. The seat, when assembled and thoroughly sanded, can be finished to suit.

— A Simple Bench —

A bench, substantial enough to hold a machine vise, and of sufficient strength to stand the rough usage incident to this duty, is a necessity around the farm or home workshop. A very simple and cheap bench is shown in the illustration; it consists of a stout barrel, in the center of which is set a heavy post, firmly packed with gravel. A board of the desired dimension is fastened to the post top, and the vise is mounted thereon. A bench of this character does not occupy much space, and is unusually well suited for this purpose.

— Footstool —

The material necessary for the footstool shown in the illustration is as follows:

- *2 end pieces,* 1 by 10 by 15 in.
- *3 cross braces,* 1 by 4 by 12 in.
- *2 end braces,* 7/8 by 4 by 8 in.
- *1 top board,* 1/2 by 10 by 14 in.
- *1 piece of leather,* 11 by 16 in.

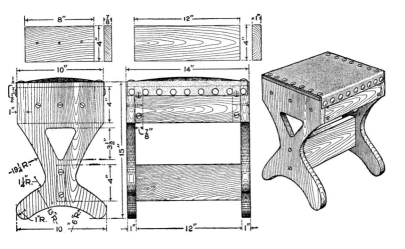

FOOTSTOOL IN MISSION FINISH WITH A LEATHER TOP.

- *Round-head wood screws and nails*

The two end pieces should be marked to a suitable pattern and may be cut out with a scroll or coping saw or, if these are not available, with a keyhole saw. The center opening should first be bored at one end and then cut out with the saw. The three long braces should be accurately squared and finished at the ends; the rigidity of the stool depending on this work. The seat consists of a box form with the open side down. The top is a ½ in. board, 8 in. wide by 12 in. long; the sides are formed by two of the long braces and the ends are the short braces. This box is securely put together with nails and then screwed in position with round-head wood screws so as to be flush with the top edge of the end pieces. The lower brace is secured in place with screws. In putting on the leather top, ½ in. should be turned under at each end and 1½ in. brought down on each side. This will provide sufficient looseness to pad the seat properly. Large round-head brass nails can be used, producing a neat appearance. The stool is then ready for a suitable stain or finish.

— EASILY MADE FOOTREST —

A comfortable and easily made footrest is made from two pieces of ¾-in. board and a pair of metal shelf brackets. The two boards, each 9 by 18 in., are screwed together at right angles to each other, and the shelf brackets are attached underneath to strengthen the construction. All corners of the boards are rounded off smoothly, and the whole is given a coat of paint, varnish, or stain, as desired. The footrest is used as shown in the drawing, and no effort is required to hold it in position.

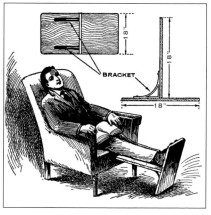

No effort is required to hold this easily made footrest in position. Two boards and a pair of metal shelf brackets are the materials required.

— WOVEN-TOP STOOL —

The material necessary for this stool is as follows:

- *4 legs,* 1¾ by 1¾ by 16 in.
- *4 bottom rails,* ⅞ by 1¾ by 16 in.
- *4 top rails,* ⅞ by 2 by 16½ in.
- *4 diagonal braces,* ⅞ by 1¾ by 6 in.

The legs are mortised so the top rails come level. The upper rails are tenoned on the sides only and beveled at the ends. For the bottom rails, the mortises are made one above the other, the rails being tenoned on all sides. The braces are cut at 45-degree angles on each end and glued into place.

In weaving the top, proceed as follows: Use a wet weaver and wrap one layer over the entire top, the strips being placed close together and tightly wound. Start the second layer at right angles to the first by going under one strip, then over

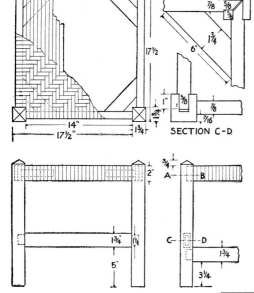

SECTION A-B

SECTION C-D

CONSTRUCTION OF THE FRAME
AND MANNER OF LAYING THE
WEAVERS FOR THE TOP.

preceding; the fifth, start over two, then under and over three, repeatedly. The sixth, and last of the series, begin over three and then continue, by threes, as before. Having finished one series, the remainder of the top should be completed in similar order. Good white shellac makes the best finish for the seat; the stool itself may be finished to suit.

three strips, under three, and so on, by threes, until that strip is finished. Start the second by going under two strips, then over three, under three, and so on, as before. The third strip should start by going under three, then over and under three, etc. Start the fourth by going over one, then under three, and over three, as in the

WEAVING THE TOP OF THE
STOOL BY USING A WET
WEAVER OF REED.

— How to Make a High Stool —

The cast-off handles of four old brooms, three pieces of board cut as shown, and a few screws will make a substantial high stool. The legs should be placed in the holes, as shown at A, and secured with screws turned through the edge of the board into the legs in the holes. The seat B should be fastened over this and the legs braced by the square piece C. Screws are turned through the legs and into the square piece to keep it in position.

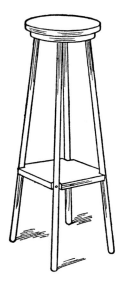

— An Enameled Armchair Made of Wooden Strips —

An armchair suitable for a dressing table was made by a handy women from pine strips. The photo- graph shows the simple and pleasing lines of the construction. Aside from the board seat, only three sizes of

THE SIMPLE CONSTRUCTION OF
THIS NEAT ARMCHAIR MAKES IT
AN ATTRACTIVE JOB FOR THE
AMATEUR CRAFTSMAN.

ones being used at exposed points. The seat is wider from side to side then from front to back. Two coats of white paint and one of white enamel give a good finish.

The dimensions may be varied to suit individual needs. Sizes suggested are: back, 32 in. high and 24 in. wide; side, 26 in. to top of arm and 19 in. wide; seat, 17 in. from floor, 18 in. from front to back, and 20 in. wide between the front supports. The stock is all planed up square to dimensions and sanded smooth. The ends should be cut squarely in a miter box, with a fine-toothed saw, and then sanded smooth, taking care not to round the ends.

wood are used, 2 by 2 in., 1 by 2 in., and ½ by 2 in. The pieces are fastened with screws, round-head brass

— A DETACHABLE CHAIR ARM —

The children in the home as well as others can make good use of a chair arm that may be attached quickly to an ordinary chair. The wide arm is clamped to the back of the chair by means of a metal strip fitted with a thumbscrew, and the upright is fixed to the arm by a hinge, making it convenient to store the device. The lower end of

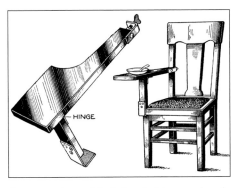

the upright is fitted with a metal angle that fits on the corner of the chair.

DESKS *and* TABLES

— A PARLOR TABLE —

The material required for the parlor table illustrated is as follows:

- *1 tabletop,*
  1 by 26 by 41 in.
- *1 bottom shelf,*
  1 by 15 by 35 in.
- *2 side rails,*
  ¾ by 4 by 33 in.
- *2 end rails,*
  ¾ by 4 by 21 in.
- *2 top cross braces,*
  1 by 4 by 19½ in.
- *4 feet,*
  1¾ by 4 by 4 in.
- *2 posts,* 6 by 6 by 26 in.
- *2 side corner strips,*
  1 by 1 by 31½ in.
- *2 end corner strips,*
  1 by 1 by 17½ in.

DESIGN OF A TABLE THAT WILL APPEAR WELL IN THE DIFFERENT OAK FINISHES AS WELL AS IN MAHOGANY.

The bottom shelf can be made of two pieces of 1-in. material, 8 in. wide, carefully glued together and reinforced on the underside with two crosspieces glued and screwed to it. The foot pieces are secured to the bottom shelf so as to project 1 in. on the ends and side. In case a center support is deemed advisable, another foot piece can be added. But unless the floor is very level, rocking may result. The uprights, or posts, are made from solid 6- by 6-in. lumber, 26 in. long, carefully squared at the ends and tapered to 4 in. square at the upper end. If desired, the posts can be made of boards cut and fastened together to form a hollow tapered post. In either case, they should be set in about 4 in. from each side of the bottom shelf and fastened to it by means of screws. The rail pieces for the tabletop should be cut and fitted with mitered joints at the corner to form a rectangular frame, 21 by 33 in. This is glued to the top and may be toenailed to it. But to provide a more secure bracing, a 1-in. square strip of material is fastened all around the inside edge of the rails, flush with their upper edge. The top is screwed to this. In order to prevent tipping when the top is resting on the 4- by 4-in. ends of the posts, two cross braces are provided. These should be screwed to the outer end sides of the posts and beveled off on their upper edges to fit the tabletop. They should be of such length as to have a tight fit between the side rails, and are fastened to these by means of finishing nails driven from the outside. Gluing and toenailing can also be used to secure the top more firmly to the braces; care should be taken that no nails cut through the tabletop. After thoroughly sanding and smoothing off the table, it can be finished to suit.

— A Folding Wall Desk —

To provide an inexpensive desk in a shop, where space was quite limited, the folding wall desk shown in the sketch was devised. It was cut from a packing box and the hinged lid built up of boards of better quality. To give a good writing surface, a piece of heavy cardboard was fastened to the writing bed with thumb tacks and may be renewed whenever necessary. The inside of the desk was fitted with filing compartments arranged to care for a large variety of shop forms and stationery. An inkwell holder made of a strip of sheet metal was fixed to the end of the desk and the bottle suspended in it, there being space for additional bottles also. The hinged lid is provided with a hasp and padlock.

When not in use, the desk may be tilted upward and locked against the wall with small catches. By using a T-square against the left edge of the writing bed, a convenient drafting table for shop sketching is provided.

The detailed construction for the making of the desk from stock lumber, by boys or amateur workers with tools, may be carried out as follows: Determine upon the size of the proposed desk. Convenient dimensions are 30 in. long, 18 in. wide, 7 in. high at the back, and 4 in. high at the front. Use ⅞-in. softwood; pine and poplar are suitable. Cut and shape all

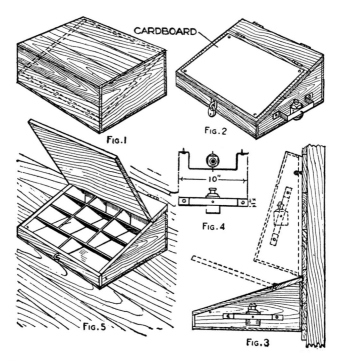

CARDBOARD

FIG. 1

FIG. 2

10"

FIG. 4

FIG. 3

FIG. 5

THE PACKING BOX, FROM WHICH THE DESK WAS MADE, IS SHOWN IN
FIG. 1. THE DOTTED LINES INDICATED WHERE IT WAS CUT TO
GIVE THE SLANTING WRITING SURFACE. THE DEVICE IN ITS
NORMAL POSITION IS SHOWN IN FIG. 2, HOOKED AGAINST
THE WALL IN FIG. 3, AND WITH THE LID RAISED,
SHOWING THE COMPARTMENTS, IN FIG. 5.

the pieces before beginning the assembling of the parts. The wood should be planed smooth and may be sanded lightly when the construction is completed, before applying a finish. A simple arrangement of the pieces so they can be nailed together is that shown in the sketch, which was used in making the box. First shape the pieces for the sides, 5¼ in. wide at the larger end, 2¼ in. wide at the smaller, and 16¼ in. Clamp the boards together or tack them with two wire nails while shaping them so that they will be exactly alike. Make a piece 5½ in. wide and 30 in. long for the back, and one the same length and 2½ in. wide for the front. Nail them to the ends, as shown, permitting the slight excess material to project over the upper edges of the sidepieces. Trim off this extra stock with a plane so that the upper surfaces of the front and back conform to the slant of the sidepieces. Make a strip 4 in. wide for the upper edge of the desk, to which the writing bed is hinged. Cut pieces for the bottom and nail them in place.

Before nailing down the upper hinge strip the interior fittings should be made. Use wood not thicker than ½ in., and fit the pieces into place carefully, nailing them firmly through the outer faces of the desk. A better method is to make the pigeonholes or compartments with a piece off the thin stock on the ends of the partitions so that the compartments are built up as a unit and slid into the desk, no nails being necessary to hold them.

The lid should be made of sound, dry stock and glued up of strips about 3 in. wide to prevent it from warping or twisting easily. If the person making the desk has the necessary skill, it is best to fix a strip 2 in. wide at each end of the writing bed to hold the pieces together and to keep the bed in shape.

The holder for the inkwell is made of a 1-in. strip of metal, bent to the shape shown in Fig. 4 and drilled to fit small screws. A can is supported in the holder and the bottle rests in it.

The desk may be finished by painting it or giving it a coat of shellac and one of varnish, either after it has been stained to match adjoining woodwork or in the natural color.

— ADJUSTABLE AND PIVOTED BED TABLE ATTACHED TO A BEDPOST —

A table arrangement that can be clamped handily to the bedpost and swung out of the way or removed altogether when not in use is a convenience that has a wide use in the home. A device of this kind, which requires no floor support and can be folded compactly for storage, is shown in the illustration. The table proper consists of a ⅞-in. board, of suitable size, the edges of which are banded with metal or thin wooden strips. The board is supported on a frame of iron rod bent to the form indicated in the dotted lines and clamped with 1/16 in. brass clamps. The end of this frame rod is bent at an angle and pivoted in a metal bracket. A cotter pin guards against accidental loosening of the joint. The clamping device is made of 1/4- by 1 1/4 in band iron, and is bent to fit loosely around the bedpost. A brass plate, A, is fitted inside of the main piece B, as shown. A thumbscrew is threaded into the piece B, its point engaging the brass plate, which acts as a guard. In fastening the piece B on the bedpost, the thumbscrew is set and the wing nut also tightened.

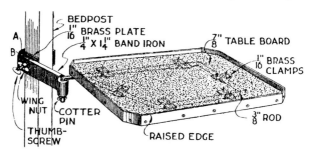

THIS HANDY TABLE CLAMPS ONTO THE BEDPOST AND CAN BE SWUNG ASIDE CONVENIENTLY OR REMOVED ALTOGETHER.

MISSION POSSIBLE

— MISSION CANDLESTICK —

Even though a candlestick is one of the simplest of the smaller household furnishings, it nevertheless can be made a very attractive feature. For the illustrated mission design, a base, 4 by 4 by 7/8 in., should be provided. This is cut, with the grain, for a 1/2 in.-wide groove, 1/4 in. deep, and extending from one side to within 1/2 in. of the opposite side. In this groove is to fit the handle, which is made from a piece of 1/2- by 2 1/4- by 3 3/4-in. stock. It is provided with a finger-grip hole 3/4 by 1 1/4 in. at one end. Its upper edge should be marked off from the

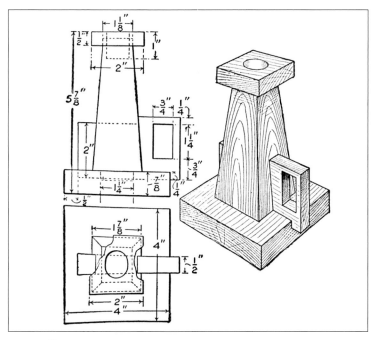

MISSION CANDLESTICK OF PLEASING DESIGN, WHICH WILL
COMPLEMENT OTHER FURNITURE OF THIS CLASS.

center pedestal and fitted to it. The pedestal can be made from stock 1⅞ by 1⅞ by 5 in. A tenon, ¼ in. long by 1¼ in. square, is formed on the lower end. This tenon is to fit a mortise in the center of the base. A slot ½ in. wide is cut centrally in the pedestal and 2 in. above the lower end, to fit the handle. The upper end of the pedestal is cut straight for ¼ in. and squared off to 1⅛ in. This

is to serve as a tenon to fit a corresponding mortise in the ½- by 2-in. square top. The sides of the pedestal are evenly tapered off from the 1⅞-in. square base to the lower end of the 1⅛-in. square tenon, at the top.

The parts, before assembling, should be thoroughly sanded, as considerable difficulty would otherwise be experienced. No nails or screws need be used, because good glue will keep the parts together equally well. When completely assembled, a hole should be drilled through the top and into the pedestal to fit the size of candle to be used. A carefully applied mission stain and varnish will give a proper finish to the candlestick.

How to Make a Mission Library Table

The mission library table, the drawings for which are given here, has been found well proportioned and of pleasing appearance. It can be made of any of the several furniture woods in common use, such as selected quarter-sawn white oak, which will be found exceptionally pleasing in the effect produced.

If a planing mill is at hand, the stock can be ordered in such a way as to avoid the hard work of planing and sanding. Of course, if mill-planed stock cannot be had, the following dimensions must be enlarged slightly to allow for "squaring up the rough."

For the top, order 1 piece 1⅛ in. thick by 34 in. wide by 46 in. long. Have it S-4-S (surfaced on four sides) and "squared" to length. Also, specify that it be sanded on the top surface, the edges, and ends.

For the shelf, order 1 piece ⅞ in. thick by 22 in. wide by 42 in. long, with the four sides surfaced, squared, and sanded the same as for the top.

For the side rails, order 2 pieces ⅞ in. thick by 6 in. wide by 37 in.

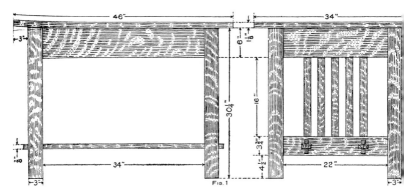

Fig. 1

THIS PICTURE IS DRAWN FROM A PHOTOGRAPH
OF THE MISSION TABLE DESCRIBED IN THIS ARTICLE.

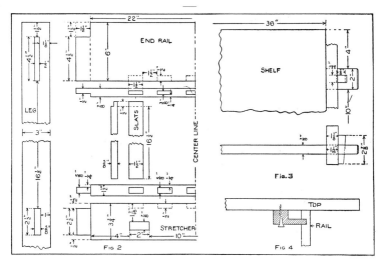

long, S-4-S and sanded on one side. For the end rails, 2 pieces ⅞ in. thick by 6 in. wide by 25 in. long. Other specifications as for the side rails.

For the stretchers, into which the shelf tenons enter, 2 pieces 1⅛ in. thick by 3¾ in. wide by 25 in. long, surfaced and sanded on four sides. For the slats, 10 pieces ⅝ in. thick by 1½ in. wide by 17 in. long, surfaced and sanded on four sides. For the keys, 4 pieces ¾ in. thick by 1¼ in. wide by 2⅞ in. long, S-4-S. This width is a little wide; it will allow the key to be shaped as desired.

The drawings obviate any necessity for going into detail in the description. *Fig. 1* gives an assembly drawing showing the relation of the parts. *Fig. 2* gives the detail of an end. The tenons for the side rails are laid off and the mortises placed in the post, as are those on the end. Care must be taken, however, not to cut any mortises on the post, below, as was done in cutting the stretcher mortises on the ends of the table. A good plan is to set the posts upright in the positions they are to occupy relative to one another and mark with pencil the approximate positions of the mortises. The legs can then be laid flat and the mortises accurately marked out with a fair degree of assurance that they will not be cut where they are not wanted, and that the legs shall "pair" properly when effort is made to assemble the parts of the table.

The table ends should be glued up first and the glue allowed to harden, after which the tenons of the shelf may be inserted and the side rails placed.

There is a reason for the shape, size, and location of each tenon or mortise. For illustration, the shape of the tenon on the top rails permits the surface of the rail to extend almost flush with the surface of the post, at the same time permitting the mortise in the post to be kept away from that surface. Again, the shape of the ends of the slats is such that, though they may vary slightly in length, the fitting of the joints will not be affected. Care must be taken in cutting the mortises to keep their sides clean and sharp and to size.

In making the mortises for the keyed tenons, the length of mortise must be slightly in excess of the width of the tenon—about ⅛ in. of play to each side of each tenon. With a shelf of the width specified for this table, if such allowance is not made so that the tenons may move sideways, the shrinkage would split the shelf.

In cutting across the ends of the shelf between the tenons, leave a hole in the waste so that the turning saw or compass saw can be inserted. Saw within 1/16 of the line, after which this margin may be removed with a chisel and mallet.

Fig. 3 shows two views of the keyed tenon and the key. The mortise for the key is to be placed in the middle of the tenon. It will be noted that this mortise is laid out 1 1/16 in. from the shoulder of the tenon, while the stretcher is 1⅛ in. thick. This is to ensure the key's pulling the shelf tightly against the side of the stretcher.

Keys may be made in a variety of shapes. The one shown is simple and structurally good. Whatever shape is used, the important thing to keep in mind is that the size of the key and the slat of its forward surface where it passes through the tenon must be kept the same as the mortise made for it in the tenon.

The top is to be fastened to the rails by means either of wooden buttons, *Fig. 4,* or small angle irons.

There are a bewildering number of mission finishes upon the market. A very satisfactory one is obtained by applying a coat of brown Flemish water stain, diluted by the addition of water in the proportion of 2 parts water to 1 part stain. When this has dried, sand with Number 00 paper, being careful to "cut through." Next, apply a coat of dark brown filler; the directions for doing this will be found upon the can in which the filler is bought. One coat usually suffices. However, if an especially smooth surface is desired a second coat may be applied in a similar manner.

After the filler has hardened, a very thin coat of shellac is to be put on. When this has dried it should be sanded lightly and then one or two coats of wax should be properly applied and polished. Directions for waxing are printed upon the cans in which the wax is bought. A beautiful dull gloss so much sought by finishers of modern furniture will be the result of carefully following these directions.

— A MISSION BRACKET SHELF —

The shelf consists of six pieces of wood, A, B, C, D, E and F. The material can be of any wood. I have one made of mahogany finished in natural color, and one made of poplar finished black. The dimensions given in the detail drawings are sufficient for anyone to make this bracket. The amount of material required is very small and can be made from scrap or purchased from a mill, surfaced and sanded. The parts are put together with dowel pins.

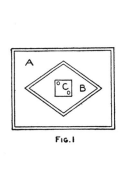

FIG. 1

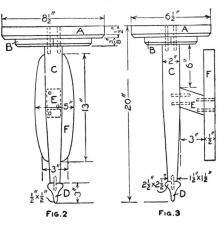

FIG. 2   FIG. 3

DETAILS OF THE WALL BRACKET

EMBELLISHMENTS

— A COLONIAL MIRROR FRAME —

Black walnut or mahogany is the most effective wood to use in making this simple but artistic frame. It requires a very small amount of stock, and what is used should be of a good quality and carefully worked to the given dimensions with keen tools. The stock required for the frame is as follows:

Black walnut or mahogany
- 2 pieces, 27½ in. long by 1 ⅜ in. wide by ¾ in. thick
- 1 piece, 22 in. long by 1⅜ in. wide by ¾ in. thick
- 1 piece, 9¼ in. long by 1⅜ in. wide by ¼ in. thick

White holly
- 1 piece 27½ in. long by 1½ in. wide by 1/16 in. thick

Picture board
- 1 piece, 25 in. long by 9 in. wide by ⅛ in. thick.

The dimensions for the walnut and mahogany pieces are rough sizes, oversize to allow for planing to the dimensions given in the sketch. The white holly may be procured smoothly planed on both sides and of the exact thickness required. The

picture backing may be purchased in almost any store that sells frames. It is usually rough pine and inexpensive.

The first operation is to plane the frame pieces on one side and edge, using great care to ensure both being perfectly straight and the edge square with the face. Gauge for, and plane to, the thickness required, although this need not be exactly ⅝ in. as called for, but if the stock will stand 11/16 in. or ¾ in. Do not take the time to cut it down to ⅝ in. The little cross rail must be exactly ⅛ in. thick, because it is to be let ⅛ in. into the rabbet cut for the glass, which makes it come ⅛ in. back from the face of the frame when it is in place. Plane all of these pieces to the width 1⅛ in.

For cutting the rabbet a plow, or a ¾-in grooving, plane is the best tool to use. But if neither is available, a rabbet plane can be used. Be sure to plane the rabbet square and to the lines gauged for the depth and width.

To groove the pieces for the holly strips a special tool is required. This may be made of a piece of soft sheet

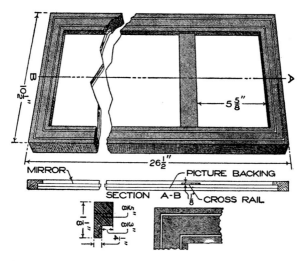

MIRROR

SECTION   A-B

PICTURE BACKING

CROSS RAIL

AN INLAY OF HOLLY MAKES AN EXCEEDINGLY PRETTY FRAME
OF COLONIAL DESIGN FOR A MIRROR.

steel or iron, which must be of a thickness to correspond to that of the holly. A piece 2½ in. long, and of almost any width, will answer the purpose. File one edge of the metal straight, and cut saw teeth in it by filing straight across with a small saw file. Remove the burr raised by the filing by rubbing each side on an oilstone. Drill two holes in it for fastening with screws to a piece of hardwood. The wood serves as a fence, and if properly fastened to the metal, the teeth should cut a groove 1/16 in. deep and 3/16 in. from the edge. The holly strip should fit the groove

tightly so that it can be driven home with light taps of a hammer. It is smart to try the tool on a bit of waste wood first to see if it cuts the groove properly.

The holly is cut into strips ⅛ in. wide with a slitting gauge. An ordinary marking gauge, with the spur filed flat on each side to make a sharp, deep line, will do very well for this work. The gauging is done from both sides of the piece to make the spur cut halfway through from each side. Before the slitting is attempted, one edge of the piece is first straightened. This is readily accomplished with a fore plane, laid on its side and used as a shoot plane. The strip to be planed is laid flat on a piece of ⅞-in. stock with one edge projecting slightly. This raises it above the bench and allows the fore plane to be worked against the projecting edge.

The strips should be applied to the groove to test the fit, and if found to be tight, they must be tapered slightly by filing or scraping the sides. If the fit is good, hot glue may be run into the grooves with a sharp stick, and the strips driven into place. They will project above the surface slightly, but no attempt should be made to plane them off flush until the glue has become thoroughly hardened. Then use a sharp plane and finish with a scraper and No. 00 sandpaper.

The miters are cut in a miter box or planed to the exact 45-degree angle on a miter shoot board. Before gluing the corners, the recesses are cut for the cross rail, but it must not be put in place until the corners of the frame have been fastened and the glue given time to dry.

The frame may be given either a dull or bright finish. The dull finish gives a rich appearance and is very easy to apply. Give the completed frame one coat of white shellac. When it is dry, rub the surface with very fine sandpaper until is has a smooth finish. Finish with any of the prepared waxes, being careful to follow the directions furnished.

Before putting the board back of the mirror, be sure to place two or three sheets of clean paper on the silvered surface. The picture board is fastened with glazier's points or with small bung-head wire nails. The back is finished by gluing a sheet of heavy wrapping paper to the edges of the frame. If the wrapping paper is moistened with a damp cloth before it is applied, it will dry out smooth and tightly drawn over the back.

— A Jardinière Pedestal —

The pedestal may be made of any close-grained wood, such as basswood or maple, if the stain is to be walnut or mahogany, but it can also be constructed of quarter-sawn oak and finished in a waxed mission or varnished surface. The material required is as follows:

- *1 top*, 12 by 12 by ⅞ in, S-2-S
- *2 caps*, 6 by 6 by ⅞ in., S-2-S

- *1 upright*, 18 by 4 by 4 in., S-4-S
- *1 base*, 8 by 8 by ⅞ in., S-2-S.

The top is centered and a circle, 11½ in. in diameter, is drawn upon it and sawn out. The caps are also centered, and circles drawn upon them, 5½ in. and 3½ in. in diameter. Saw them out on the larger circles and center them in a wood lathe, and turn out the wood in the smaller circles to a depth of ½ in. The upright is then centered in the lathe and turned to 3½ in. in diameter for its full length.

The base and foot pieces are cut out as shown, fitted together, and fastened with screws from the underside. One of the caps is mounted in the center on the base and the other cap in the center on the underside of the top. The upright is then placed in the turned-out parts of the caps and either glued or fastened with screws.

If lightwood is used, the finish can be walnut or mahogany. A very pretty finish can be worked out in pyrography, if one is familiar with that work.

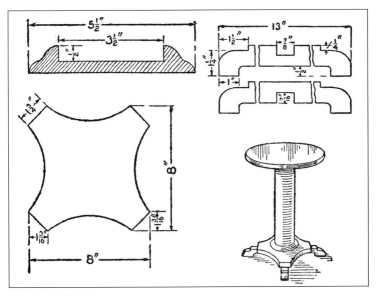

THE PEDESTAL CAN BE MADE OF A WOOD SUITABLE FOR FINISHING TO MATCH OTHER FURNITURE.

— A Turntable Stand
for Potted Flowers —

Potted flowers, if kept in the house, tend to grow toward the light. From time to time the pot should be turned. The turntable stand shown in the sketch was designed to do this more readily. It is made up of a low, four-legged taboret upon which a 12-in. disk of 1-in. wood is fixed with a screw. A thin wooden washer, sanded and shellacked, ensures easy turning. Rectangular boxes or circular jars look equally good upon the stand, the beauty of which depends much upon its workmanship and finish.

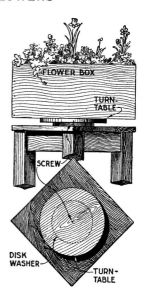

— Stand for a Test-tube
Flower Vase —

A test-tube vase, containing a single blossom, adds color and a certain individual touch to the businessman's desk, or it may be used with effectiveness in the home. A simple wooden stand, finished to harmonize with the surroundings, may be made easily and affords a support and protection for the test tube. The sketch shows a small stand of this type, made of oak, in the straight-line mission style. It may be adapted to other woods and to various designs in straight or curved lines.

The base is 2½ in. square and rests on two cross strips, 1 in. wide. All the material may be about ¼ in. thick, but it is desirable to have the base and cap pieces of thicker wood. The uprights may be of ⅛ to ¼ in.

wood, and are notched together as shown. They are 1 in. wide and 6¼ in. long, a portion being cut to receive the test tube. The cap is 1½ in. square, and its edges are chamfered slightly, as are those on the upper edge of the base. The pieces are fitted together with small brads

used as hidden dowels and the joints are glued. Brads may be used to nail the pieces together, and they should be sunk into the wood, the resulting holes filled carefully. The stand should be stained a dark color or left natural and given a coat of shellac or varnish.

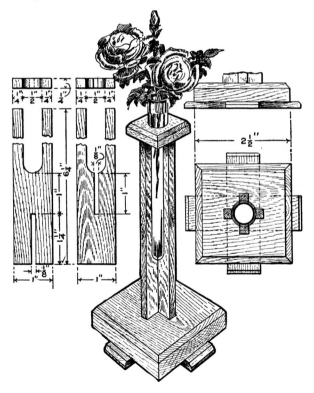

THE STAND PROVIDES A SUPPORT AND PROTECTION FOR THE TEST-TUBE VASE ON THE OFFICE DESK OR IN THE HOME.

— TURN-DOWN SHELF FOR A SMALL SPACE —

The average amateur photographer does not have very much space in which to do his work. The kitchen is the room ordinarily used for finishing the photographs. In many instances there will not be space enough for any extra tables, and so a temporary place is prepared from boxes or a chair on which to place the trays and chemicals. Should there be space enough on one of the walls, a shelf can be made to hang down out of the way when not in use. A shelf constructed on this order may be of any length to suit the space or of such a length for the purpose intended. A heavy piece of wood about 1½ in. thick and 4 to 6 in. wide is first fastened to the wall at the proper height with nails, or much better, large screws.

The shelf is cut and planed

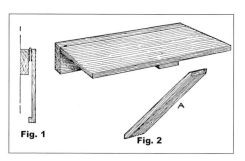

Fig. 1

Fig. 2

TURN-DOWN SHELF.

smooth from a board 12 in. wide and about 1 in. thick. This board is fastened to the piece on the wall with two hinges, as shown in *Fig. 1*. A small cleat is nailed to the outer and under edges of the board and in the middle, as shown. This is used to place a support under the outer edge of the shelf. The support A, *Fig. 2*, should be long enough to extend diagonally to the floor or top of the baseboard from the inner edge of the cleat when the shelf is up in its proper place.

{ CHAPTER 3 }

IN *the* GARDEN

—

SMALL GARDEN PROJECTS

— DEVICE FOR PACKING EARTH IN
TRANSPLANTING —

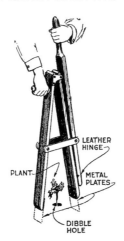

When tomato or cabbage plants are to be set out in considerable numbers, the simple implement shown here makes stooping over to press the dirt about the plants unnecessary. After a row of plants has been set in dibble holes and watered, the soil can be packed about their roots quickly while one is standing upright. The jaws of the device are activated by means of the hinged lever.

LEATHER HINGE

PLANT

METAL PLATES

DIBBLE HOLE

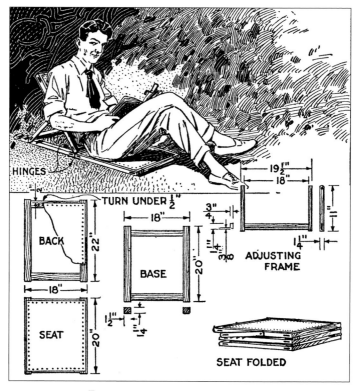

HINGES

TURN UNDER ½"

BACK

18"

22

SEAT

20"

18"

BASE

20"

1½"
¼

19½"
18"

ADJUSTING
FRAME

1¼"

SEAT FOLDED

THIS SEAT IS USEFUL OUT OF DOORS
AND ALSO FOR SPECIAL PURPOSES INDOORS.

— A FOLDING GROUND SEAT WITH BACKREST —

Those who enjoy sitting or lying upon the grass while reading will find the device shown in the illustration convenient and comfortable. With this, one may enjoy the coolness of the ground without

harm to the person or clothing. The adjustable backrest supports the body in various positions. The device is light, compact, and readily transported. It is useful also in the home and elsewhere. By placing it across the bed, or on a bunk, a good substitute for an extra chair is provided. The seat proper may be folded under and the backrest used as a prop for reading in bed.

Oak is a suitable wood, and other common woods may be used. First construct, according to the dimensions given, three rectangular frames with mortise-and-tenon joints. Cover the seat and back frames with heavy duck, turning it in ½ in. at the edges. The base is an open frame, provided with adjusting notches spaced 2 in. apart. Next make the adjusting frame, as detailed. Hinge the back and the seat to the base, and fasten the adjusting frame to the back with screws, permitting it to fold for convenient storage, as shown.

— PRACTICAL BRACKET FOR GARDEN HOSE —

Care in the storage of a garden hose will pay the owner in the longer life of it, and the homemade bracket shown in the sketch suggests a convenient method of caring for the hose. A portion of a barrel was sawn off at one of the hoops and reinforced

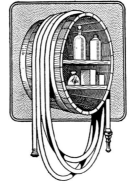

by nailing the hoops and inserting shelves, after which it was nailed to the wall. The hose may be coiled over it in shape to be easily carried to the lawn or garden for use. The shelves provide space for an oilcan for the lawn mower and other accessories.

— PORTABLE HEAD AND BACK REST —

A convenient and readily portable head and back rest, for use on beach or lawn, is made from several hardwood strips and a length of canvas, combined as in the sketch. The long side strips are mortised at the center and the crosspiece is provided with a corresponding tenon at each end, as in the drawing. The lower ends of the sidepieces are pointed. Near the upper end of each crosspiece, a hole is drilled for a piece of rope, which passes through them and through the hem provided at one edge of the canvas strip. The rope is secured to the outside of the strips with knots.

In use, the rest is placed at an angle, as shown. The pointed sidepieces are forced into the ground, the person sitting on the extended canvas. When not in use, the seat may be taken apart and rolled in a small bundle.

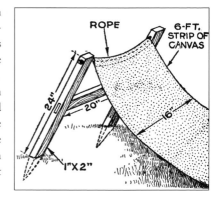

— QUICKLY MADE LAWN TENT —

A very simple way of erecting a lawn tent for the children is to take a large umbrella such as used on delivery wagons and drive the handle into the ground deep enough to hold it solid. Fasten canvas or cotton cloth to the ends of the ribs and let it hang so the bottom edge will touch the ground. Light ropes can be tied to the ends of the ribs and fastened to stakes driven in the ground in a tentlike manner to make the whole more substantial and to stand against a heavy wind.

This makes an exceptionally fine tent, as the umbrella is waterproof. Also, there is more room to stand up in than in a tent that is in the shape of a wigwam.

— A SIMPLE RAIN GAUGE —

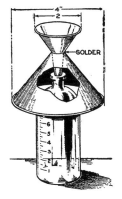

A rain gauge, by which one can ascertain with fair accuracy the precipitation over a certain period, is made from a graduated bottle and two tin funnels. The spout of the larger funnel is removed and that of the smaller one is inserted into the opening and soldered, as indicated. The spout of the smaller funnel is placed in the neck of the bottle. In order to determine the amount of precipitation, the bottle must be graduated in fractions of an inch, and this may be done by marking the bottle with a file, or by making a scale on paper and gluing it to the glass, afterward coating it with varnish. In use, the gauge should be set in the open.

— AN EFFECTIVE CHERRY PICKER —

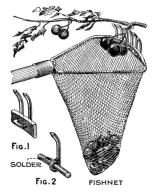

An effective implement can be easily made for picking cherries rapidly with a minimum of climbing. A frame is made of stiff wire or light iron rod, the ends being brought together and forced tightly into a handle of the proper length. On the front of the frame a series of picking fingers or hooks is fastened, about ¼ in. apart, so that the fruit cannot pass between them. *Figs. 1* and *2* illustrate two methods of attaching the hooks. Solder should be used in both cases to make the fingers rigid. The device is completed by attaching a bag of close-woven fish netting to catch the fruit as it is plucked from the tree.

The Birds *and the* Bees

— A Catproof Bird Table —

Our bird table is a source of great enjoyment, particularly since the birds feel secure from cats or other enemies because of the construction of this ornament in our garden. The sketch shows the arrangement of the table braced at the top of a 6-ft. post. Shrubbery surrounds the table and a light evergreen climber clings to the post, yet does not give the cats a good foothold.

Experience has taught us that birds in general prefer breadcrumbs to other varieties of food, and they are also fond of cracked wheat. The linnets like oranges particularly. We cut an orange in two and place the halves on the table. It is amusing to see the birds balance on one side of the orange while they peck at the fruit. Soon the orange peel is almost entirely emptied. We provide a small basin of fresh water on the table, and the birds use it as a drinking cup as well as a bathtub.

— Hollow-log Birdhouses —

Birdhouses that are far more attractive than almost any kind made of boards are easily made by those who delight in watching their feathered friends, using sections of hollow logs.

The type shown in the drawing is made from a length of log mounted on a pole. The piece of log is thoroughly cleaned of all rot and is held in place between the circular bottom platform and the solid top with long bolts, as indicated in the illustration.

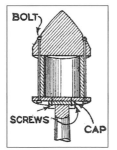

The thickness of the walls will be determined to some extent by the amount of sound wood in the interior of the log, although if this is too thick, it can be cut down by using a carpenter's gouge. Holes are drilled through the sides, and the interior may be divided into several compartments by suitable partitions.

Most pleasing proportions are obtained with a birdhouse of the type shown when the section of log forming the body of the house is about 2 in. longer than its diameter, the height of the cap or top being made a little less than that of the walls. Such a birdhouse can be mounted on the end of a pole. Or it can be mounted by putting a screw eye into the center of the cap and suspending the house from a tree branch.

— CLAY FLOWERPOTS USED FOR BIRDHOUSES —

A novel use of the common garden flowerpot may be made by enlarging the small opening at the bottom with a pair of pliers and carefully breaking the clay away until the opening is large enough to admit a small bird.

Place the pot, bottom side up, on a board 3 in. wider than the diameter of the largest pot used and fasten it to the board with wood cleats and brass screws. Fit the cleats as close as possible to the sides of the pot. One

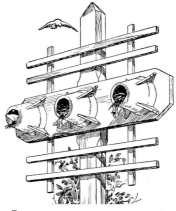

POTS FASTENED TO THE BOARD.

or more pots may be used, as shown on the sketch.

The board on which the pots are fastened is nailed or screwed to a post or pole 10 or 12 ft. in height. The board is braced with lath or similar strips of wood, making a framework suitable for a roost. In designing the roost, the lath can be arranged to make it quite attractive, or the braces may be of twigs and branches of a tree to make a rustic effect.

— Bee Feeder for Winter Use —

The use of a feeder, like that shown in the sketch, makes the feeding of bees in winter convenient. Syrup is fed to the bees from inverted glass jars, the openings of which are covered with muslin. The jars are encased in a packing of chaff in a wooden covering. The wood box is made to fit over the hive as shown in the sketch, and a 2-in. strip is nailed over the joint.

The device is made as follows: Use wood smoothed on both sides, pine, basswood, or other softwood being satisfactory. Make two pieces, ⅞ in. thick, and the same size as the top of the hive. Into one of these cut two round holes, as shown, to fit the necks of the jars. Make two pieces 6 ¾ in. wide for the sides and two for the ends, the length being suited to the hive, the dimensions given in the

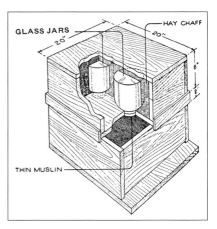

SYRUP IS FED TO THE BEES IN WINTER AND PROTECTED FROM THE COLD BY THE FEEDING JARS ENCLOSED IN THE BOX.

sketch being suggestive only. Make four strips 2 in. wide and long enough to fit the four sides of the box. Nail the pieces of the box together, as shown, nailing the sides over the end pieces and the top over the frame of sides and ends. Pack chaff into the box and, after filling the jars with syrup and covering their openings with muslin, pack the jars into the box so that their openings will be level with the bottom through which the holes have been cut. Fasten the board, with holes for the jars, into place with screws so that it may be removed when it is desired to remove the jars for refilling. Nail the 2-in. strips around the lower edge of the box so as to cover the joint between the box and the hive. The feeder is then fitted into place, the bees feeding from the surface of the muslin. The chaff prevents the syrup from congealing in cold weather and so it is always available for the bees. The use of this simple device will prove economical and practical in keeping bees over the winter, assuring them a good food supply, with little effort on the part of the keeper.

LOCKS, GATES *and* FENCES

— DOUBLE-SWING GATE WITH COMMON HINGES —

Ordinary hinges can be easily bent and so placed on posts that a gate can be swung in either direction. As shown in the illustration, hinges can be made to fit either round or square posts. The gate half of the hinge is fastened in the usual way. The post half is bent and so placed that the hinge pin will be approximately on a line between the centers of the posts. The gate and post should be beveled off to permit a full-open gateway.

POST AND GATE ARE CUT AWAY BACK OF THE HINGE TO ALLOW THE GATE TO SWING BACK.

— SELF-CLOSING GATE —

This gate is suspended from a horizontal bar by chains, and swings freely about a 1-in. gas pipe, placed vertically in the center of the gate. The chains are of the same length, being fastened equidistant from the pipe, the upper ends farther out than the lower. The distance depends on the weight of the gate and the desired force with which it should close. Any of the numerous styles of latches can be used, if desired.

THE GATE WILL SWING IN EITHER DIRECTION AND COME TO A REST WHERE IT CLOSES THE OPENING.

— PORCH GATE FOLDS INTO HOLLOW PILLAR —

The porch is a convenient play spot for the children but must be properly safeguarded to prevent not uncommon accidents and injury by falls. The folding gate shown in the sketch provides a substantial barrier to the head of the stairs and may be quickly folded out of the way. It is hardly noticeable when set in the side of the pillar and does not mar the finish or general effect of the latter.

The gate is made of strips of band iron, although wood may be used. The strips are fastened with bolts or rivets, and the forward end is fitted to the section of the pillar, which forms the cover for the recess in which the gate is housed. The cover is hooked to the opposite pillar when the gate is opened. Any suitable height may be chosen for the gate but, for the purpose suggested, 24 to 30 in. is satisfactory. The device may be adapted to a variety of other uses by providing a box or chamber for the collapsed gate, when no hollow recess is otherwise available.

THE GATE IS FOLDED WHEN NOT IN USE AND IS CONCEALED IN THE HOLLOW PORCH PILLAR.

— LOCKING DEVICE FOR LATCH HOOK ON GATE OR DOOR —

The troublesome opening of a latch hook on a gate or door, permitting intruders to enter or possibly injuring the door in the wind, can be easily overcome by fitting a small catch over the hook, as indicated in the sketch. The U-shaped device is cut from a piece of tin and fastened on the screw over which the hook is set. When locked, it is pushed back over the head of the hook, and cannot be easily jarred out of place.

— PORTABLE SECTIONAL POULTRY FENCING —

Sectional poultry fencing has several advantages over stationary fencing: It can be easily moved, the poultry yard being made larger, smaller, or shifted; and an area may be planted to a crop and gradually included in the yard, furnishing greens for the poultry. Also, the tenant who does not care to put down permanent equipment will find sectional fencing desirable.

Sections are practical to about 18 ft. long,

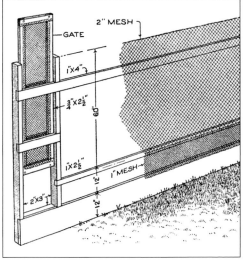

POULTRY FENCING MADE IN PORTABLE SECTIONS HAS SEVERAL ADVANTAGES OVER A STATIONARY BARRIER.

and should be 7 ft. high for the lighter breeds of poultry. If the fencing is to be used for grown stock only, the fine-mesh wire below may be omitted and 2-in. mesh used. Some sections should be fitted with gates,

and the top batten should be set down about 1 ft. so as not to afford footing for the poultry. The sections are lashed together with wire and supported by an occasional post, or guyed to buildings for supports.

— AN ANIMAL-PROOF GATE LATCH —

One of the farmer's worries is the possibility of his stock opening the gates of their pasture

and gaining access to his own or his neighbor's crops. Horses and cattle speedily learn to open gates fitted with an ordinary latch, and when they do this, it usually means retrieving the stock—and paying for the damage.

A simple latch, that is proof against such animal intelligence, consists of a notched wooden bar fitting against a similar notch in one of the rails of the gate. This bar is provided with a handhold and the end slides into a mortise cut into the gatepost. The latch is held in position by guides fastened to each side of the gate.

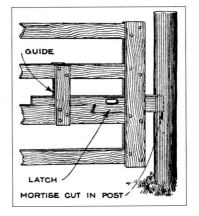

— ❖ ❖ ❖ —

THE GREAT OUTDOORS

—

THE TRICKS *of* CAMPING OUT: PART I

— THE CAMPING OUTFIT —

To enjoy a vacation in the woods thoroughly, it is essential that the camper be provided with the right kind of an outfit. The inexperienced are likely to carry too much rather than too little to the woods—to include many unnecessary luxuries and overlook the more practical necessities. However, camp life does not mean that one must be uncomfortable but rather implies plain and simple living close to nature. An adequate shelter from the sun and rain, a comfortable bed, a good cooking kit, and plenty of wholesome food are the important things to consider. No man or woman requires more, and if unwilling to share the plain fare of the woodsman, the pampered ones should be left at home. The grouchy, complaining individual makes, of all persons, the very worst of camping companions.

The Choice of Tent

There are tents and tents, but for average outings in what may be con-

THE OLD HAND AT THE CAMPING GAME PREFERS TO CUT POLES ON THE CAMPSITE AND SET THEM UP ON THE OUTSIDE FOR THE CAMPFIRE TENT

sidered a permanent camp, the regulation wall, or army, tent is generally used to make a comfortable shelter. It is a splendid utility tent, with generous floor space and plenty of headroom. For the permanent camp, the wall tent is often provided with a fly, which may be set up as an extra covering for the roof or extended over the front to make a kind of porch. An extension may also be purchased to serve the same purpose. The 7-by- 9-ft. wall tent will shelter two persons comfortably, but when the camp is seldom moved, the 9-by-12-ft. size, with a 3½-ft. wall, will afford more room. The regulation 8-oz. duck is heavy enough. Or the same tent may be obtained in tan or dark green khaki, if preferred. In any case the tent should have a sod cloth, from 6 to 12 in. wide, extending around the bottom and sewed to the tent. An extra piece of canvas or floor cloth is desirable, but this as well as the fly are extras, and while convenient, are by no means necessary. The wall tent may be erected with the regular poles, or it may be ordered with tapes along the ridge and erected by suspending between it two trees. The old hand at the camping game rarely uses the shop poles supplied with most tents, but prefers to cut them at the camping site and rig them up on the outside, one slender pole fastened with tapes along the ridge and supported at either end in the crotch formed by setting up two poles, tripod or shear fashion.

The "Baker" style is a popular tent with a large sleeping capacity, yet folds compactly. The 7-by-7-ft. size, with a 2-ft. wall, makes a good comfortable home for two and will shelter three or even four, if

required. The entire front may be opened to the fire by extending it to form an awning, or it may be thrown back over the ridge to form an open-front lean-to shelter.

The "Dan Beard," or campfire tent, is a modification of the Baker style, having a slightly steeper pitch with a smaller front opening. The dimensions are practically the same as the Baker, and it may be pitched

THE WALL TENT MAY BE ERECTED WITH THE REGULAR POLES OR, WHEN ORDERED WITH TAPES ALONG THE RIDGE, IT CAN BE SET UP WITH OUTSIDE TRIPOD OR SHEAR POLES.

THE FORESTER'S TENT IS QUICKLY ERECTED BY USING THREE SMALL SAPLINGS, ONE ALONG THE RIDGE AND ONE ON EACH SIDE OF THE OPENING TO FORM A CROTCH FOR THE RIDGEPOLE.

by suspending it between two trees, by outside poles, or the regular poles may be used.

For traveling light by canoe or pack, a somewhat lighter and less bulky form of tent than the above styles may be chosen, and the woodsman is likely to select the forester's or ranger types. The ranger is a half tent with a 2-ft. wall, and the entire front is open; in fact, this is the same as the Baker tent without the flap. If desired, two half ranger tents with tapes may be purchased and fastened together to form an A, or wedge, tent. This makes a good tent for two on a hike, as each man carries his own half and is assured a good shelter in case one becomes separated from his companion and a tight shelter when the two make camp together.

The forester's tent is another excellent one with good floor space and folding up very compactly. It is a 9-by-9-ft. tent weighing about 5½ lb. when made of standard-weight fabric. It may be had with or without hood, and is quickly erected by using three small saplings, one along the ridge, running from peak to ground, and one on each side of the opening, to form a crotch to support the ridgepole, shear fashion. These tents are not provided with sod or floor cloths, although these may be ordered as extras if wanted.

The canoe, or "protean," tents are good styles for the camper who travels light and is often on the move. The canoe tent has a circular front, while the protean style is made with a square front, and the wall is attached to the back and along the two sides. Both tents are quickly set up, either with a single inside pole or with two poles set shear fashion on the outside. A 9-by-9-ft. canoe or protean tent with a 3-ft. wall makes a comfortable home in the open.

Whatever style of tent is chosen, it is smart to pay a fair price and obtain a good quality of material and workmanship. The cheaper tents are made of heavier material to render them waterproof while the better grades are fashioned from lightweight fabric of close weave and treated with a waterproofing process. Many of the cheaper tents will give fair service but the workmanship is often poor, the grommets are apt to pull out, and the seams rip after a little hard use. All tents should be waterproofed, and each provided with a bag in which to pack it.

THE CANOE OR PROTEAN TENTS ARE GOOD STYLES FOR THE CAMPER WHO TRAVELS LIGHT AND IS OFTEN ON THE MOVE, AND THEY CAN BE QUICKLY SET UP WITH A SINGLE INSIDE POLE.

ning in during a heavy rain. This is a good idea for the permanent camp, but is not often necessary if the soil is sandy or porous or where a sod cloth is used.

It is rarely necessary to carry the regular poles to the campground and they may be omitted except when en route to a treeless region. The wall and other large tents may be pitched in several ways. In some places, the woodsman cuts a straight ridgepole about 3 ft. longer than the tent and two crotched uprights, 1 ft. or more longer than the height of the tent. The ridgepole is passed through the opening in the peak of the tent or fastened to the outside of the ridge with tapes sewn to the cloth. The two upright stakes are then firmly planted in the ground, one at the back and the other in front, and the ridgepole is lifted and dropped into these crotched supports. Set up the four corner guys first to get the tent in shape, then peg down the side guys and slide them taut so that all of them will exert an

THE RANGER'S OR HIKER'S TENT COMES IN HALVES. EACH HALF MAY BE USED INDEPENDENTLY AS A LEAN-TO SHELTER FOR ONE MAN, OR BOTH JOINED TOGETHER TO MAKE ROOM FOR TWO PERSONS.

How to Pitch a Tent

It is, of course, possible to pitch a tent almost anywhere, but for the sake of comfort it is wise to select a site with natural drainage. Many campers dig a shallow trench around the tent to prevent water from run-

even pull on the tent. Another good method for setting up the side guys is to drive four crotched stakes, each about 4 ft. long, somewhere near 3 ft. from each corner of the tent, and drop a fairly heavy pole in the rest so formed, then fasten the guy ropes to this pole. When a sod cloth is provided it is turned under on the inside, the floor cloth is spread over it, and the camp duffel distributed along the walls of the tent to hold it down and prevent insects and rain from entering.

To overcome the disadvantage of placing the poles in the center of the entrance, the uprights may be formed by lashing two poles together near the top to make a crotch and spreading the bottoms to form a pair of shears. Poles may be dispensed with entirely, providing the tent is ordered with tapes for attaching a rope to suspend the ridge of the tent between two trees. In a wooded country this manner of setting a tent is generally preferred.

Where a wall tent is used in a more permanent camp, it is a good plan to order a fly a couple of sizes larger than the tent. This should be set up by using separate poles and rigged some 6 or 8 in. higher than the ridge of the tent, thus affording an air space to temper the heat of the sun and also serving to keep things dry during long heavy rains.

The Camping Kit

The camping kit, including the few handy articles needed in the woods, as well as the bedding and cooking outfit, may be either elaborate or simple, according to the personal experience and ideas of the camper. In making up a list of things you'll need for your kit, remember that only comparatively few articles are really essential for a comfortable vacation in the wilderness. A comfortable bed must be reckoned one of the chief essentials, and one may choose a deluxe couch—the air mattress or sleeping pocket—use an ordinary sleeping bag, or court slumber on one of the several other styles of camp beds. The fold-over combination bed, the stretcher bed, or a common bag made of ticking 6½ ft. long by 2 ft. wide, which is stuffed with bows or leaves, will suffice for the average person. Folding camp cots, chairs, tables, and other so-called camp furniture have their places in the large, fixed camps, but the woodsman can manage to live comfortably without them. A good pair of warm blankets should be included for each person, providing the sleeping bag is not

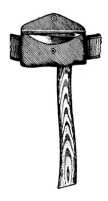

THE BELT AX.

taken along. The regulation army blankets are a good choice reasonable in price, or the blankets used at home may be pressed into service.

A good ax is the woodsman's everyday companion, and a good-weight tool, weighing 3 or 4 lbs., and a smaller one of 1½ lbs., should be carried. When going light, the belt ax should suffice.

The oil lantern is only suited for the fixed camp, since the fuel is difficult to transport unless it is placed into screw-top cans. The "Stonebridge" and other folding candle lanterns are the most convenient for the woods and give sufficient light for camp life.

The aluminum cooking outfits are light in weight, nest compactly, and will stand many years of hard usage. But like other good things, they are somewhat expensive. A good substitute in tin and steel may be obtained for half the price, having the good feature of nesting within each other but, of course, not being quite so light nor so attractive in appearance as the higher-priced outfits. Both the aluminum and steel outfits are put up in canvas carrying bags, and an outfit for two includes a large and a small cooking pot, coffeepot, frying pan with folding or detachable handle, two plates, cups, knives, forks, and spoons. Outfits may be bought for any number of persons, and almost all sporting-goods stores carry them.

FOLDING CANDLE LANTERN

The Camper's Outfit

The personal outfit should include only the most useful articles, and each member of the party should be provided with a dunnage bag of canvas to hold bedding and clothing, and a smaller, or "ditty," bag for keeping other toilet and personal belongings that most everyone finds necessary for everyday comfort. A mending kit, containing a few yards of silk, linen, and a twist; a length of mending cotton; buttons; a few needles and pins, both safety and the common kinds, should not be overlooked. The veteran usually stows away a bit of wire, a length of strong twine, a few nails and tacks, rivets, etc., for emergency use. It is surprising to the novice how handy these several odds and ends are found while in camp. A compact tin box will form a convenient place to keep them will take up little room in the dunnage bag. A medicine case and a first-aid outfit are well worth packing; the smallest cases containing a few of the common remedies will fully meet the camper's needs.

When carrying food by canoe or pack basket, the canoe duffel and provision bags are a great convenience, enabling the camper to carry different foodstuffs in a compact and

FOOD BAGS WITH FRICTION-TOP TINS TO FIT THEM.

sanitary manner. Food bags may be had in different sizes, and friction-top tins may be purchased to fit them. One or more of these liquidproof containers are desirable for transporting lard, butter, pork, ham, and other greasy necessities. The food bags slip into the larger duffel bags, making a very compact bundle for stowing away in a canoe or pack harness.

Carrying List for Camp Outfit

For permanent camps, take the wall tent with fly, although the Baker or campfire styles are also good. When traveling light by canoe, the canoe or protean tent is recommended. When going very light by pack, use the forester's or ranger's tent. Sod and floor cloths and mosquito netting are optional.

The cooking kit may be of aluminum or steel, all items nesting within the largest pot. Include a folding baker, or reflector, with bread board in a canvas bag, a wood saltbox, and a watertight can for matches.

Furniture for the permanent camp consists of a full-sized ax—double-blade or tomahawk style with straight handle—in a protecting case, whetstone, and file for keeping the ax in shape. A shovel and saw will be needed when a cabin is built. A can-

teen may be included, but is not required on most trips. A folding candle lantern is the best for the average trip, but an oil, or acetylene, lantern may be used in a fixed camp. Cots, folding chairs, tables, hangers, etc., are useful only in fixed camps.

A pack basket with a waterproof canvas lid and cover, having straps to go over the shoulders, is a general favorite with woodsmen and guides. Canvas packs or dunnage bags may be used if preferred. There are two sizes of food bags, one holding 5 lbs. and another of 10-lb. capacity, with drawstrings at the top. These are the best for carrying provisions.

THE COOKING KIT MAY BE OF ALUMINUM OR STEEL, ALL NESTING WITHIN THE LARGEST POT, AND MAY INCLUDE A FOLDING BAKER, OR REFLECTOR, WITH BREAD BOARD IN CANVAS BAG, A WOOD SALTBOX, AND A WATERTIGHT CAN FOR MATCHES.

A PACK BASKET WITH A WATER-
PROOF CANVAS LID AND COVER.

Pack harness, with a tumpline to go across the forehead, is needed when the outfit must be carried on portages, etc. This may be omitted when pack baskets are used. Packing cases of fiber may be used for shipping the outfit to the camping ground, but ordinary trunks, or wood boxes, will answer as well.

The Personal Outfit

An old ordinary suit that is not worn too thin is sufficient. Corduroy is too heavy for the summer and too cold for winter, and canvas is too stiff and noisy for the woods. Cotton khaki is excellent for the summer and all-wool khaki, or mackinaw coat and trousers are comfortable for winter. Wool is the best material for undergarments in all seasons. Two sets of garments will be sufficient, as the washing is done at night. Be sure the garments are large enough to allow for shrinkage. Lightweight cashmere is the best material for socks during the summer; use a heavier weight for the winter. Three pairs of ordinary-weight and one pair of heavyweight socks will be sufficient. A medium-weight gray flannel overshirt, with breast pockets having button flaps, is the woodsman's choice. On short and light trips one shirt will do. A lightweight, all-wool gray or brown sweater is a good thing to carry along. It is easily wetted through and a famous briar catcher, yet most woodsmen carry one.

The regulation army poncho is more suited to the woods than a rubber coat or oilskins. The larger-size poncho is more bulky to pack, but may be used as a shelter by rigging it up with poles, lean-to fashion. A poncho makes a good ground blanket also.

A medium wide-brimmed hat, in gray or brown, is better than a cap. A gray, or brown, silk handkerchief should be included to wear around the neck to protect it from the sun and cold. Only a few novices will carry one, but not so with the regular woodsman. The moccasin is the only suitable footwear for the woods. The "puckaway," with extra sole, is known to most woodsmen. A pair of larrigans—ankle-high moccasins with single soles—is suitable to wear about the camp.

Each member of the party carries a pair of woolen blankets. Army blankets in tan color are serviceable and inexpensive.

A good, tempered knife should be worn at the belt, preferably one without a hilt and having a blade 5 or 6 in. long.

A small leather pouch containing a few common remedies, such as quinine, laxative, etc.; and a small first-aid kit should be included in each camper's personal pack. Also, a small leather pouch containing an assortment of needles, darning cotton, buttons, and a length of heavy silk twist is a handy companion.

A few sheets of paper and as many envelopes, a notebook, pencil, and a few postcards are usually carried, together with an almanac page of the months covering the intended trip.

The compass is by far the most useful instrument in the woods, but any reliable and inexpensive watch may be carried.

THE COMPASS.

Many woodsmen carry a small hatchet at the belt, and on trips when but the few necessities are carried, the belt ax takes the place of the heavier-weight tool. The tomahawk style gives two cutting edges and is therefore the best tool to carry. A leather or other covering case is needed to protect the blades.

A small tin box containing an assortment of rivets, tacks, a bit of string, brass wire, a few nails, a couple of small files, a tool holder with tools, a sheet of sandpaper, a bit of emery cloth, and any other small articles that the sportsman fancies will come in handy may be carried.

THE TRICKS *of* CAMPING OUT: PART II

— COOKING IN THE WOODS —

Cooking in the woods requires more of a knack than equipment, and while a camp stove is good enough in a permanent camp, its weight and bulk make this article of camp furniture unsuited for transportation by canoe. Patent cooking grates are less bulky, but the woods-man can learn to do without them very nicely. However, the important item that few woodsmen care to do without is the folding baker, or reflector. The baker is folded flat and carried in a canvas case, including baking pan and kneading board. The largest size, with an 18-in. square pan, weighs about 5 lb., and the smallest, with an 8-by-12-in. pan in aluminum, only 2 lb. In use, the reflector is placed with the open side close to the fire, and cooking is accomplished evenly and well in any

A COOKING RANGE FASHIONED FROM TWO GREEN LOGS LAID IN
A V-SHAPE WITH A FEW STONES BUILT UP AT THE WIDE END
OVER WHICH A FIRE IS MADE OF HARDWOOD STICKS

A GREEN POLE PLACED IN A FORKED STICK PROVIDES
A POT HANGER FOR A NOONDAY MEAL

kind of weather. Bread, fish, game, or meat is easily and perfectly cooked, and the smaller size is large enough for a party of two or three.

The campfire is one of the charms of the outdoors, and if it is built right and of the best kind of wood, cooking may be done over it as well as over a forest range. Many woodsmen prefer to build a second and smaller fire for cooking, and although I have never found this necessary—excepting in large camps where a considerably quantity of food must be prepared—the camper can suit himself, for experimenting is, after all, a large part of the fun of living in and off the woods.

A satisfactory outdoor cooking range may be fashioned by roughly smoothing the top and bottom sides of two green logs and placing them about 6 in. apart at one end, and about 2 ft. apart at the opposite end.

At the wide end a few stones are built up, and across these, hickory, ash, and other sticks of hardwood are placed. The reflector is placed close to the coals at this end, and the fire is built between the logs, the broiling and frying being done at the narrow-end opening. Woods that burn slowly when green should be used for back logs and end logs; chestnut, red oak, butternut, red maple, and persimmon being best adapted for this purpose.

The hardwoods are best for cooking and heating because they burn more slowly, give out considerable heat, and burn down to a body of glowing coals. Softwoods are quick to catch fire, burn rapidly, and make a hot fire but burn down to dead ashes. Hickory is by far the best firewood of the north, in that it makes a hot fire, is long-burning, and forms a large body of coals that gives an even and intense heat for a considerable length of time. Next to hickory comes chestnut; the basket oaks, ironwood, dogwood, and ash are the woodsman's favorites. Among the woods that are easy to split are the red oak, basket oak, white oak, ash, and white birch. A few woods split more easily when green than after seasoning, and

A LIMB SUPPORTED AT AN ANGLE OVER THE FIRE IS ANOTHER MEANS OF HANGING THE POT.

among them are hickory, dogwood, beech, sugar maple, birch, and elm. The most stubborn woods to split are the elder, blue ash, cherry, sour gum, hemlock, sweet gum, and sycamore. Of the softer woods, the birches make the best fuel; black birch in particular makes a fine campfire and it is one of the few woods that burn well when green. The dry bark of the hemlock makes a quick and hot fire, and white birch takes fire quickly even when moist. Driftwood is good to start a fire with, and dry pine knots—the limb stubs of a dead pine tree—are famous kindling. Green wood will, of course, burn better in winter when the sap is dormant. And trees found on high ground make better fuel than those growing in

moist bottomlands. Hardwoods are more plentiful on high ground, while the softer woods are found in abundance along the margins of streams.

For cooking the noonday meal, a small fire will suffice to boil the pot and furnish the heat sufficient to make a fry. Simply drive a forked stick in the ground and lay a green stick in the fork with the opposite end on the ground with a rock laid on it to keep it down, and hang the pot on the projecting stub left for this purpose. A long stick with projecting stubs, planted in the ground to slant over the fire at an angle, will serve as well. Let the pot hang about 2 ft. from the ground, collect an armful of dry twigs and plenty of larger kindling sticks. Now shave three or four of the larger sticks and leave the shavings on the ends. Stand them up beneath a pot, tripod fashion, and place the smaller sticks around them to build a miniature wigwam. While the pot is boiling, get a couple of bed chunks, or andirons, 4 or 5 in. in diameter, set and level these on each side of the fire, and put the frying pan on them. When the pot has boiled, there will be a nice bed of coals for frying that will not smoke the meal.

When the woodsman makes "one-night stands," he will invariably build the fire and start the kettle boiling while he or a companion stakes the tent. As soon as the meal is prepared, a pot of water is started boiling for dish washing.

For roasting and baking with the reflector, a rather high fire is needed. A few sticks, a yard or more long, resting upright against a back log or rock, will throw the heat forward. When glowing coals are wanted one can take them from the campfire, or split uniform billets of green, or dead, wood about 2 in. thick and pile them in the form of a hollow square, or crib. The fire is built in the center of the crib and more parallel sticks are laid on top until it is a foot or more higher. The crib will act as a chimney, and a roaring fire will result, which upon burning down will give a glowing mass of coals.

Camp cookery implies the preparation of the more simple and nutritious foods, and in making up a list it is wise to include only the more staple foodstuffs, which are known to have these qualities. Personal ideas are certain to differ greatly, but the following list may be depended upon and will serve as a guide.

Provisions List

The items in this list will be sufficient for two persons on an outing of two weeks. Carry in a stout canvas food bag 12 lb. of common wheat flour. The self-raising kind is good but the common flour is better. It is good to bring about 6 lb. of yellow or white cornmeal to be served as a johnnycake, hot, cold, or fried mush. It is fine for rolling a fish in for frying. Rice is very nutritious, easily digested, and easy to cook. It is good when boiled with raisins. When cold, it can be fried in slices. About 3 lb. will be sufficient. Oatmeal is less sustaining than rice but it is good for porridge or sliced when cold and fried. Take along about 3 lb. About 2 lb. of the self-raising buckwheat flour should taken along, as it is the favorite for flapjacks or griddlecakes.

Beans are very nutritious and about 2 lb. of the common baking kind will be required to boil or bake with the salt pork. For soups, take 2 lb. of split peas. They can also be served as a vegetable. Salt pork is a stand-by, and 5 lb. of it is provided and carried in friction-top tins or a greaseproof bag. It should be parboiled before adding to the beans or when fried like bacon. The regulation meat of the wilderness is bacon, and 5 lb. of it is carried in a tin or bag. Carry along 3 lb. of lard in a tin or bag, for bread-making and frying. About 3 lb. of butter are carried in a friction-top tin. For making rice puddings, take along 1 lb. raisins. About 1 lb. of shredded codfish is good for making fish balls. Other small articles, such as ½ lb. of tea, 1 lb. of coffee, 3 lb. of granulated sugar, 1 pt. of molasses, 1 pt. of vinegar, 4 cans of condensed milk, 1 can of milk powder, a good substitute for milk, 1 can egg powder, good for making omelets or can be scrambled, 1 lb. salt, 2 oz. pepper, 1 package each of evaporated potatoes, onions, and fruits, and 3 packages of assorted soup tablets.

This list is by no means complete, but it will suffice for the average person on the average trip, since the occasional addition of a fish or game will help to replenish the stores. When going very light by pack, only the most compact and nutritious foods should be selected. While on short, easy trips the addition of canned goods will supply a greater variety.

— WOODCRAFT —

While shooting, fishing, and camping are chapters in the book of woodcraft, the word is generally defined to mean the knack of using the compass, the map, and in making use of the natural signs of the woods when traveling in the wilderness. If the camper keeps to the beaten paths and does not stray far from the frequently used waterways, he needs no compass, and sufficient knowledge of the ways of the woods may be acquired from the previous articles. But if the camper ventures into an unknown region, the value of more intimate knowledge increases as the distance from civilization lengthens, because it will enable him to keep traveling in the desired direction and prevent the "insane desire to circle," should one discover he has lost the trail.

— The Emergency "Snack" and Kit —

The woodsman well knows that it is an easy matter to stray farther from camp than he intended to when starting out, and that it is a common enough occurrence to lose one's bearings and become temporarily lost. To prepare for this possible emergency and spend a comfortable night away from the camp, he carries in his pocket a little packet of useful articles and stows away a tiny package containing a small amount of nutritious food. When leaving camp for a day's hunting and fishing, the usual lunch is, of course, included. But in addition to this, the woodsman should carry a couple of soup tablets, a piece of summer sausage, and some tea. Wrap this in oiled silk and pack it in a flat tin box. It will take up very little room in the pocket.

The emergency kit is merely a small leather pouch containing a short fishing line, a few fishing hooks, 1 ft. of surgeon's adhesive plaster, needle and thread, a few safety pins, and a small coil of copper or brass wire. These articles, with a gun and few spare cartridges, or rod, a belt knife, match safe, compass, map, a little money, pipe, and tobacco make up the personal outfit without which few woodsmen care to venture far from camp. In addition to the above, I carry a double-edge lightweight ax or tomahawk in a leather sheath at the belt and a tin cup strung to the back of the belt, where it is out of the way and unnoticed until wanted.

— The Compass —

A small pocket compass affixed to a leather thong should be carried in the breast pocket and fastened to a button of the shirt. An instrument costing $1 will be accurate enough for all purposes. Many of the woodsmen do not use a compass, but even the expert woodsman gets lost sometimes, and it may happen that the sun is obscured by clouds, thus making it more difficult to read the natural signs of the wilderness. The compass is of little value if a person does not know how to use it. It will not tell you in what direction to go, but when the needle is allowed to swing freely on its pivot the blue end always points to magnetic north. True north lies a degree or more to either side. In the west, for instance, the needle will be attracted a trifle to the east, while on the Atlantic coast it will swing a trifle to the west of true north. This

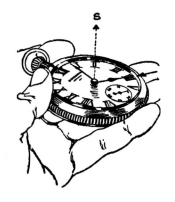

magnetic variation need not be taken into account by the woodsman, who may consider it to point to the true north, for absolute accuracy is not required for this purpose. However, I would advise the sportsman to take the precaution of scratching on the back of the case these letters: B=N, meaning blue equals north. If this is done, the novice will be certain to remember and read the compass right no matter how confused he may become on finding that he has lost his way. The watch may be used as a compass on a clear day by pointing the hour hand to the sun. The point halfway between the hour hand and 12 will be due south.

The compass needle is attracted to iron and steel, therefore keep it away from the gun, hatchet, knife, and other metal articles. Hold the compass level and press the stop, if it has one, so that the needle may swing free. Note some landmark as a prominent tree, high cliff, or other conspicuous object lying in the direction of travel, and go directly to this object. Consult the compass frequently when making a detour or when the landmark passes out of sight. When this mark is reached, select another farther on and continue the travel, always picking out new marks along the line indicated by the compass. When making camp, consult a map, study it, and so gain a good general idea of the surrounding country. When leaving camp, take the bearings from the compass. By so doing a person will know in what direction he is traveling, and when the course is changed, keep the general direction in mind. When climbing a hill or making detours, take a mental note of the change in direction and the bearings will not be lost.

— MAPS —

The maps of the U.S. Geological Survey are drawn to a scale of 2 in. to the mile and cost 5 cents each. On the back of each map are printed the symbols showing the character of the land, the contours, roads, and all important rivers and lakes in the district. For convenience, the map should be pasted on a backing of cotton cloth and then cut up into handy sections. Number the sections from left to right and paste a key to the pieces on the back of one of them.

— NATURAL SIGNS —

When traveling through underbrush the woodsman cannot see far ahead, and so plots a true course by noting the position of the sun. For example, here in the northern hemisphere, the sun rises just south of east and sets somewhere south of due west. Therefore, if a person is going north, he should keep the sun on his back and to the right shoulder in the morning hours, full on the back at noon, and on the back and over the left shoulder throughout the afternoon.

If the day is cloudy, set the point of a knife blade on the thumbnail, twist it around until the full shadow is cast on the nail, thus indicating the position of the sun.

The direction of the wind is apt to change, and for this reason is an unreliable guide. The so-called signs of the woods, such as the tips of evergreen trees pointing north, bark being thicker on the north side of trees, or moss growing thicker on the north side of the trees, are by no means to be depended upon. There is absolutely nothing in these signs. However, every woodsman is aware that the foliage of trees grows somewhat thicker on the south side, and that the branches are rather shorter and more knotty on the north side. But these and other signs are scarcely infallible, and if they were, few tenderfeet would recognize them.

When traveling by night, look for the Big Dipper or Great Bear, as the two end stars are known as the pointers, pointing to the north star.

— MARKING THE TRAIL —

crooked and wind about the trees and rocks, while the logging road is fairly straight and broad. Of course, tote roads lead nowhere in particular, but all logging roads are sure to come to a fork and lead to water. When breaking a new trail, blaze it by taking a single clip from a tree from the side it is approached, and on the opposite side make two blazes, indicating the way from the camp. If this is done a person will always know the way back if the trail

Wh. en traveling over old and blind trails look for the old blaze marks, and if doubtful about them, make new ones by breaking down the brushes every 15 or 20 ft., the bent part pointed in the direction of travel. If a road is encountered, it is easy to tell if it is a tote or logging road because tote roads are is crossed from side to side. This is the rule of the wilderness, but it is not always observed to the letter, for many woodsmen blaze their trail by clipping the trees as they pass them. Be sure to blaze your own trail correctly, and when you come to a place where two roads or trails fork, set a stick to indicate the right direction.

When a person becomes lost in the woods, as every woodsman is sure to do sometimes, sit down and think it over. Many times a person is nearer camp and companions than it is possible to realize, and if a straight direction is taken, a lumber road or a stream will be found that will give one his bearings. Above all, do not become frightened. If the emergency kit and lunch have not been forgotten, a day and night in the woods alone is not a hardship by any means. Avoid wasting energy by rushing madly about and forgetting to blaze the trail that is being made. Bend the points of the brushes down in the direction of travel. Do not shoot the last cartridge to attract attention, and do not shout until hoarse. Sit down and build a fire of green wood, damp leaves, or moss so that it will smoke. Build a second fire a short distance from the first. This is the recognized signal of the one who is lost. The afternoon may be windy, but the wind is certain to die away at the sundown, and then smoke rising from the fires will visible from a considerable distance. When an experienced woodsman gets lost he merely camps on the spot and awaits the next day for picking up the trail.

TENTS *and* SHELTERS

— CAMPS AND HOW TO BUILD THEM —

There are several ways of building a temporary camp from material that is always to be found in the woods. Whether these improvised shelters are intended to last until a permanent camp is built or only as a camp on a short excursion, a great deal of fun can be had in their construction. An evergreen tree with branches growing well down toward the ground furnishes all the material. By chopping the trunk almost through, so that when the tree falls the upper part will still remain attached to the stump, a serviceable shelter can be quickly provided. The cut should be about 5 ft. from the ground. Then the boughs and branches on the underside of the fallen top are chopped away and piled on top. There is room for several persons under this sort of shelter, which offers fairly good protection against any but the most drenching rains.

The wigwam sheds rain better, and where there are no suitable trees that can be cut, it is the easiest camp to make. Three long poles with the tops tied together and the lower ends spaced 8 to 10 ft. apart make the frame of the wigwam. Branches and brush can easily be piled up and woven in and out on these poles so as to shed a very heavy rain.

The brush camp is shaped like an ordinary "A" tent. The ridgepole should be about 8 ft. long and supported by crotched uprights about 6 ft. from the ground. Often the ridgepole can be laid from one small tree to another. Avoid tall trees on account of lightning. Eight or ten long poles are then laid slanting against the ridgepole on each side. Cedar or hemlock boughs make the best thatch for the brush camp. They should be piled up to a thickness of a foot or more over the slanting poles and woven in and out to keep them from slipping. Then a number of poles should be laid over them to prevent them from blowing away.

In woods where there is plenty of bark available in large slabs, the bark lean-to is a quickly constructed and serviceable camp. The ridgepole is set up like that of the brush camp. Three or four other poles are laid slanting to the ground on one side only. The ends of these poles should be pushed into the earth and fastened with crotched sticks. Long poles are then laid crossways of these slanting poles, and the whole can be covered with brush as in the case of the brush camp or with strips of bark laid overlapping each other like shingles. Where bark is used, nails are necessary to hold it in place. Bark may also be used for a wigwam, and it can be held in place by a cord wrapped tightly around the whole structure, running spiralwise from the ground to the peak. In the early summer, the bark can easily be removed from most trees by making two circular cuts around the trunk and joining them with another vertical cut. The bark is easily pried off with an ax, and if laid on the ground under heavy stones, will dry flat. Sheets of bark, 6 ft. long and 2 or 3 ft. wide, are a convenient size for camp construction.

The small boughs and twigs of hemlock, spruce, and cedar, piled 2 or 3 ft. deep and covered with blankets, make the best kind of a camp bed. For a permanent camp, a bunk can be made by laying small poles close together across two larger poles on a

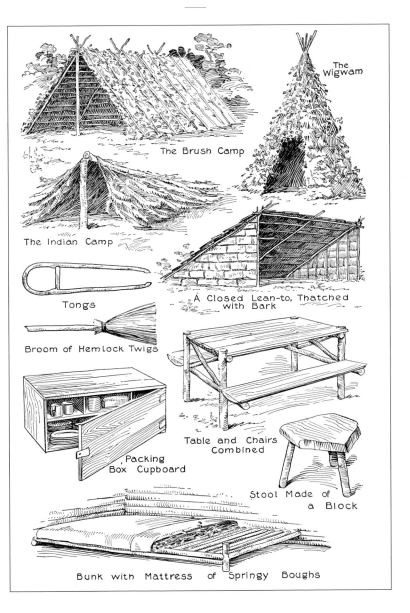

The Wigwam

The Brush Camp

The Indian Camp

A Closed Lean-to, Thatched with Bark

Tongs

Broom of Hemlock Twigs

Packing Box Cupboard

Table and Chairs Combined

Stool Made of a Block

Bunk with Mattress of Springy Boughs

rude framework. Evergreen twigs or dried leaves are piled on this, and a blanket or a piece of canvas stretched across and fastened down to the poles at the sides. A bed like this is soft and springy and will last through an ordinary camping season. A portable cot that does not take up much room in the camp outfit is made of a piece of heavy canvas 40 in. wide and 6 ft. long. Four-inch hems are sewn in each side of the canvas, and when the camp is pitched, a 2-in. pole is run through each hem and the ends of the pole supported on crotch sticks.

Freshwater close at hand and shade for the middle of the day are two points that should always be looked for in a selecting a site for a camp. If the camp is to be occupied for any length of time, useful implements for many purposes can be made out of such material as the woods afford. The simplest way to build a crane for hanging kettles over the campfire is to drive two posts into the ground, each of them a foot or more from one end of the fire space, and split the tops with an ax so that a pole laid from one to the other across the fire will be securely held in the split. Tongs are very useful in camp. A piece of elm or hickory, 4 ft. long and 1½ in. thick, makes a good pair of tongs. For a foot in the middle of the stick, cut half of the thickness away and hold this part over the fire until it can be bent easily to bring the two ends together. Then fasten a crosspiece to hold the ends close together, shape the ends so that anything that drops into the fire can be seized by them, and a serviceable pair of tongs is the result. Any sort of a stick that is easily handled will serve as a poker. Hemlock twigs tied around one end of a stick make an excellent broom. Movable seats for a permanent camp are easily made by splitting a log, boring holes in the rounded side of the slab, and driving pegs into them to serve as legs. A short slab or plank can easily be made into a three-legged stool in the same way.

Campers usually have boxes in which their provisions have been carried. Such a packing box is easily made into a cupboard, and it is not difficult to improvise shelves, hinges, or a lock for the camp larder.

A good way to make a camp table is to set four posts into the ground and nail crosspieces to support slabs cut from chopped wood logs to form a top. Pieces can be nailed onto the legs of the table to hold other slabs to serve as seats, affording accommodation for several persons.

— HOMEMADE SHOULDER-PACK TENT —

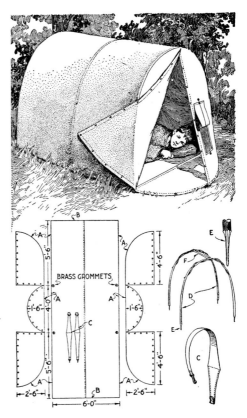

Affter sleeping under various kinds of canvas coverings and not finding any of them entirely to my liking, I made the tent shown in the illustration, which proved quite satisfactory. It is of light weight, easily set up or taken down, and when buttoned closely is practically rain-, wind-, and bug-proof. The cost of materials necessary for making it is slight. I use it not only as a sleeping tent but also as a carryall in packing camping equipment. The canvas is supported by frames made of pliable branches cut in the woods.

The layout for the canvas is shown in the detailed drawings. The sections for the ends are made of three pieces, one for the ground and two, divided vertically, for the end covering. The ground section of the main portion of the tent and the covering are made in one piece, 6 ft.

STAKES, ROPE BRACES, AND SUPPORTING POLES ARE NOT REQUIRED FOR THIS SHOULDER-PACK TENT, THE SUPPORTS BEING CUT AT THE CAMP.

wide, joined at the middle as shown. The adjoining edges A are sewn together and the edges B, which are set at the ridge of the tent, are sewn after the other pieces are joined. Brass grommets are fitted in the canvas, as indicated, and the points of the supporting frames pass through them in driving the supports into the ground. The shoulder straps C are placed so that they are in position when the tent is folded and rolled into a pack. Other equipment may be placed inside of it. The tent supports D are pointed at the ends E and are twisted together at the top. The ridgepole F steadies them and holds the canvas at the middle.

To set up the tent, lay the canvas flat on the ground and place the supports, twisted together, through the grommets. Spring them into the ends of the canvas and insert the ridgepole by springing it between the supports. The canvas is 8-oz. duck, and the fastenings used are snap buttons; buttonholes, buckles, or harness snaps may also be used.

— CARE AND STORAGE OF CAMP EQUIPMENT —

A slovenly sportsman misses much of the joy of the man who takes pride in giving his outfit proper care, not only during its period of use but also during the winter, when occasional overhauling serves to keep one in touch with sports of other seasons. And a real joy it is, each article recalling an experience as one examines it minutely for possible rust spot, scratch, or injury.

Tents usually come in for much abuse, which shortens their life considerably. Cotton duck molds quickly and rots if left rolled up damp. Care should be taken, therefore, to ensure its perfect dryness before storing. Silk and silk-composition tents, being thoroughly waterproof, are almost as dry after a rain or dew as before, so may be packed for moving at any time. But all tents and tarpaulins should be washed and dried carefully after the season's use.

Blankets absorb much moisture and should be shaken and spread out over bushes to dry in the sun at least once a week. In the cold nights of late summer, the increased warmth of blankets after drying is considerable.

Pack straps and ropes should not be left exposed to the weather. They speedily become hard or brittle. Squirrels like the salt they can obtain by chewing the leather, and if left on the ground in a rabbit country the straps are soon cut into bits. Hang the leather goods in the peak of the tent, keep them away from fire, and oil them occasionally.

A canoe should not be left in the water overnight, or at any time when it is not in use. Simply because use makes it wet, a canoe should not be left so, anymore than a gun should left dirty or an ax dull. If on a cruise with a heavy load, pile the stuff on shore at the night camp and turn the canoe over it. If a canoe is permitted to remain in the water unnecessarily, or its inside exposed to rain, it soon becomes water soaked and heavy for portage, besides drying out when exposed to the sun and developing leaks.

Small punctures in the bottom of a canoe may be mended with spruce, tamarack, or pine gum, melted into place with a glowing firebrand, held close, while blowing at the spot to be repaired. Torn rags of canvas-covered bottoms may be glued with the softer gum of new "blazes," gathered with a knife or a stick.

While traveling on shallow streams, the bottom of a board canoe develops a "fur" of rubbed-up shreds. Every night these should be cut short with a sharp-pointed knife to prevent a shred from pulling out and developing into a large splinter. The paddles, and the setting pole, unless shod with iron, become burred at the ends and require trimming down to solid wood.

The track line, if in use, is wet most of the time. Unless dried frequently it becomes rotten. Every tracker knows the grave danger with a rotten line in a rapids.

During the winter the canoe should be scraped and sandpapered, bulges nailed down, permanent repairs made to the covering, and the canoe painted on the exterior and varnished on the interior.

The average fisherman is an enthusiast who needs no urging in the matter of caring for his outfit, and the user of firearms should profit by this example. Even if not a shot has been fired from a gun all day, moisture from the hands or from the dampness in the woods or marshes may cause rust spots or corrode the bore. Rub an oily rag through the bore and over the outside of the gun every evening before laying it aside.

Cleaning rods are safer and more thorough in cleaning the bore than the common mouse string, which may break when drawing a heavy piece of cloth through, causing much difficulty. A wooden rod, preferably of hickory, is best, although the metal rod is stronger for use in small bores. But care must be taken not wear the muzzle unduly. The hunting weapons should be carefully overhauled before storing them and given a coat of oil to protect the metal parts from rust.

— CAMP SHELTER AFFORDS PROTECTION FROM MOSQUITOES —

LITHE BRANCHES CUT IN THE WOODS ARE USED FOR FRAMEWORK, WHICH IS COVERED WITH MOSQUITO NETTING.

When it is undesirable to stay in a camping tent, on warm nights or during the day when a siesta is taken, a mosquito shelter can be made of materials readily available at most camping places. The arrangement, as shown, is made as follows: Procure a number of pliable switches about ¾ in. in diameter and 8 or 10 ft. long—willow or similar growths. Sharpen the butts and force them into the ground in two rows, 3½ ft. apart. Bend the tops together and tie them in arches of the same height, as indicated. Next, tie a ridge binder the entire length. Cover the frame with mosquito netting, providing an entrance at one end. The shelter shown is for one person but may easily be made larger. The fly, supported on a rope between posts or trees, affords shade.

— A Hammock Sleeping Tent —

A COMFORTABLE SLEEPING TENT IS PROVIDED BY THE ARRANGEMENT SHOWN IN THE SKETCH.

Compactness in transportation and general serviceableness are features of the hammock tent shown in the illustration. It is made by sewing a piece of canvas to the sides of an ordinary "dog," or shelter, tent and may be made of a piece of canvas or tarpaulin. The tent is suspended by the ridge from a heavy rope supported on trees or posts. It is kept taut on the sides by tent ropes attached to stakes driven in the ground.

This form of tent is particularly convenient in providing a good sleeping place in very small space. It is free from dampness, and the camper is provided with a comfortable rest free from prowling animals, with the use of a cot.

— A Set of Folding Tent Poles —

Motor tourists and others who realize the necessity of traveling light, and with their tent and other equipment stowed away as compactly as possible, will appreciate the merits of the folding tent poles illustrated.

The poles are made of flat bar iron cut into convenient lengths and assembled by means of bolts and

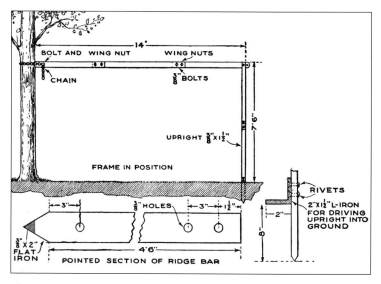

A SET OF SECTIONAL TENT POLES, THE VALUE OF WHICH IS REALIZED
BY MOTOR TOURISTS AND CAMPERS WHO MUST TRAVEL WITH THEIR
EQUIPMENT STOWED IN THE MOST COMPACT MANNER.

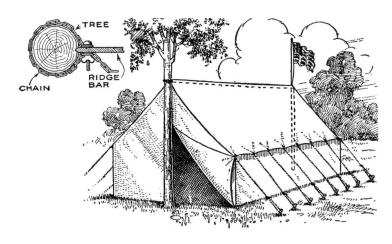

wing nuts. One section of the horizontal bar is sharpened at one end and provided with a suitable length of chain for securing it to a tree or post. The bottom section of the end pole is pointed and provided with an L-shaped piece, about 8 in. from the end, to serve as a stop and assist in driving it into the ground. After the supports have been assembled and erected, the tent is put up, pegged, and guyed in the usual manner. The bars should be given at least one coat of paint to prevent rust.

The same idea can be applied to the construction of a set of wooden poles if it is found undesirable to make use of the metal sections. However, in this case some form of slip or strap joint should be used so that it will not be necessary to make the ends of the sections overlap each other, which would make an unsightly joint in a wooden pole. The entrance to the tent may be made at either end.

— Portable Tent Made from an Umbrella and Paper Muslin —

Picnickers desiring to go in bathing are often handicapped by the lack of a convenient place to change clothes. An umbrella and some paper muslin provide a light portable tent that is practical and inexpensive for such uses. Cut the dark paper muslin into as many 9-ft. lengths as there are sections of the umbrella. Sew these strips together. At each seam tie a string about a yard long and a stout cord 15 ft. long to the handle to hold up the tent. For use, open the umbrella, invert it, and to each rib tie one of the strings. Then tie one end of the cord to the handle of the umbrella and suspend it from a tree or other support, as shown, weighting or tying down the other end.

— COMBINATION TENT AND PACK COVER —

FOR THE SPORTSMAN OR VACATIONIST "ROUGHING IT" IN THE WOODS OR TRAVELING "LIGHT" IN A CANOE, THE TENT SHOWN IN THE DRAWING NOT ONLY PROVIDES A SHELTER AT NIGHT BUT SERVES AS A COVER FOR HIS PERSONAL EFFECTS.

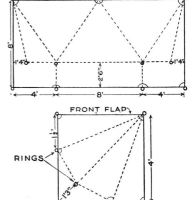

Sportsmen and vacationists "roughing it" and carrying their own beds and boards on their backs, or in a canoe, will appreciate the obvious advantages afforded by a tent that also serves as a cover for the owner's camp effects when not used as a shelter.

There are two methods of making the tent illustrated: One is to use a rectangular tarpaulin, or other suitable material, which is twice as long as the width. Make a strong hem around all edges and sew brass or iron rings, as indicated, at the ends of the dotted lines. The fly, or front flap, is made separately from a square piece of material, the dotted lines showing the folds of the shelter when it is set up. It is unnecessary to do any cutting of material in making a tent of this type.

The alternative method requires more or less cutting of the material, which is cut along the dotted lines as a pattern. The separate pieces are sewn together, with the seam inside. This makes a regulation tent, and by making a few paper models of different sizes it is an easy matter to get the right proportions for a tent of different dimensions from that illustrated. The tent in the drawing is a good average size, and a piece of material 8 ft. wide and 16 ft. long is needed for making it. It is not necessary for the cloth to be in a single piece, but this is an advantage. In using yard-wide goods, the strips are sewn together with heavy waxed thread, the seams running lengthwise of the 16-ft. piece. To reinforce the tent at the corners, where the greatest strain comes when the tent is pegged and the guys in place, it is a good plan to sew patches of cloth on both sides where the rings are sewn on. The tent is amply large for two occupants. When set up it is 8 ft. wide, 6 ft. deep, 7½ ft. high at the front, sloping to a height of 2½ ft. at the back wall.

For a light summer tent, a heavy grade of unbleached cotton cloth is a good choice, although if heavier material is wanted, regulation canvas duck of several weights can be used.

— A Cave House of Boughs and Thatch —

There is a singular romance attaching to cave dwellers, or troglodytes, which never ceases to fascinate a boy. This is possibly because pirates and other favorite characters of fiction hold forth and store their booty in caves. Cave houses are dangerous because the earth is likely to cave in on the workers, but the house described in this article offers an acceptable substitute.

Two forked sticks are securely set into the ground and a ridgepole laid across the forks, as shown. The sides are formed by placing a number of small poles, or saplings, at an angle to the ridgepole. Additional strength is obtained by burying the bottom ends of the poles in the ground. A number of poles are arranged in a semicircle

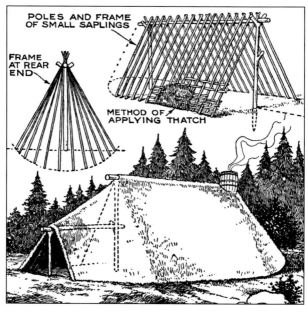

POLES AND FRAME OF SMALL SAPLINGS

FRAME AT REAR END

METHOD OF APPLYING THATCH

LIVING IN CAVES HOLDS A SINGULAR FASCINATION FOR BOYS, BUT IT IS DANGEROUS. THIS CAVE HOUSE CAN BE BUILT ANYWHERE AND IS A PERFECTLY SAFE "ROBBERS'" DEN.

at the rear of the frame, the poles resting in the crotch of the rear upright and ridgepole. The house is completed by covering it with boughs, thatch, bark, or sod. If thatch is used, it is necessary to nail or tie poles horizontally to the frame, or smaller boughs may be woven between the side poles, basket fashion. Begin applying the thatch at the bottom and work toward the top. When the bottom row of thatch has been applied, another row is put on so that the rows overlap until the top is reached. A hole is left at one end in the roof to permit escape of smoke from the fire, which is built directly underneath. If the front upright has a crotch about the center, a small extension may be added to the house, built in the same manner as the house itself, so that the young "pirates" and "smugglers" will have to crawl into their dwelling after the approved fashion.

— Tent for Permanent Camp —

The interior of an ordinary wall tent may be made more comfortable by setting the tent over a wooden wall, 2 or 3 ft. high, and fastening the guy ropes to a raised railing at the sides, as shown in the drawing. The front end of the wall is provided with a doorframe to which a screen door is attached. A short tent pole is attached over the center of the doorframe to support the front end of the ridgepole; a longer pole will be required at the rear to allow for the height the tent is elevated. Additional ventilation may be obtained by fitting smaller doors in the wall, at each side of the entrance. A window-shade roller to which a strip of canvas is tacked may be fitted at the top of the door to prevent rain from blowing in, and for additional privacy. The tent is attached to the wooden wall by hooking the grommets or eyelets on the bottom edge of the canvas over screw hooks.

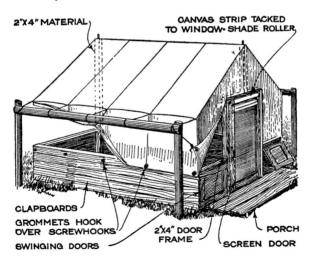

THE INTERIOR OF AN ORDINARY WALL TENT MAY BE GREATLY ENLARGED BY SETTING THE TENT ON TOP OF WOODEN WALLS; A SCREEN DOOR KEEPS OUT INSECTS.

— ERECTING TENTS WITHOUT POLES —

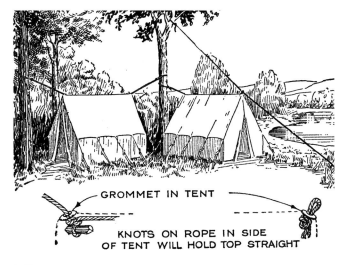

GROMMET IN TENT

KNOTS ON ROPE IN SIDE
OF TENT WILL HOLD TOP STRAIGHT

THE DISADVANTAGES OF TENT POLES ARE ALWAYS APPARENT
TO THE CAMPER, BUT POLES ARE UNNECESSARY
NUISANCES, AS THE DRAWING SHOWS.

Although many a camper has observed and remarked upon the well-known fact that tent poles are a nuisance, it has possibly never occurred to many of them that it is quite possible to erect a tent without poles, using ropes instead. The ridgepole is eliminated by a rope running through the inside of the tent. The ends of this rope are brought through the grommets provided at each end of the tent for the spikes of the end poles, and a knot is tied under each grommet or eyelet, to prevent the tent from sagging in the center. The outer ends of the rope are attached, at the proper height between two trees, as in the drawing. Should there be only one tree available, one end of the tent rope is tied to the tree; the front end of the tent is supported by a rope running from a branch of the tree to a stake that is firmly driven into the ground somewhat in front of the tent and in line with its center.

— Screen Door for Tent —

While homes are provided with screen doors to prevent entrance of insects, the tent dweller unwillingly entertains a variety of pestiferous insect life, and assumes that an enterprising colony of hornets in his tent is the thing to be expected. By equipping the tent with a screen door, the camper is enabled to show a light in his tent after dark without permitting insects to enter. A light wooden frame is made and covered with wired cloth or mosquito netting, as shown in the drawing. A stake is driven at one corner of the tent, to which a corner of the door is attached with screw eyes and a wire link, the upper corner being similarly attached to the end pole.

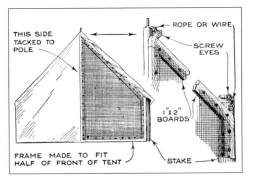

A SCREEN DOOR FOR THE CAMPER'S TENT IS OPENED BY LIFTING, THE UPPER EDGE BEING HINGED.

— How to Make a Bell Tent —

A bell tent is easily made and is nice for lawns, as well as for a boy's camping outfit. The illustrations show a plan of a tent 14 ft. in diameter. To make such a tent, procure unbleached tent duck, which is the very best material for the purpose. Make 22 sections, shaped like *Fig. 3*, each 10 ft. 6 in. long and 2 ft. 2 in. wide at the bottom, tapering in a straight line to a point at the top. These dimensions allow for the laid or lapped seams, which should be double-stitched on a machine. Sew the last seam only for a distance of 4 ft. from the top, leaving the rest for an opening. At the end of this seam stitch on an extra gusset piece so that it will not rip. Fold back the edges of the opening and the bottom edge of the bell-shaped cover and bind it with wide webbing, 3 in. across and having eyelets at the seams for attaching the stay ropes. Near the apex of the cover cut three triangular holes 8 in. long and 4 in wide at the bottom and hem the edges. These are ventilators. Make the tent wall of the same kind of cloth 2 ft. 2 in. high. Bind it at the upper edge with webbing and at the bottom with canvas. Also stitch on

round galvanized iron, 6 in. diameter. Stitch the canvas at the apex around the hoop and along the sides. Make the apex into a hood and line it with stiff canvas. The tent pole is 3 in. in diameter and should be in two sections, with a socket joint and rounded at the top to fit into the apex.

In raising the tent, fasten down the wall by means of loops of stout

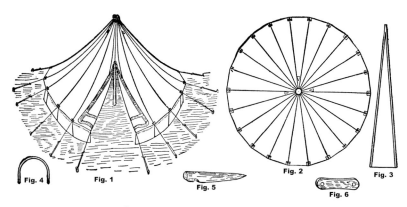

AN INEXPENSIVE HOMEMADE TENT.

coarse canvas 6 in. wide at the bottom, and fill the space between the ground and the wall when the tent is raised with canvas edging. Stitch the upper edge of the wall firmly to the bell cover.

For the top of the tent have the blacksmith make a hoop of ½ in.

line fastened to its lower edge and small pegs driven through them into the ground, *Fig. 4*. Run the stay ropes from the eyelets in the circular cover to stakes *(Fig. 5)* stuck in the ground. Use blocks, as in Fig. 6, on the stay ropes for holding the ends and adjusting the length of the ropes.

PROVISIONS *and* TOOLS

— CAMP WATER BAG —

While out on a camping trip, I devised a way to supply the camp with cool water. A strip of heavy canvas was cut about 2 ft. long and 1 ft. wide, and the edges were sewn up to make a sack 1 ft. square. In one upper corner a large porcelain knob insulator was sewn in for a mouthpiece; the groove around it makes a watertight joint with the cloth. Two metal rings were sewn in the cloth at the top for attaching a strap to carry it. The side and top seams were made as tight as possible.

In use, this sack was filled with as cool water as possible and tightly corked. It was then hung in the shade where a breeze would strike it. The water gradually seeped through the cloth and this, in evaporating, kept the contents cool. This sack also came in handy while fishing or on the road.

— A TABLE BOX FOR CAMPERS —

A very useful combination packing box and camp table may be made from a coffee or other large box. If a box with a three-ply top is available, it makes a neat appearance, but this is not essential. A box 14 in. deep, 20 in. wide, and 29 in. long, outside

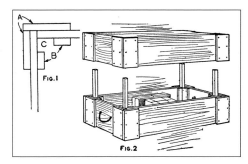

THE STRIPS IN THE CORNERS OF THE BOXES FORM SOCKETS FOR THE LEGS.

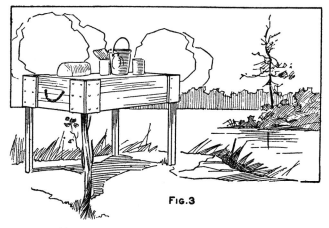

FIG. 3

EACH HALF OF THE BOX INVERTED IS USED
AS A TABLETOP ON THE LEGS.

measurements, is convenient. It will slip under the seat of a spring wagon and is of such a size that a person's knees will pass under it when used as a table.

Saw the box in two on the center-line of the narrow way, making two uncovered boxes of the same size and depth. The corners of each box should be well braced on the outside, as shown in A, *Fig. 1*. The strips B are fastened to the inside of the box to form sockets, C, for the legs. The strips are ½ in. thick, 1¼ in. wide, and as long as the box is deep. Four legs, about 12 in. long and of such size as to fit in the sockets, are used for holding the boxes together in transit. Rope handles are fastened in the ends of each box, and a hook and eye are used to lock them together.

To pack the boxes place one half open side up and insert the legs, as shown in *Fig. 2*. Then fill it and extend the packing to the level of the leg ends; slip the other half of the box on the legs and fasten the two with the hooks. If properly roped, such a box will be taken as baggage. Canvas and other articles that will be removed at once upon arrival in camp, rather than pro-visions, should be packed in this box so that it can be converted into a table with the least possible work.

To make one table or two of the box, remove the packing legs and insert long legs in the sockets of each section. A set of eight legs, 30 in. long, takes up very little space and can be carried diagonally in the bottom of the box. A piece of oilcloth can be wrapped around them and used later as a cover for the table. The legs should fit loosely in the sockets to provide for swelling in damp weather. Ordinarily they can be wedged to make them rigid. The table is shown in *Fig. 3*.

— A Camper's Salt-and-Pepper Holder —

A camper will find a very clever way to carry salt and pepper by using a piece cut from a joint of bamboo. A piece is selected with the joint in the center, and the ends are stoppered with corks.

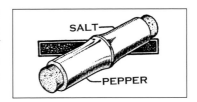

— Kitchen for Hikers —

The kitchen illustrated was constructed with a view to providing all the needs of a commissary department for 36 boys for a period of four days, either on a hike or in a permanent camp. Because it is placed on two wheels, which are removed when the kitchen is in use, it can be moved from one day's camp to another by attaching it to the rear of a horse-drawn wagon by means of a shaft. When the wheels

THE KITCHEN OUTFIT COMPACTED INTO ITS CABINET, MOUNTED ON WHEELS AND UNDER TRANSPORT.

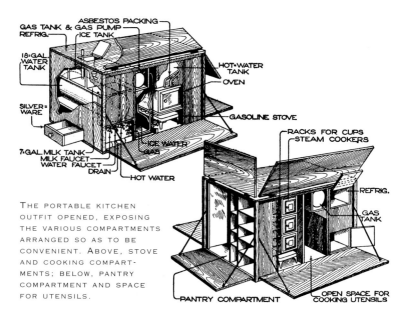

THE PORTABLE KITCHEN OUTFIT OPENED, EXPOSING THE VARIOUS COMPARTMENTS ARRANGED SO AS TO BE CONVENIENT. ABOVE, STOVE AND COOKING COMPART- MENTS; BELOW, PANTRY COMPARTMENT AND SPACE FOR UTENSILS.

are removed the entire outfit rests on legs, which are swung down from the bottom. The sides and one end are opened by swinging one half up and resting it on the top, while the other half swings down to a horizontal position where it is used as a work board, making all parts easily accessible.

The outside dimensions of the kitchen, when closed and in the form of a large box on wheels, are 5 ft. 3 in. long, 3 ft. wide, and 2½ ft. high. The main feature of this entire kitchen is its compactness. At the

front, and extending about 1 ft. back, is a kitchen cabinet where the plates, sugar, salt, flour, etc., are kept in separate compartments. Here also are found the necessary cooking utensils such as bread knives, butcher knives, cleaver, cooking spoons, pancake turner, sieves, large forks, lemon squeezer, etc. Small boxes and packages of baking powder, cocoa, etc., are placed on the shelves of galvanized iron. This entire compartment, as well as all others where food is handled and prepared, is lined with No. 28 gauge galvanized iron.

Which makes sanitation a feature also.

Upon passing around to one side there can be seen a large three-shelved oven, 21 in. wide, which is heated by a gasoline burner. Between the burner and the bottom of the oven are located coils of pipe for heating water, and these coils are connected to a tank of 7-gal. capacity located just above the oven. An air valve and glass gauge are attached to the tank.

The next compartment to the rear is a large storage space, extending all the way through the kitchen, and a 2½-gal. forged-copper gasoline tank occupies a shelf in the upper portion of this space. At the rear end along this side are located nickel-plated faucets that are connected to the hot-water tank mentioned, a 7-gal., white-enameled milk tank above, an 18-gal. cold-water tank, and an ice-water tank, used when distilled-water ice can be secured. These faucets drain into a small sink, which, in turn, drains off through an ordinary sink drain to a hole dug in the ground beneath it. Practically the entire rear end of the kitchen is occupied by the large water tanks, ice box, and milk tanks, with the exception of a small space at the bottom where the silverware is kept in a drawer.

On the other side, and to the rear, two compartments above and below the large water tank form excellent storage space for ham, bacon, sausage, preserves, butter, etc., which need to kept in a cool place. Next in line is the other end of the large storage space, which extends through from the other side. Pans, pails, canned goods, larger packages, etc., are kept in this space.

Immediately to the rear of the kitchen cabinet, on this side, are located compartment shelves where the tin cups are kept. Adjoining this is found a three-compartment steam cooker. By having the cups and plates near this steam cooker, which is also heated by a gas burner, there is less danger from rust, as they are kept thoroughly dried. Wherever there is a gasoline burner the compartment in which it is located is not only lined with galvanized iron, but sheets of nonflammable material are placed on the inner side so that the heat will not ignite the interior packing or the woodwork. The tanks are accessible from the top of the kitchen for filling and cleaning and are packed with ground cork.

The kitchen has shown its efficiency by giving satisfactory service in camps of many members.

— A Canoe Stove —

Limited space and the rocking motion of salmon-fishing boats in a heavy sea on the Pacific coast brought about the construction of the canoe stove shown in the illustration. It is made of a discarded kerosene can whose form is a square. A draft hole is cut in one side of the of rocking can cause the vessel to slide from the stovetop, and as the stove is weighted with sand, it cannot be easily moved from the place where it is set in the canoe.

The use of such a stove in a canoe has the advantage that the stove can be cleaned quickly, as the ashes and

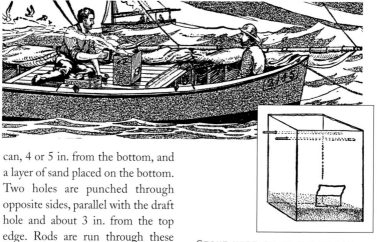

can, 4 or 5 in. from the bottom, and a layer of sand placed on the bottom. Two holes are punched through opposite sides, parallel with the draft hole and about 3 in. from the top edge. Rods are run through these holes to provide a support for the cooking utensil. The smoke from the fire passes out at the corners around the vessel.

The main reason for making this stove in this manner is to hold the cooking vessel within the sides extending above the rods. No amount

STOVE MADE OF AN OLD OILCAN WITH EXTENDING SIDES AND WEIGHTED WITH SAND FOR USE ON A FISHING BOAT HOLDS THE COOKING VESSEL SAFELY IN A SEA

fire can be dumped into the water and the stove used for a storage box. The whole thing may be tossed overboard and a new one made for another trip.

— UTENSIL RACK FOR CAMPFIRE —

A compact, simple device for holding cooking utensils steady over a campfire is shown in the sketch. It may be collapsed into a small bundle and is of light weight, factors that are important in camping equipment.

The device consists of two sections of pipe, A, supported on rods, B, having eyes bent at their upper ends. The

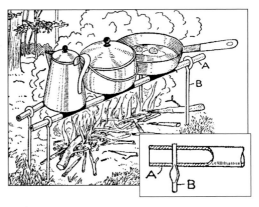

IRON PIPES HELD BY POINTED STEEL RODS PROVIDE A SIMPLE AND SATISFACTORY SUPPORT FOR COOKING UTENSILS IN THE CAMP.

lower end of the supports is pointed and may be driven into the ground so as to spread the pipes more at one end than at the other, thus providing support for large as well as small utensils.

— HANDLING CAMP KETTLES —

Removing a kettle from the campfire demands considerable care and caution if burned fingers are to be avoided and the contents of the kettle prevented from spilling and possibly extinguishing the fire.

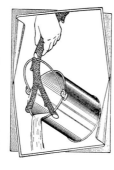

Fortunately, there is usually a forked stick of the right size to be found somewhere nearby, and this is converted into a safe handle by cutting three notches in it, as indicated in the drawing. This prevents the handle and edge of the kettle from slipping. Using this handy little device, it is unnecessary to touch the handle until it is entirely cool, because the kettle can be removed from the fire and the contents poured out in the manner shown.

— HOLDING AX HEADS IN PLACE —

It is not always possible to tell when an ax head is fastened securely enough to prevent the possibility of an accident, especially when using a heavy ax in winter. But by using the simple method shown in the drawing, the ax may be made permanently safe.

A pin is made of $1/16$-in. sheet iron to the pattern shown, and after the head has been wedged in place, the pin is driven in until the shoulder bears against the head. A screw is then driven into the handle through the hole in the pin; this will keep the head from flying off, even if the wedges loosen and drop out.

— CAMP STOVE MADE FROM THREE HINGES —

The novel camp stove shown in the drawing is made from three common strap hinges. The hinges are fastened together at the center ends with a small bolt, and the other ends are sunk into the ground. The bolt should be flatheaded and should be screwed up tightly to make the hinge supports as rigid as possible. This stove may be folded up when not in use, and occupies but little space in the camping equipment.

— QUICKLY MADE DIPPER FOR CAMP USE —

When without a dipper or other means for handling water while camping, recourse may be had to an old trick of hunters and trappers, who make serviceable dippers from the bark of trees. A piece of birch bark, stiff paper, or other material is cut about 8 by 10 in., as indicated. The flat piece is bent longitudinally in the center and then slightly along the diagonal lines. To form the dipper, hold the finger at X and push forward on the material inside the triangle until it assumes the shape shown in the drawing. A split stick is forced over the folds

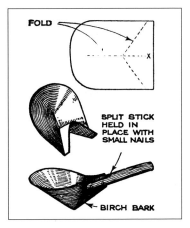

and held in place with small nails or even pins.

— A CAMP PROVISION BOX —

While on a camping and canoeing trip recently, I used a device that added a touch of completeness to our outfit and made camp life really enjoyable. This useful device is none other than a provision, or "grub," box.

From experience, campers know that the first important factor in having a successful trip is compactness of outfit. When undertaking an outing of this kind it is most desirable to have as few bundles to carry as possible, especially if one is going to be on the move part of the time. This device eliminates an unnecessary amount of bundles, thus making the trip easier for the campers, and doubly so if they intend canoeing part of the time. And, apart from its usefulness as a provision container, it affords a general repository for the small articles that mean so much to the camper's welfare.

The box proper may be made in any convenient size, so long as it is

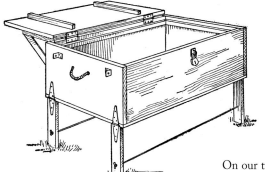

THE PROVISION BOX READY FOR USE IN CAMP, THE COVER TURNED BACK ON THE BRACKETS AND THE LEGS EXTENDED.

brackets, upon which the top rests when open, fold in against the back of the box when not in use. The same may be said of the legs. They fold up alongside the box and are held there by spring brass clips.

On our trips we carry an alcohol stove on which we do all of our cooking. The inner side of the top is covered with a sheet of flameproof material, this side being uppermost when the hinged top is opened and resting on the folding brackets. The stove rested on this material, thus making everything safe. The cover is large enough to do all the cooking on, and the box is so high that the cooking can be attended to without stooping over, which is much more pleasant than squatting before a campfire getting the eyes full of smoke. The legs are hinged to the box in such a manner that all of the weight of the box rests on the legs rather than on the hinges, and are kept from spreading apart by wire turnbuckles. These, being just bolts and wire, may be tucked inside the box when on the move. The top is fitted with unexposed hinges and

not too cumbersome for two people to handle. The dimensions given are for a box I used on a canoe trip of several hundred miles; and from experience I know it to be of a suitable size for canoeists. If the camper is going to have fixed camp and have his luggage hauled, a larger box is much to be preferred. A glance at the figures will show the general proportions of the box. It may be possible, in some cases, to secure a strong packing box near the required dimensions, thus doing away with the trouble of constructing it. The distinguishing features of this box are the hinged cover, the folding legs, and the folding brackets. The

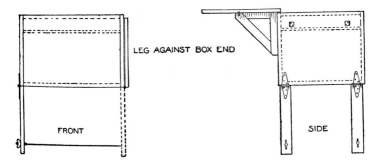

LEG AGAINST BOX END

FRONT

SIDE

THE BRACKETS FOR THE COVER AS WELL AS EACH OF THE FOUR
LEGS FOLD AGAINST THE SIDES OF THE BOX IN SUCH A
MANNER AS TO BE OUT OF THE WAY, MAKING THE BOX
EASY TO CARRY AND STORE AWAY IN A SMALL SPACE.

with a lock to make it a safe place for storing valuables.

In constructing the cover it is wise to make it so that it covers the joints of the sides, thus making the box waterproof from the top, if rain should fall on it. A partition can be made in one end to hold odds and ends. A tray could be installed, like the tray in a trunk, to hold knives, forks, spoons, etc., while the perishable supplies are kept underneath the tray. Give the box two coats of paint and shellac the inside.

The wire braces for the legs are made as follows. Procure four machine bolts, about ¼ in. in diameter and 2 in long—any thread will do—with wing nuts and washers to fit. Saw or file off the heads and drill

a small hole in one end of each bolt, large enough to receive a No. 16 galvanized iron wire. Two inches from the bottom of each leg drill a hole to take the bolt loosely. Determine the exact distance between the outside edges of the legs when the box is resting on them. Make the wire braces 1 in. longer than this distance so that the bolts will protrude through the holes in the legs and allow for putting on the nuts and washers. Screwing up on the nuts draws the wire taut, thus holding the legs firm.

The size of the top determines the dimensions of the folding brackets that support it when open. These brackets may be solid blocks of wood, but a lighter and more serviceable bracket is constructed as follows.

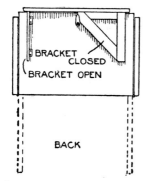

DETAIL OF THE TURNBUCKLE, BUTTON TO HOLD THE BRACKETS, AND THE SPRING CLIP FOR HOLD- ING THE LEGS ON THE SIDE OF THE BOX.

If the top is 20 in. wide and 30 in. long, make the brackets 10 by 13 in. Constructing the brackets so that their combined length is 4 in. shorter than the total length of the box facil- itates their folding against the back of the box when not in use. This point is clearly shown in the drawing. Our brackets were made of ½ in. oak, 1½ in. wide, and the joints halved together. They are hinged to the back of the box as shown, and when folded are held in place by a simple catch. The weight of the lid is sufficient to hold the brackets in place when open, but to make sure they will not creep when in use insert a ¼ in. dowel in the end of each so that it protrudes ¼ in. Drill two holes in the top to the depth of ¼ in. so that when the top rests on the brackets, these holes engage with the dowels. In hinging the brackets to the back see that they are high enough to support the lid at right angles to the box.

The box here shown is made of ⅞ in. white pine throughout. The legs are ⅞ by 2½ by 18 in. They are fas- tened to the box with ordinary strap hinges. When folded up against the box they do not come quite to the top, so the box should be at least 19 in. high for 18-in. legs. About 2 in. from the bottom of the legs drive in a brad so it protrudes ⅛ in., as shown. This brad engages in a hole in the spring brass clip when folded up as shown in the illustration.

If in a fixed camp, it is a good idea to stand the legs in tomato cans partly full of water. This prevents ants from crawling up the legs into the box, but it necessitates placing the wire braces higher on the legs.

Our box cost us nothing but the hardware because we knocked some old packing boxes to pieces and planed up enough boards to make the sides. Of course, the builder need not adhere to these dimensions; he can make the size to suit his require- ments. The finish is a matter of per- sonal taste.

CAMP FURNISHINGS

— A SPRINGY HAMMOCK SUPPORT MADE OF BOUGHS —

In many camping places, balsam branches, or moss, are available for improvising mattresses. Used in connection with a hammock or a bed made on the spot, such a mattress substitute provides a comfort that adds to the joys of camping. A camp hammock or bed of this kind is shown.

Then cut two poles, 2 in. in diameter and 3½ ft. long, and two smaller poles, 3 ft. long. Also cut two forked poles, 4½ ft. long, for the diagonal braces. Place two of the long poles crossing each other as shown, 1 ft. from the ground. Set up the second pair similarly. Fix the crossbars into place, in the crotches, the ends of the

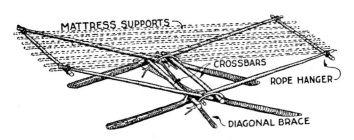

THE CAMP BED CAN BE "KNOCKED DOWN," OR TRANSPORTED CONSIDERABLE DISTANCE AS IT STANDS.

To make it, cut four 6-ft. poles, of nearly the same weight and 1 in. diameter at the small end. These saplings should have a fork about 2½ ft. from the lower ends, as resting places for the crossbars, as shown.

crotch branches being fastened under the opposite crossbar. The end bars are fixed to the crossed poles by means of short rope loops. The mattress is placed on springy poles, 7 ft. long and 2 in. apart, alternating thick

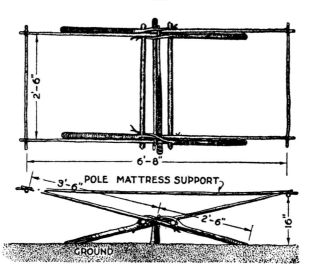

THE POLES ARE SELECTED CAREFULLY AND SET UP WITH STOUT CROSS
BRACES AT THE MIDDLE AND LIGHTER ONES
FOR THE MATTRESS SUPPORT.

and thin ends. The moss is laid over the poles, and the balsam branches spread as thickly. Blankets may be used as cover.

— CAMP LANTERN MADE OF TIN CAN —

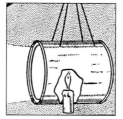

Campers and others who have need of an emergency lantern may be interested in the contrivance shown in the sketch, which was used in preference to other lanterns and made quickly when no light was at hand. It consists of an ordinary tin can, in the side of which a candle has been fixed. A ring of holes was punched through the metal around the candle and wires were placed at the opposite side for a support. The glistening interior of the can reflects the light admirably.

— MAKESHIFT CAMPER'S LANTERN —

While out camping, our only lantern was accidentally smashed beyond repair and it was necessary for us to devise something that would take its place. We took an empty tomato can and cut out the tin 3 in. wide for a length extending from a point 2 in. below the top and to within ¼ in. of the bottom. Each side of the cutout A was bent inward in the shape of a letter S, in which was placed a piece of glass. Four V-shaped notches were cut as shown in B, near to the top of the can, and their points turned outward. A slit was cut in the bottom, shaped as shown in C, and the pointed ends thus formed were turned up to make a place for holding the base of a candle. A larger can was secured and the

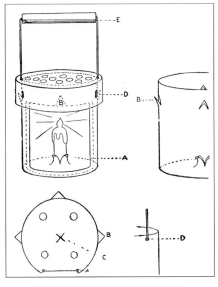

LANTERN MADE OF OLD CANS.

bottom perforated. This was turned over the top of the other can. A heavy wire was run through the perforations and a short piece of broom handle used to make a bail.

— HOW TO MAKE A CAMP STOOL —

The stool, as shown in *Fig. 1*, is made of beech or any suitable wood with a canvas or carpet top. Provide four lengths for the legs, each 1 in. square and 18½ in. long; two lengths, 1⅛ in. square and 11 in. long for the top, and two lengths ¾ in. square, one 8½ and the other 10½ in. long, for the lower rails.

The legs are shaped at the ends to

fit into a ⅝-in. hole bored into the top pieces as shown in *Fig. 2,* the distance between the centers of the holes being 7⅝ in. in one piece and 9⅝ in. in the other. The lower rails are fitted in the same way, using a ½ in. hole bored into each leg 2½ in. up from the lower end.

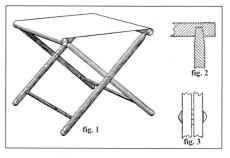

CAMPSTOOL DETAILS

Each pair of legs has a joint for folding and this joint is made by boring a hole in the middle of each leg, inserting a bolt and riveting it over washers with a washer placed between the legs as shown in *Fig. 3.* The entire length of each part is rounded off for the sake of neatness as well as lightness.

About ½ yd. of 11-in. wide material will be required for the seat, and each end of this is nailed securely on the underside of the top pieces. The woodwork may be stained and varnished or plain varnished, and the cloth may be made to have a pleasing effect by stenciling in some neat pattern.

— A HANGER FOR THE CAMP —

A garment or utensil hanger can be easily made for the camp in the following manner: Procure a long leather strap, about 1¼ in. wide, and attach hooks made of wire to it. Each hook should be about 4 in. long and of about No. 9 gauge wire. Bend a ring on one end of the wire and stick the other end through a hole punched in the center of the strap. The ring will prevent the wire from passing through the leather, and it should be bent in such a manner that the hook end of the wire will hang downward when the width of the strap is vertical. These hooks are placed about 2 in. apart for the length of the strap, allowing sufficient ends for a buckle and holes. The strap can be buckled around a tree or tent pole.

— A Bed for a Camp —

A quickly made bed for a camp is shown in the illustration. The corner posts consist of four forked stakes driven into the earth so that the crotches are on a level and about 1 ft. from the ground. Poles are laid in the crotches, lengthwise of the bed, and canvas covering double-lapped over them. If desired, the

CANVAS BED MADE ON TWO POLES LAID IN THE CROTCHES OF FORKED STAKES.

canvas can be stitched along the inside of the poles.

— A Variety of Camp Furnishings —

When on a camping trip, nothing should be carried but the necessities, and the furnishings should be made up from materials found in the woods. A good spring bed can be made up in the following manner: Cut two stringers from small, straight trees, about 4 in. in diameter, and make them about 6 ft. long. All branches are trimmed off smooth, and a trench is dug in the ground for each piece, the trenches being 24 in. apart. Small saplings, about 1 in. in diameter and as straight as can be found, are cut and trimmed of all branches and nailed across the stringers for the springs. Knots, bulges, etc., should

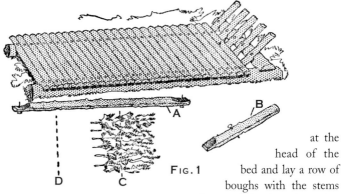

Fig. 1

A CAMP BED MADE OF SAPLINGS WITH SEVERAL LAYERS OF BOUGHS FOR THE MATTRESS.

be turned downward as far as possible. The ends of each piece are flattened, as shown in A, *Fig. 1*, to give it a good seat on the stringers.

A larger sapling is cut, flattened, and nailed at the head of the bed across the stringers, and to it a number of head-stay saplings, B, are nailed. These head-stay pieces are cut about 12 in. long, sharpened on one end, and driven a little way into the ground, after which they are nailed to the head crosspiece.

In the absence of an empty mattress tick and pillow cover that can be filled with straw, boughs of fir may be used. These boughs should not be larger than a match and crooked stems should be turned down. Begin

at the head of the bed and lay a row of boughs with the stems pointed toward the foot. Over this row, and half-lapping it, place another row so that the tops of the boughs lay on the line C, and their stems on the line D. The process is continued until the crosspiece springs are entirely covered, and then another layer is laid in the same manner on top of these, and so on, until a depth of 6 or 8 in. is obtained. This will make a good substitute for a mattress. A pillow can be made by filling a meal bag with boughs or leaves.

A good and serviceable table can be constructed from a few fence boards or boards taken from a packing box. The table and chairs are made in one piece, the construction being clearly shown in *Fig. 2*. The height of the ends should be about 29 in., and the seats about 17 in. from

FIG. 2

FIG. 3

A TABLE MADE OF PACKING-BOX MATERIAL AND
A WASH-BASIN STAND OF THREE STAKES.

from a sapling, into them. The extending ends are supported on legs of the same material. The seat is made of a slab with the rounding side down.

A clothes hanger for the tent ridgepole can be made as shown in *Fig. 5*. The hanger consists of a piece 7 in. long, cut from a 2-in. sapling, nails being driven into its sides for hooks. The upper end is fitted with a rope that is tied over the ridgepole of the tent.

the ground. The other dimensions will be governed by the material at hand and the number of campers.

A wash-basin support can be made of three stakes, cut from saplings and driven into the ground, as shown in *Fig. 3*. The basin is hung by its rim between the ends of the stakes.

Wherever a suitable tree is handy, a seat can be constructed as shown in *Fig. 4*. Bore two 1-in. holes 8 in. apart in the trunk, 15 in. above the ground. Drive two pins, about 12 in. long and cut

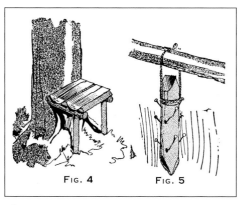

FIG. 4

FIG. 5

A SEAT AGAINST THE TRUNK OF A TREE, AND
A CLOTHES HANGER FOR THE TENT RIDGE-
POLE.

— A Shaving Lamp and Mirror for the Camp —

To make shaving possible in camp at night or with little daylight, a small mirror was provided with an electric flashlight. The mirror was set to swing free in a wooden support. The light was fastened slightly above and behind the mirror, and swings at its base so that it can be tipped upward or downward, throwing the light correspondingly. A piece of wood 1¼ by 3½ in., and as long as

the mirror frame is wide, serves as a base. The arms will hold the mirror far enough in front of the lamp to allow room in which to swing. The body of the lamp is set on a block and held between two wooden pieces into which a band of iron was set near the top. The uprights move in an arc, pivoting at their lower fastening on screws.

Two *for the* Price *of* One

— Combination Camp-Kitchen Cabinet and Table —

The combination camp-kitchen cabinet and table is the result of not being able to take the members of my family on an outing unless they could have some home conveniences on the trip. Perhaps the sketch and description may help solve the same problem for others. The table will accommodate four persons comfortably, and extra compartments may be added if desired. The cabinet, when closed, is strong and compact and is well made with a snug-fitting cover. It is bugproof and the contents will not be injured greatly, even if drenched by rain or a mishap in a craft.

For coffee, tea, sugar, salt, etc., I used small screw-top glass jars. They are set in pocket shelves at both ends. When closed, one can sit on the box or even walk on it if necessary when in the boat. If an armful or two of coarse marsh grass is spread over it, the contents will keep quite cool even when out in the hot sun. When open for use, the metal tabletop F is supported on metal straps, E, which also act as braces and supports for the table leaf, G, on each side of the box. This

THIS OUTFIT PROVIDES ACCOMMODATIONS FOR FOUR PERSONS AND FOLDS COMPACTLY.

affords plenty of table surface, and one can easily get at the contents of the cabinet while cooking or eating. The legs, D, are stored inside of the box when closed for traveling. They are held in place under metal straps when in use and held at their upper ends by the metal plate and blocks, B and C. The bent metal pieces, A, on the ends of the top, spring over the blocks at B and C and form the handles.

— A Chair Swing —

A comfortable porch or lawn swing can be easily and quickly made with a chair as a seat, as follows. Procure some rope of sufficient strength to bear the weight of the person, and fasten one end securely to one of the front legs of the chair and the other end to the same side of the back, as shown in the illustration, allowing enough slack to form a right angle. Another piece of rope of the same length is then attached to the other side of the chair. The supporting ropes are tied

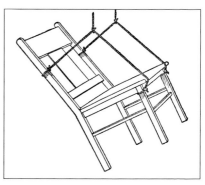

THE ROPES ARE TIED TO THE CHAIR SO THAT IT WILL BE HELD IN RECLINING POSITION.

to these ropes and to the joist or holding piece overhead.

— How to Attach a Sail to a Bicycle —

This attachment was constructed for use on a bicycle to be ridden on the well-packed sands of a beach, but it could be used on a smooth, level road as well. The illustration shows the main frame to consist of two boards, each about 16 ft. long, bent in the shape of a boat, to give plenty of room for turning the front wheel. On this main frame is built up a triangular mast to carry the mainsail and jib, having a combined area of about 40 sq. ft. The frame is

fastened to the bicycle by numerous pieces of rope.

Sailing on a bicycle is very much different from sailing in a boat, because the bicycle leans up against the wind instead of heeling over with it as the boat does. It takes some time to learn the supporting power of the wind, and the angle at which one must ride makes it appear that a fall is almost sure to result. A turn must be made by turning out of the wind, instead of, as in ordinary

BICYCLE SAILING ON A BEACH.

sailing, into it. The boom supporting the bottom of the mainsail is then swung over to the opposite tack, when one is traveling at a good speed.

— SAIL FOR A BOY'S WAGON —

Every boy who loves a boat and has only a wagon can make a combination affair in which he can sail even though there is no water for miles around. One boy accomplished this as shown in the illustration, and the only assistance he had was in making the sails.

The box of the wagon is removed and the boat deck

THE SAIL WAGON WILL TRAVEL AT A GOOD SPEED IN A STIFF BREEZE.

bolted in its place. The deck is 14 in. wide and 5 ft. long. The mast consists of an old rake handle, 6 ft. long; the boom and gaff are broomsticks, and the tiller is connected with wire to the front axle, which gives perfect control of the steering. The sails are made of drilling.

On brick pavement, the sail wagon can easily pull along two other normal wagons with two boys in each, making in all five boys. Of course a good steady wind must be blowing. With two boys it has made a mile in five minutes on pavement.

— MOTORIST'S FOLDING LUNCHBOX AND TABLE —

For the automobile outing, when lunch is taken along, a compact and substantial combination lunchbox and table can be made along the lines of the one illustrated. In use, the top and bottom hinged covers open horizontally. A pivoted block attached inside one end of the box frame helps to stabilize the outfit. The legs are pivoted on a small iron rod and open downward. They are held rigidly vertical by means of wire braces attached to the underside of

A CLEVERLY DESIGNED COMBINATION TABLE AND LUNCHBOX FOR AUTOMOBILE EXCURSIONS.

the cover, the ends of the wires fitting into a hole on the outside edge of each leg. The legs are provided with buttons on the underside so that, when folded up in their slots, the buttons can be turned, locking the legs and forming a continuous cover.

OUTDOOR HELPERS

— A WOODSMAN'S LOG RAFT —

Making a raft for crossing a stream or other small body of water is often a diversion for campers who have the usual supply of camp tools and materials. The woodsman is sometimes confronted with a different situation: He has only a hand ax as his tool equipment, and to construct a fairly safe raft of crude materials becomes necessary in order to pursue his course. Logs are readily available, and he may be fortunate enough to find willow withes, various stringy kinds of bark, or even coarse seaweed. If they are not available, the practical woodsman, particularly of the northern regions, builds a raft of logs pinned together firmly with poles and pointed wooden spikes cut on the spot. The method, as shown in the illustration, is simple and interesting. It may be of service in the woods even when other methods of binding the logs into a raft are

possible, and as a practical test of woodcraft for the amateur or boy camper it is of interest. The sketch shows the completed raft, bound together by wooden pins notched into the poles, and the inset details show the manner in which the poles are clamped by the crossed pins.

This method of construction may be applied to a variety of rafts for carrying small or large loads. In selecting the material for the raft, several points must be considered. Dry logs are preferable to wet or green ones, and if the latter are used, a relatively larger raft will be needed to carry a certain load. For one passenger, three logs 9 to 12 in. in diameter, 12 to 16 ft. long, and spaced to a width of 5 ft. will provide a stable raft. Poles may be laid across the raft to give sufficient footing. For heavier loads, the logs should be about the same length and diameter but spaced

THE INVENTIVE WOODSMAN BUILDS HIS LOG RAFT OF SIMPLE MATERIALS
GATHERED AT THE RIVERBANK; THE LOGS AND POLES ARE NOTCHED
TOGETHER FIRMLY AND HELD WITH WOODEN PINS.

closer together and laid to form a raft of considerably greater width and buoyancy.

Select a shore sloping gently into the water, if possible, and cut the logs and poles as near this place as is convenient. Cut the logs and roll them to the bank, alternating the butts, if there is any considerable difference in the diameter of the ends. Cut a supply of poles of about 3 in. diameter and of the length necessary to reach across the proposed raft. Then cut a number of pins of hardwood 1 ft. long and sharpened on one end as shown in the detailed sketch.

Roll the first log—one of the largest—into the water until it is nearly floating. If it is bowed or crooked, place the "humped" side toward the outer edge of the raft. Chop notches 2 in. deep in the top of the log about 1½ ft. from the ends, and squarely across. Place a pole in the notch with its end projecting slightly beyond the log, and cut a double notch in the upper edge of the pole, as shown in the detail sketches, so that when the pins are driven into the log they will rest diagonally in the notches cut into the poles. Make rifts in the log with the ax, cutting as though to split off a slab of bark and wood, rather than toward the center of the log, and drive two of the pins into place. Properly done, this will make a remarkably strong joint. Fasten a second pole at the other end of the log and prop up both poles so as to permit the next log to be rolled into the water under the poles.

Notch the second log before slipping it finally into place. Alternate ends only of the inner logs need to be fastened. If time is important, some of the logs may be left unfastened provided they are held tightly between the logs that are pinned. Shove the raft out into the water as each log is added. If there is a strong current it is desirable to guy the raft with a pole to the bank, downstream. The last log, which should also be a large one, is then floated down and pinned at both ends.

The raft may then be floated and is ready to be covered with light poles or brush to provide dry footing and place for the dunnage. The dunnage is placed near the forward end of the raft, and the person controlling it sculls with a pole at the rear.

— BIRCH-BARK LEGGINGS MADE IN THE WOODS —

An excellent pair of leggings for use in brush and forest land can be made in a few minutes from birch bark cut in the woods. Select a suitable tree, about 6 or 8 in. in diameter, and cut into the heavy bark to obtain two rolls around the circumference of the tree,

taking care not to cut deep enough to injure it. Fit these sections around the legs leaving 6-in. portions overlapping. Trim the bark to the proper shape and soak it in water to soften the grain. Place the bark close to the fire until it curls. The leggings are then ready to use.

— Attachment for Glasses Aids Marksman —

The elderly marksman, on account of changing eyesight, often finds himself handicapped by the limitations of focus. If he uses glasses to overcome a tendency to far-sightedness, the target and front sight are clear but the rear sight is more or less indistinct. If "nearsighted" glasses are used, the target and front sight are blurred while the rear sight is clear and sharp. The little device shown in the drawing, which one sharpshooter has found eliminates these troubles, is made from a narrow piece of card-

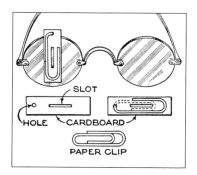

board having a narrow slot cut in the center; it is held to the lens of the "sighting" eye by a wire paper clip.

— A Mirror an Aid in Rowing a Boat —

The young oarsman is apt to experience difficulty in keeping a straight course until he has had some practice. Rowing a boat in a narrow channel calls for considerable skill to hold a course in midstream. A variation of force in pulling the oars almost instantly results in the

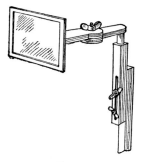

THE MIRROR ATTACHED TO THE BOAT.

rowboat making a landfall on one of the other of the banks.

The skilled oarsman does not need an appliance that the beginner might welcome. With the aid of a mirror conveniently supported at a suitable angle and height before the oarsman's face, the water, the shores, and approaching boats may be seen with distinctness. The mirror may be set directly in front or a little distance to one side, as shown in the sketch.

— WEBFOOT ATTACHMENTS FOR SWIMMERS —

In order to make the feet more effective in swimming, webfoot devices are frequently used. A simple arrangement for this purpose is shown in the illustration. It consists of three thin sections of metal or wood fastened together on the back side with spring hinges, which tend to remain open thereby keeping all the sections spread out in one straight surface. The center section should be cut to conform closely to the shape of the foot or it will produce considerable resistance during the inward stroke of the foot and tend to stop the forward movement of the swimmer. Straps should be provided for attaching the device to the foot; one to fit

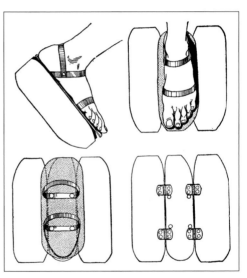

DEVICE FOR ATTACHING TO THE FEET TO WORK LIKE WEBFEET.

across the toes and the other adjusted around the ankle by a buckle.

When using the device, the upward or forward stroke of the legs will cause the wings to brush against the water, creating sufficient resistance to overcome the slight force of the springs, thereby pushing the wings parallel with the direction of the stroke. During the opposite, or pushing, stroke, the resistance of the water combined with the opening tendency of the hinges will quickly spread the wings out flat, greatly increasing the effectiveness of the feet.

— DUCK DECOYS MOUNTED ON A FOLDED FRAME —

The duck hunter who wishes to economize by making some of his equipment will be interested in the folding frame for duck decoys, shown in the illustration. It is made of two strips, ¾ in. by 2 in. by 3 ft. 6 in., of softwood, and fitted with a bolt at the middle so that it may be folded for convenience in carrying. The decoys are cut from a sheet of tinned metal and are painted to resemble the game.

DUCK DECOYS MOUNTED ON A FOLDING FRAME MAY BE MADE BY THE HUNTER.

— ❖ ❖ ❖ —

{ CHAPTER 5 }

TOYS, GAMES, *and* OTHER AMUSEMENTS

—

THE ONE TOY *that* GUARANTEES *a* HAPPY CHILDHOOD

— HOMEMADE ELECTRIC-LOCOMOTIVE MODEL AND TRACK SYSTEM: THE MOTOR —

The electric locomotive described may be constructed by boys having average mechanical ability and the necessary tools. However, in any piece of mechanical construction care must be taken to follow the instructions. The material required is inexpensive and the pleasure derived

from such a toy is well worth the time used in its construction.

The making of the outfit may be divided into three parts, the first of which is the motor; second, the truck that is to carry the motor and the body of the car; and third, the track system upon which the engine is to

reversed to make the locomotive travel forward or backward. The armature and field are constructed of sheet-iron stampings, riveted together.

The detailed construction of the armature and its dimensions are shown in *Fig. 2*. The shaft upon which the armature core and commutator are to be rigidly mounted is made of a piece of steel rod, $7/32$ in. in diameter. A portion of this rod, $2\frac{1}{4}$ in. long, is threaded with a fine thread, and two small brass or iron nuts are provided to fit it. The ends of the rod are turned down to a diameter of $\frac{1}{8}$ in. for a distance of $\frac{1}{8}$ in. These are to fit in the bearings that are to be made later.

operate. A side view of the locomotive is shown in *Fig. 1*.

The motor is of the series type, having its field and armature terminals connected to the source of electrical energy through a special reversing switch. By this means, the rotation of the armature may be

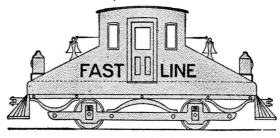

Fig. 1

SIDE VIEW OF A LOCOMOTIVE DESIGNED TO BE
OPERATED WITH EITHER END FORWARD.

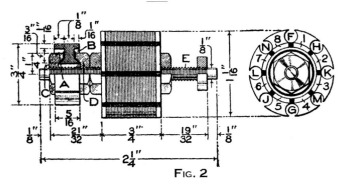

FIG. 2

HOW THE ARMATURE CORE IS MADE OF SOFT-IRON
DISKS FOR THE LAMINATION.

Cut from thin sheet iron a sufficient number of disks 1⅛ in. in diameter, to make a pile exactly ⅝ in. thick when they are securely clamped together. Drill a hole in the center of each of these disks of such a size that they will slip on the shaft snugly. Remove the rough edges from the disks and see that they are flat. Cut two disks of the same size from a piece of 1/16-in. spring brass, and drill a hole in the center of each so that they will slip onto the shaft. Place all these disks on the shaft, with the brass ones on the outside, and draw them up tightly with the nuts provided. Be sure to get the laminated core in the proper position on the shaft by observing the dimensions given in the illustration, *Fig. 2.*

After the disks have been fastened, clamp the shaft in the chuck of a lathe and turn down the edges of all the disks so that they form a smooth cylinder, 1 1/16 in. in diameter. Draw a circle on the side of one of the brass disks, 3/32 in. from the edge, while the shaft is held in the chuck. Divide this circle into eight equal parts and make a center-punch mark at each division. Drill eight holes through the core lengthwise with a 3/16-in. drill. If the centers of the holes have been properly located, all the metal on the outside will be cut away, as shown in the end view at the right in *Fig. 2.* The width of the gaps F, G, H, etc., thus formed, should be about 1/16 in. Smooth off all the edges with a fine file after the holes are drilled.

A cross-sectional view of the commutator is shown at the extreme left, *Fig. 2.* It is constructed as follows:

Clamp one end of a rod of copper or brass, ⅞ in. in diameter and 1¼ in. long, in the chuck of a lathe. Turn the other end down to a diameter of ¾ in., and drill a ½-in. hole through it at the center. Cut away the metal from the end to form a disklike recess.

Cut off a disk, 5/16 in. thick measuring from the finished end, from the piece of stock. Place this disk in a chuck, with the unfinished end exposed, and cut away the metal in a dish form, as shown at B. Cut small slots, into which the ends of the wires used in the winding are to be soldered, as shown in 1, 2, 3, etc., in the right-hand view of *Fig. 2*. Obtain two brass nuts, about ¼ in. in thickness, and turn their edges down so that they correspond in form to those shown in C and D. Divide the disk ring, just made, into eight equal parts by lines drawn across it through the center. Cut eight slots at these points, in the rim of the disk. These cuts should be through the rim. Fill each of the slots with a piece of mica insulation.

Place one of the nuts on the shaft, and then a washer of mica insulation, shown by the heavy lines, near A and B; then the ring, a second piece of mica, and last the nut, C. The latter should be drawn up tightly so that the insulation in the slots in the disk is opposite the drilled slots in the armature core, as shown in the right-hand view of *Fig. 2*. After the disk has been fastened securely, test it to learn whether it is insulated from the shaft. This is done by means of a battery and bell connected in series, one terminal of the circuit being connected to the disk and the other to the shaft. If the bell rings when these connections are made, the ring and shaft are not insulated. The disk must then be remounted, using new washers of mica insulation. Mica is used because of its ability to withstand a higher degree of heat than most other forms of insulation.

Each of the eight segments of the dished disk should be insulated from the others. Make a test to see if the adjacent commutator segments are insulated from each other, and also from the shaft. If the test indicates that any segment is electrically connected to another, or to the shaft, the commutator must be dismantled and the trouble corrected.

The armature is now ready to be wound. Procure ⅛ lb. of No. 26 gauge insulated copper wire. Insulate the shaft, at E, with several turns of thin cloth insulation. Also insulate similarly the nuts holding the armature core and the inside nut holding the commutator. Cut several pieces from the cloth insulation wide enough to cover the walls of the slots in the core, and long enough to extend at least 1/16 in. beyond the core at the ends. Insulate slots F and G thus, and wind 15 turns of the wire around the core lengthwise, passing the wire back through the slot F, across the back end of the core, then forward the front end through slot G, and back through F, and so on. About 2 in. of free wire should be provided at each end off the coils.

In passing across the ends of the armature, all the turns are placed on one side of the shaft, and so as to pass on the left side, the armature being viewed from the commutator end. The second coil, which is wound in the same grooves, is then passed on the right side, the third on the left, and so on. After this coil is completed, test it to see if it is connected to the armature core. If such a condition is found, the coil must be rewound. If the insulation is good, wind the second coil, which is wound in the same slots, F and G, and composed of the same number of turns. Insulate the slots H and J, and wind two coils of 15 turns each in them, observing the same precautions as with the first two coils. The fifth and sixth coils are placed in slots K and L, and the seventh and eighth in slots M and N.

The arrangement of the half coils, slots, and commutator segments is given in detail in *Fig. 3*. Each coil is reduced to one turn in the illustration, in order to simplify it. From an inspection of this diagram it may be seen that the outside end of the second coil in the upper row of figures, at the left end, is connected to the inside end of the fourth coil at segment 1, in the lower row of figures, representing the segments

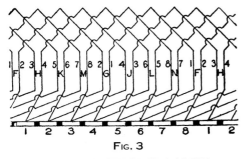

FIG. 3

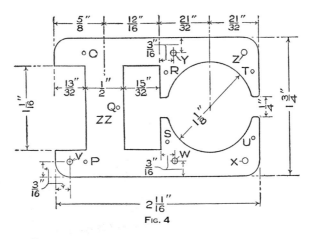

FIG. 4

PATTERN FOR THE FIELD STAMPINGS, SEVERAL PIECES
BEING USED TO MAKE THE DESIRED THICKNESS.

of the commutator. The outside end of the fourth coil is connected with the inside end of the sixth coil, at segment 2; the outside end of the sixth coil is connected with the inside end of the eighth coil at segment 3; the outside end of the eighth coil is connected to the inside end of the coil 1 at segment 4; the outside end of the coil 1 is connected to the inside end of the coil 3 at segment 5; the outside end of the third coil is connected to the inside end of the fifth coil at segment 6; the outside end of the fifth coil is connected to the inside end of the seventh coil at segment 7; the outside end of the seventh coil is con-

nected to the inside end of the second coil at segment 8, and the outside end of the second coil is connected to segment 1, completing the circuit.

In winding the coils on the core, their ends should be terminated close to the commutator segments to which they are to be connected, in order to simplify the end connections. After all the coils are wound and properly tested, their ends may be connected as indicated. They are then soldered into the slots in the ends of the commutator segments. The completed winding is given a coating of shellac.

The dimensions and form of the field stampings are given in *Fig. 4.* A

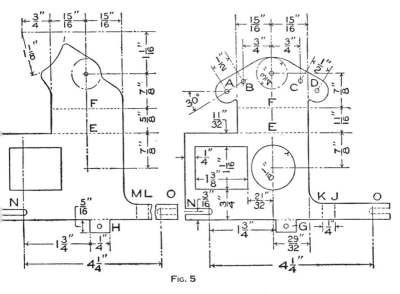

FIG. 5

DETAIL OF THE FIELD-STRUCTURE SUPPORTS, ONE BEING FOR
THE LEFT SIDE AND THE OTHER FOR THE RIGHT.
THE SUPPORTS ARE SHOWN IN PLACE BELOW.

number of these are cut from thin sheet iron to make a pile ⅝ in. thick when clamped together. The dimensions of the opening to carry the armature should be a little less than that indicated in the sketch, as it will be necessary to true it up after the stampings are fastened together. Use one of the stampings as a pattern and drill seven small holes in each, as indicated by the letters O, P, Q,

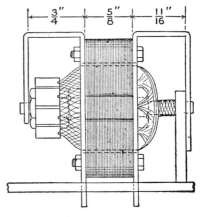

FIG. 6

R, S, T, and U. Fasten them together with small rivets, and true up the opening for the armature to a diameter of 1⅛ in. Drill five ⅛-in. holes, as indicated by the letters V, W, X, Y, and Z, to be used in mounting the pieces, which are to form the armature bearings, brush supports, and base of the motor.

Cut two rectangular washers from a piece of thin fiber insulation with outside dimensions of 1⅛ in. and 1¼ in., and inside opening, ½ in. by ⅝ in. Cut open these washers and slip them in position on the portion of the field marked ZZ. Wrap two turns of the cloth insulation about this part, which is to form the field core, and wind the space full of No. 18 gauge enamel-insulated copper wire. Give the completed winding a coat of shellac. The terminals of this winding should be brought out through two holes drilled in one of the fiber washers, one near the core and the other near the outer edge. It is better to have the field terminals at the lower end of the part ZZ than at the upper end.

Now cut two pieces from 1/16 in. sheet brass, similar to those shown in *Fig. 5*. Place them on opposite sides of the laminated field structure, shown in *Fig. 4*, and carefully mark the position of the holes, V, W, X, Y, and Z, as indicated in *Fig. 4*, and drill ⅛-in. holes where the marks were made. Lay out and drill ⅛ in. holes, A, B, C, and D, *Fig. 5*. Bend the upper portion of the pieces at right angles to the lower portion, along the dotted lines E, and then bend the end of the horizontal portions down along the dotted lines F, until they are parallel with the main vertical parts of the pieces. The latter should be bent so that one forms the left support and the other the right, as shown in *Fig. 6*.

Bend the projections G and H at right angles to the vertical main parts. The parts at the bottom are bent, one back along the dotted line J and forward on the line K; the other forward on the line L and back on the line M. The pieces are then mounted on the side of the field structure, as shown in *Fig. 6;* the supports are fastened in place with five small bolts. The grooves N and O, in *Fig. 5*, are used in mounting the motor on the axles of the truck. They will not be cut until after the truck is constructed.

The brush holders are made of two pieces of hexagonal brass, each 1 in. in length, having a ⅛-in. hole drilled in one end to a depth of ⅞ in., and a threaded hole in the other end, for a small machine screw, as shown in *Fig. 7*. Two holes are drilled and threaded in one side of each of these pieces. These holders are to be

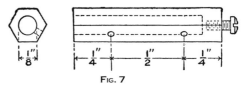

FIG. 7

DETAIL OF THE BRUSH HOLDERS, ONE INCH LONG, WITH HOLES AS SHOWN.

mounted by means of screws, through the holes A, B, C, and D, *Fig. 5*. Each holder must be insulated from its support. The distance of the holder from its support should be such that the opening in its end is in the center of the commutator. The brushes are made of very fine copper gauze, rolled to form a rod. They are made long enough to extend about ½ in. into the holder when they are resting on the commutator. A small

spiral spring is placed on the holder, in back of the end of the brush, and will serve to keep the latter in contact with the commutator.

Temporary connections are made, and the motor is tested with a six-volt battery. The construction of the motor may be modified as to the length of shaft, and other minor details, and may be used for other purposes by fitting it with pulleys, a countershaft, or other transmission devices.

— THE LOCOMOTIVE TRUCK AND CAB —

Successful operation and construction that is feasible, yet of a reasonable standard of workmanship, are the essentials of the locomotive truck and cab described as the second feature of the locomotive and track system under consideration. The materials suggested are those found to be satisfactory, but substitutes may be used if caution is observed. The completed locomotive

is shown in *Figs. 1* and *2*. The outward aspect only is presented and, for the sake of clarity, the portions of the motor and driving rigging attached to it that project below the cab are omitted. These parts are shown assembled in *Fig. 12*, and in detail in the succeeding sketches.

The locomotive, apart from the motor, consists of two main portions: the truck and the cab. Consideration

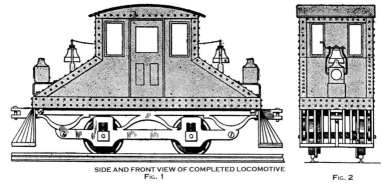

SIDE AND FRONT VIEW OF COMPLETED LOCOMOTIVE
FIG. 1   FIG. 2

THE CONSTRUCTION OF THE CAB IS SUGGESTIVE ONLY, AND THE INVEN-
TIVE BUILDER MAY DESIGN ONE IN CONFORMITY WITH THE MATERIALS
AVAILABLE OR WITH THE INDIVIDUAL BUILDER'S TASTE.

will be given first to the building of the truck and the fitting of the motor into it. The mechanical and operative features are to be completed before beginning work on the cab, which is merely a hood fixed into place with screws, set onto the wooden cab base.

Begin the construction with the wheels shown in *Fig. 3*. Make the axles of ⅛ in. round steel rod, cut 3 3/16 in. long.

Turn four wheels of ⅜-in. brass. Drill a ⅛-in. hole in two of them so that they may be forced on the slightly tapered ends of the axle. Drill a ¼-in. hole in each of the other wheels and solder a collar, A, *Fig. 3*, on the inside surfaces of them. Two fiber bushings, B, should be provided

to fit in the ¼-in. openings in the wheels and to fit tightly on the ends of the axles. This insulates the wheels on one side of the truck from those on the other. If the rails forming the track are insulated from each other, the current supplied to the motor may pass in on one rail to the two insulated wheels, then to a brush, which bears on the brass collar A, through the windings of the motor, through the reversing switch to the other set of wheels, and back to the source of energy over the other rail, as shown in *Fig. 15*.

The wheels of the truck should fit on the axles tightly, because no means other than the friction will be employed in holding them in posi-

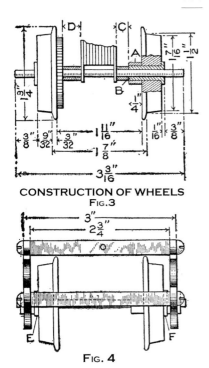

CONSTRUCTION OF WHEELS
Fɪɢ.3

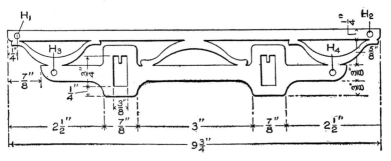

Fɪɢ. 4

tion. If the ends of the axles are tapered slightly, the wheels may be forced into place and will stay firmly. Do not force them on until the truck is finally assembled.

The truck frame should be constructed next, and its details are shown in *Figs. 4* and *5*. Make two sidepieces of 1/16 in. brass, 9¾ in. long by 1⅝ in. wide, cutting out portions as shown, in order to reduce the weight. This also gives the appearance of leaf springs.

Sᴜᴄᴄᴇssꜰᴜʟ ᴏᴘᴇʀᴀᴛɪᴏɴ, ʙᴀsᴇᴅ ᴏɴ ꜰᴇᴀsɪʙʟᴇ ᴄᴏɴ-sᴛʀᴜᴄᴛɪᴏɴ ᴀɴᴅ ᴀ ʀᴇᴀsᴏɴᴀʙʟᴇ sᴛᴀɴᴅᴀʀᴅ ᴏꜰ ᴡᴏʀᴋᴍᴀɴsʜɪᴘ, ɪs ᴛʜᴇ ꜰɪʀsᴛ ᴄᴏɴsɪᴅᴇʀᴀᴛɪᴏɴ ɪɴ ᴛʜᴇ ʟᴏᴄᴏᴍᴏᴛɪᴠᴇ. Tʜᴇ ᴅɪᴍᴇɴ-sɪᴏɴs sʜᴏᴜʟᴅ ʙᴇ ᴏʙsᴇʀᴠᴇᴅ ᴄʟᴏsᴇʟʏ ɪɴ ᴏʀᴅᴇʀ ᴛʜᴀᴛ ᴛʜᴇ ᴘᴀʀᴛs ᴍᴀʏ ʙᴇ ᴀssᴇᴍʙʟᴇᴅ sᴀᴛɪsꜰᴀᴄᴛᴏʀɪʟʏ.

SIDE OF TRUCK
Fɪɢ. 5

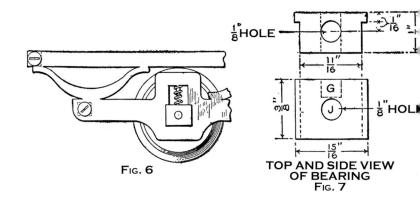

FIG. 6

$\frac{1}{8}$" HOLE

$\frac{11}{16}$"

$\frac{3}{8}$"

G

J

$\frac{1}{8}$" HOL

$\frac{15}{16}$"

$\frac{1}{16}$"

TOP AND SIDE VIEW
OF BEARING
FIG. 7

The two rectangular openings are to accommodate the axle bearings. They should be cut to precise dimensions and their edges should be squared off. Extensions, $1/16$ in. wide, are provided at the middle of the upper edges of each of these openings. They are to hold the upper end of the coil springs, which are set to rest in the holes cut into the bearings, as shown at G, *Fig. 7*, and also in assembled form, *Fig. 6*.

Next, drill four $1/8$ in. holes in each of the sidepieces, as indicated at the letters H1 to H4, *Fig. 5*. For the cross supports use four pieces of brass rod, $1/4$ in. square, and square off the ends to a length of $2\frac{3}{4}$ in. Drill holes in the center of the ends and tap them for $1/8$ in. machine screws. Join the side and crosspieces

as shown in *Fig. 4*. Two fiber washers about $1/16$ in. thick should be placed on each axle at E and F, to hold the wheels from contact with the sidepieces.

Details of a bearing for the axles are shown in *Fig. 7*. The hole G carries the lower end of the coil spring and the hole J is the bearing socket for the axle. Four spiral springs, having an outside diameter of $1/8$ in. and a length of $1/2$ in. when extended, should be provided. The extensions on the sides of the bearings fit against the inner faces of the sides of the truck. They hold the bearings in position and prevent them from falling out.

The base of the cab is made of wood, dimensioned as in *Fig. 10*. The center of the piece is cut away so as to provide a space for the motor,

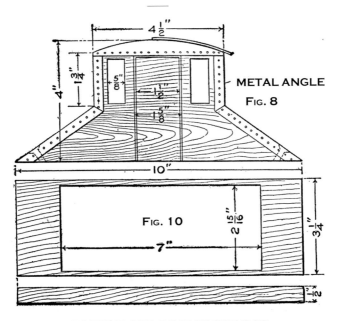

4 ½"

1 ¾"

4"

⅝"

1 ½"

1 ⅝"

METAL ANGLE

FIG. 8

10"

FIG. 10

2 15/16"

3 ¾"

7"

1 ½"

BOTTOM OF LOCOMOTIVE CAB

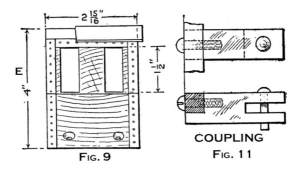

2 15/16"

E

4"

1 ½"

FIG. 9

COUPLING

FIG. 11

which extends above the upper edge of the truck as shown in *Fig. 12*. This block is fastened in place by four screws through the upper crosspieces at the ends of the truck. The base should be made and fitted into place temporarily so as to be available in observing how the motor and its fittings are placed in relation to it. For convenience in assembling the parts of the truck and setting the motor, it may be removed readily.

Assembling the truck, including the motor, probably requires the most painstaking effort of any part of the construction of the locomotive. Too great care cannot be taken with it, as the dimensions are carefully worked out and failure to observe them may cause errors sufficient to make the locomotive unserviceable. Before undertaking this work it would be wise to examine carefully the arrangement of the parts as shown in *Fig. 12*. The upper view shows the relation of the driving gears in mesh and the lower view shows the machinery of the truck as seen from above.

The power from the motor is

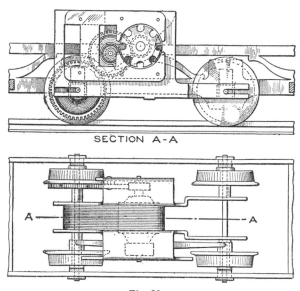

SECTION A-A

Fig. 12

INSTALLATION OF THE MOTOR, SHOWING GEARS
AND SWITCH CONTACT SPRING.

transmitted to one set of wheels by means of a small gear on the armature shaft engaging an intermediate gear, which in turn engages a large gear attached to the inside of one of the truck wheels. The center of the armature shaft is 1⁵/₁₆ in. from the center of the power axle, when both axles are in the slots provided in the motor frame, *Fig. 12*. The gears for the transmission may now be selected. The gear on the armature shaft should be as small, and that on the axle as large, as practicable. The intermediate gear should be of such a size that it will close the space between the small gear on the armature shaft and the large one on the axle. Gears suitable for the transmission may be purchased at a clock store for a small sum. If gears of exactly the proper size cannot be obtained readily, the position of the intermediate gear may be adjusted to produce a proper meshing of the gears.

Mount the small gear on the end of the armature shaft away from the commutator so that there will be about 1/16 in. clearance between the outside surface and the shoulder at the end of the shaft. Fit it on tightly so that no other means of fastening will be necessary. Mount the large

gear on the inside surface of one of the truck wheels as shown in *Figs. 3* and *12*. Place the axle of the truck into the proper grooves in the motor frame, and mark the position of the center of the intermediate gear, when it engages the other gear. Drill a hole in the extension on the motor frame, provided as a support, to fit a small bolt with which the intermediate gear is fastened.

Place a washer between the gear and the piece upon which it is mounted and a locknut on the threaded end of the bolt, drawing it up so that the gear has only sufficient play.

The slots in the motor frame to fit the free axle may now be cut, as shown in *Fig. 12*. Place the motor in position on the axle so that the gears all mesh properly. Fit tubes of insulating material with an outside diameter of ⅜ in. at C and D, *Fig. 3*, and as also shown in *Fig. 12*. Insulation tubes should be provided for the second axle so as to hold the motor in position and to keep the wheels in line. In mounting the various parts sufficient play should be allowed to prevent excessive friction.

The reversing switch, which is to be mounted on the underside of the motor frame, is shown in *Figs. 13*

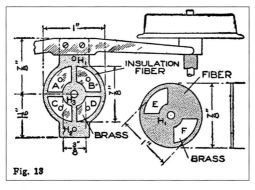

DETAILS OF THE SWITCH, SHADED PORTIONS BEING OF FIBER INSULATION.

Fig. 13

The operation of the switch is as follows: Assuming that the current enters at a terminal marked 1 and leaves at the terminal marked 2, then the direction of the current in the armature and series field will be as indicated in the diagrams. The direction of the current in the series-field winding is different in the two cases, which will result in opposite rotation of the armature.

The base of the switch is made of 1/16 in. fiber insulation; its dimensions are shown in Fig. 13. It is to be mounted on the two pieces projecting outward on the underside of the motor frame, as shown in Fig. 14. Drill a small hole in each of these projections, as indicated by the letters H1 and H2, and tap them to take a small machine screw. Next drill two holes, H1 and H2, Fig. 13, in the piece of insulation, with centers the same distance apart as those drilled in the projections. One end of this piece of insulation is extended to form a mounting for a thin brass spring, the ends of which

and 14. It is provided with a control lever that projects out from under the truck frame. A small movement of the lever will produce the necessary changes in the connections. The operation of the switch may be understood readily from the diagram shown in Fig. 15. The moving element of the switch carries two pieces of copper, E and F, which connect the four stationary pieces of copper, A, B, C, and D, when the lever attached to E and F is moved to either side of its central position. The pieces of copper that are moved— E and F—are shown outside of the stationary pieces in Fig. 15 for purposes of a diagram only, and are actually directly over the ring formed by the stationary pieces.

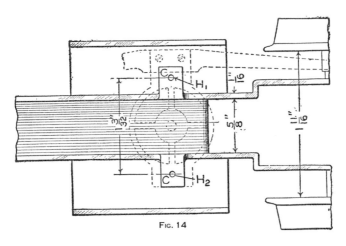

FIG. 14

VIEW OF THE UNDERSIDE OF THE MOTOR, SHOWING
HOW SWITCH IS FIXED INTO PLACE.

bear on the brass collars insulated from the axles, as shown in *Figs. 12* and *13*. The form of this spring and the method of mounting it are also shown in *Fig. 13*.

The sections that come into contact in the switch are made as follows: Mount four pieces of thin copper or brass on the fiber base with rivets having their heads countersunk. Cut a disk, 1 in. in diameter, from a piece of sheet insulation and drill a hole H1, in the center of it. Also drill a similar hole, H3, in the center of the switch base. Mount two pieces of copper or brass, E and F, on the underside of this disk. The edges and ends of all six pieces of metal should be rounded off so that the pieces E and F will move freely over those on the base. The disk, or upper part of the switch, may be attached to the base by means of a small bolt placed through the holes at the center. A small spiral spring should be placed between the disk and the lower end of this bolt so as to keep the pieces of metal on the disk in contact with those on the base. Attach a small handle to the disk so that it will extend out on one side of the truck. Fix the switch into place by bolts through the holes H1 and H2, *Fig. 14,* on the bottom of the

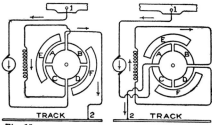

Fig. 15

DIAGRAMS OF THE REVERSING OF MOTOR BY SHIFTING SWITCH TO FORM CONTACT BETWEEN PAIRS OF BRASS SECTORS SET IN THE FIBER SWITCH BASE.

motor frame. The electrical connections should be made as shown in *Fig. 15*.

The detail of the couplers is shown in *Fig. 11*. They are made of brass fitted to the upper crosspieces and fixed to them by machine screws. "Cowcatchers" may be made for the ends of the locomotive. Sheet metal, corrugated appropriately and bent to the proper shape, will afford the easiest method of making them. Those shown in *Figs. 1* (page 180) are made of strips soldered together, and also the upper crosspieces; they are strengthened by a cross-strip at the bottom, opposite the point.

The cab is to be made apart from the truck and is to fit upon the base, as shown in *Figs. 1* and *2*. It is fixed

into place by four screws and can be removed easily for examination of the locomotive mechanism. The dimensions for the cab are shown in *Figs. 8* and *9*, and may be varied by the builder.

Sheet metal or wood may be used in the construction, and the joints soldered on the inside or riveted, as shown in the illustration. The window and door openings may be cut out or painted on. Small bells may be mounted on the ends of the cab, adding to its appearance. The headlights shown in *Figs. 1* and *2* may be cut from wood or made of sheet metal. Lightbulbs may be installed, and their voltage should correspond to that of the motive energy. The terminals for the sockets of the headlight lamps should be connected to the frame of the truck and to the spring, which bears upon the brass collars on the wheels, which are insulated from the axles, as shown in A, *Fig. 3*.

This completes the locomotive in all essential details and it is ready to be placed upon the track to be tested.

— THE TRACK SYSTEM —

Operation of the electric-loco-motive model described in the previous article is feasible only on a properly constructed track system. This equipment, including curves and switches, is to be described in this article. Two functions are to be performed by the track system: It must serve as a support and guide for the locomotive and provide a path over which the current from the source of energy is supplied to the motor within the locomotive and returned to the source. On this basis, then, the construction may be divided into two parts: the mechanical and the electrical features. If the mechanical construction is not practical and accurate, the locomotive will not operate satisfactorily. The electrical connections must be given due care also.

The track should be of uniform gauge; the joints should be solid and free from irregularities, which cause "bumping" in passing over them. The material used should be stiff, so that it will retain its form, and preferably nonrusting. The rails must be insulated from each other, and proper means must be provided for making suitable electrical connections between the various sections. The construction of a straight and a curved section of track, together with a switch and signal adaptable to various places on the system, will be considered in detail.

The straight sections may be made any suitable length. Sections 16 in. long will be found convenient, because the metal pieces forming the rails may be bent into shape easily when they are short rather than long. The possibility of various combinations of straight and curved sections in a given area is increased by having the sections shorter. The rails may be made from tinned sheet-metal strips by taking pieces 16 in. long by 1½ in. wide and bending them into the form shown in *Fig. 1*. The rails should be mounted on small wooden sleepers, ½ by ½ by 4 in., by means of small nails or preferably small screws. The distance between the centers of the rails should be 2 in. The sections of track may be fastened together at the ends by means of a special connector, shown in *Fig. 2*, made from thin metal, preferably spring brass. The type of connector shown in *Fig. 2* will not prevent the sections from pulling apart. To prevent this, a second connector similar

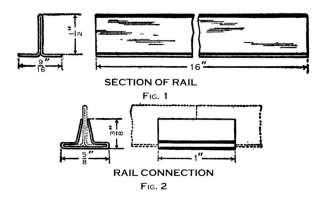

SECTION OF RAIL
Fig. 1

RAIL CONNECTION
Fig. 2

SHAPE THE RAILS FROM SHEET-METAL STRIPS, 1 1/2 INCHES WIDE BY
16 INCHES LONG, TO THE FORM SHOWN IN FIG. 1.
THE RAIL CONNECTIONS ARE FORMED
AS SHOWN IN FIG. 2.

to that shown in *Fig. 3* should be made. The sleepers at the ends of each section should have one side beveled as shown, and these edges should be exactly 1 in. from the end of the rails. A spring clip should be made, similar to that shown, which will slip down on the inside of the end sleepers and hold the sections together.

A better form of rail is shown in *Figs. 3* and *4,* but it is somewhat more difficult to construct. In this case, instead of bending the piece of metal forming the rail over on itself and closing the space entirely, the metal is bent over a round form, such as a piece of wire. The form may be removed, leaving an opening through

the upper part of the rail from end to end. This gives a better form to the tread of the rail and at the same time provides an easy means of connecting the ends of the rails, as shown in *Fig. 5*. Small metal pins, about 1 in. long and of such a diameter that they will just fit the circular opening in the top of the rail, are provided. One of these pins should be fastened in one rail at each end of a section, making sure that no rail has more than one pin in it, and that the arrangement of pins and rails corresponds in all sections. With proper care the various sections should fit together equally well, and they may be held together as shown in *Fig. 3.*

The curved sections may be made from rails similar to those described above, but some difficulty will be experienced in bending them into a curve because of the necessity of bending the lower flange on edge. The difficulty may be overcome by crimping in the inner edge of the lower flange and expanding the outer edge by hammering it on a smooth surface. The radius of the curve to which the inner rail should be bent in order to give a section of convenient length, and not too abrupt a curve, is 21 in. The circumference of such a circle is approximately 132 in.,

which, divided into eight sections, gives 16½ in. as the length of the inner rail of each section. Because the tread of the track is 2 in., the radius of the curve of the outer rail will be 23 in. The circumference of the circle formed by the outer rail is 145 in., which divided into eight sections gives 18⅛ in. as the length of the outer rail of each section. These curved rails may be mounted on sleepers, their ends being held in place, and the various sections fastened together, just as in the case of the straight sections.

Some trouble may be experienced

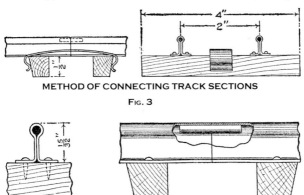

METHOD OF CONNECTING TRACK SECTIONS

Fig. 3

SECTION OF RAIL
Fig. 4

END CONNECTION OF RAILS

Fig. 5

A SPRING CLAMP FOR THE JOINTS IN THE SECTIONS IS SHOWN IN FIG. 3. AN IMPROVED FORM OF RAIL IS SHOWN IN FIG. 4, AND IN FIG. 5 IS INDICATED THE METHOD OF JOINING ITS SECTIONS.

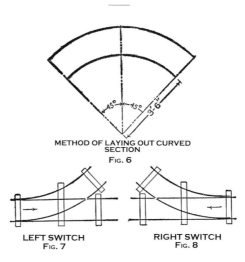

METHOD OF LAYING OUT CURVED
SECTION
FIG. 6

LEFT SWITCH
FIG. 7

RIGHT SWITCH
FIG. 8

LAY OUT THE SWITCHES AND CURVES, FULL SIZE, AND
FIT THE RAILS TO THE CURVES ACCURATELY.

in getting the curved rails properly shaped, and it would be a good plan to lay them out full size. Draw two circles on a smooth surface having diameters of 42 and 46 in., respectively, and divide each of the latter into eight equal parts. The form of the curve between these division lines and the lengths of the curves will correspond to the shape and lengths of the rails forming the curved sections of the track. The pieces should be cut slightly longer than required, and after they are bent into shape their length can be determined precisely and extra portions cut off. Each curved section will cor-

respond to ⅛ of the complete circle, or 45 degrees, as shown in *Fig. 6*.

The switches for the track may be of two kinds: left or right. They are named according to whether the car is carried to the left or right of the main track with reference to the direction in which the car moves in entering the switch. A left switch is shown in *Fig. 7*, and a right switch in *Fig. 8*, the direction of movement being indicated by arrows.

A detailed drawing of a right switch is shown in *Fig. 9*. Rail A corresponds in form and length to the outer rail of one of the curved sections previously described. Rail B corresponds to the inner rail of one of the curved sections, except that 2 ½ in. of straight rail is added at the left end. Rail C is a straight portion of rail, 18 in. in length, with a part of the base cut away at the switch. Rail D is a section of straight rail, 15½ in. in length, with the base cut away where it crosses rail A. The ends of rails D and A are hinged at the points E and F, 3¾ in. from the left end, with pins driven into the ties. The outside edges of the pieces G and H are filed off so they will fit up against the rails C and B respectively. Both the pieces G and H are attached to a strip of fiber insulating material, I, at their left-hand ends, in such a way that when the piece H is against the rail B, the piece G is away from the rail C about 3/16 in. When the end of the piece G is drawn over against the rail C, the end of the piece H is drawn away from the rail B about 3/16 in. With these two combinations the car may be made to move along the main track or to the right on a curved track. The two long sleepers J and K are to provide a mounting for the switch-control lever and signal.

The rail A is not continuous where the rail D crosses it, but is broken as shown in the figure. A small notch should be cut in the surface off the rail D where it crosses the rail A, for the flange of the car wheels to roll through when the car is moving onto or off the switch. The sections of the

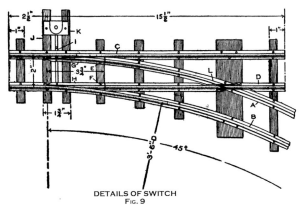

DETAILS OF SWITCH
FIG. 9

THE CROSSINGS OF THE RAILS MUST BE FITTED CAREFULLY AND THE MOVABLE SECTIONS G AND H ARRANGED TO MAKE THE PROPER CONTACTS.

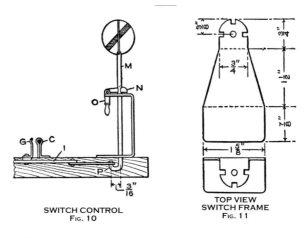

SWITCH CONTROL
Fig. 10

TOP VIEW
SWITCH FRAME
Fig. 11

THE SIGNALS INDICATE THE OPEN OR CLOSED CONDITION
OF THE SWITCH BY THE SMALL DISK, WHICH IS
REGULATED BY THE LEVER SWITCH CONTROL.

rails A and D must be connected electrically. Rail A must be connected to rail C, and rail B to rail D.

It is obvious from an inspection of *Fig. 9,* at L, that rail D will be connected to rail A when the car is on the switch, the car wheels passing over the point L, and a short circuit will result. This may be prevented by insulating the short section of the rail D at this point from the remainder of the rail, but the length of the insulated section must not be greater than the distance between the wheels on one side of the car. Otherwise the circuit through the motor would be broken. If this is the case, and the car stops on the main track with both wheels on the insulated section, it would be impossible to start the locomotive until one wheel was moved to a live part of the rail.

The switch control is shown in *Fig. 10,* and the letters C, G, and I correspond to those given in Fig. 9. A ⅛ in. rod, about 4 in. in length, is bent into the form shown at M. It is mounted in a frame, the details of which are shown in *Fig. 11.* A small arm, N, with a hinged handle, O, is soldered to the rod, after the rod is placed in position in the switch frame. The arm N and the lever P should be parallel with each other. If properly constructed, the handle O will drop into the notches in the top of the switch frame, and prevent the rod M from turning. A connection should be made from the lever P to the end of the piece I, which will result in the switch being operated when the rod M is rotated one-fourth of a turn. After this connection is made, the frame of the switch should be fastened to the ends of the long sleepers, which were provided when the track part of the switch was constructed. Two small disks, mounted at right angles to each other, will serve as signals when properly painted, or as an indication of the open or closed position of the switch. The speed of the car on the track may be controlled by inserting resistance in series with the battery or source of electrical energy, or by altering the value of the voltage between the rails, by changing the connections of the cells forming the battery. The direction of movement of the locomotive cannot be changed unless the car is turned end for end, or the connections of the armature or field winding—not both—are reversed. The switch on the bottom of the locomotive reverses these connections.

A small rheostat, which will give the desired resistance, may be constructed as follows: obtain a piece of hardwood 4 by 5 in., and ⅜ in. in

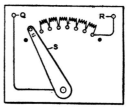

Fɪɢ. 12

thickness. Lay out a curve on this piece, as shown in *Fig. 12* by the row of small circles. Procure eight round-head brass machine screws, about ⅛ in. in diameter and ¾ in. in length, and 16 nuts to fit them. Drill eight ⅛ in. holes along the curve, spacing them ⅜ in. apart. File the heads of the screws in these holes. Make a metal arm, S, and mount it on a small bolt passing through a hole drilled at the center from which the curve was drawn, along which the screws were mounted. This arm should be of such a length that its outer end will move over the heads of the screws. Mount two binding posts, Q and R, to the bolt holding the arm S in place. Connect small resistance coils between the screws, starting with screw No. 2; screw No. 1 corresponds to an open circuit shown in contact with the arm S. Two stops, indicated by the black spots, should be provided to prevent the arm from moving back of screw No. 1 or beyond screw No. 8. The board may now be mounted on a suitable hollow base, and the rheostat is complete.

Two binding posts should be mounted on the ties of one section of the track, and one of them electrically connected to each of the two rails, which will give an easy means of making the necessary electrical connections to the source of energy. After careful examination to make certain that the locomotive is in running order, a test run may be made. If the locomotive operates properly and difficulty is experienced when it is placed upon the track, check up thoroughly on all rail connections, insulations, and other elements in the electrical equipment. Cars of a proper gauge may be coupled to the locomotive, and "runs" made as extensively as the track system will permit.

Tops, Puzzles *and* Games

— An Austrian Top —

All parts of the top are wood and they are simple to make. The handle is a piece of pine 5¼ in. long, 1¼ in. wide, and ¾ in. thick. A handle, ¾ in. in diameter, is formed on one end allow-

Parts of the top.

ing only 1¼ in. of the other end to remain rectangular in shape. Bore a ¾-in. hole in this end for the top. A ¹⁄₁₆-in. hole is bored in the edge to enter the large hole as shown. The top can be cut from a broom handle or a round stick of hardwood.

To spring the top, pass one end of a stout cord about 2 ft. long through the ¹⁄₁₆-in. hole and wind it on the small part of the top in the usual way, starting at the bottom and winding upward. When the shank is covered, set the top in the ¾-in. hole. Take hold of the handle with the left hand and the end of the cord with the right hand, give a quick pull on the cord, and the top will jump clear of the handle and spin vigorously.

— WILD TOP —

The amateur wood turner can easily make a wooden top that will hop across the floor and howl. The top consists of a hollow two-piece wooden ball, which is turned to form a piece of soft dowel. A hole is drilled through the shell of the ball at one of the center marks and fitted with a hardwood peg having a slightly rounded end,

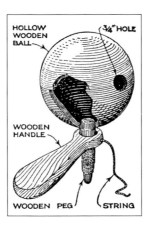

as shown. A ¾-in. hole is drilled at right angles to the peg. To spin this top, a wooden handle, such as the one shown, is required. The top string is wound around the peg and the end is brought through the hole in the handle, as indicated. A quick jerk on the string sets the top in motion and pulls it free of the handle.

— A RING-AND-PEG PUZZLE —

A short piece of board is provided with ten short wooden pegs. Eight wooden disks are drilled through the center to fit over the pegs easily; four of the disks are white and the others are either made of dark wood or painted black. When the block and disks have been made, the disks are placed on the first eight pegs, white disks alternately

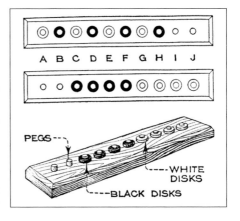

with black. The last two pegs are left vacant. The object of the puzzle is to get the four white and four black disks grouped together without leaving any pegs vacant, except two at either end. The disks must be moved two at a time and the rearrangement made in four moves, two disks at a time.

The upper drawing shows the arrangement of the disks at the commencement of the puzzle and the center one shows how the disks should appear at the conclusion. The secret of the puzzle is as follows: Move the disks B and C to the vacant pegs I and J; E and F to B and C; H and I to E and F; and A and B to H and I. This gives the necessary transposition, and the disks can be returned to their original positions by reversing the movements.

— BEWITCHED-CUBE PUZZLE —

This simple puzzle, which requires six numbered cubes, will require considerable concentration to "make it come out right." Six wooden cubes are provided and numbered on each of their six faces from 1 to 6, the order of numbering being different for each cube, as shown in *Figs. 1* and *2*.

The object is to arrange the six cubes in any shape—preferably in a straight line—as in *Fig. 3,* so that the figures 1, 2, 3, 4, 5, and 6 will appear at once on the top, bottom, front, back, right-, and left-hand faces. They will not be in consecutive order, but the six numbers must each show from every side. Separating the cubes slightly will show the right- and left-hand faces. When

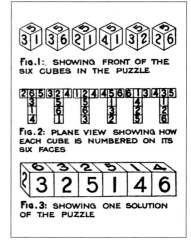

Fig.1: SHOWING FRONT OF THE SIX CUBES IN THE PUZZLE

FIG.2: PLANE VIEW SHOWING HOW EACH CUBE IS NUMBERED ON ITS SIX FACES

FIG.3: SHOWING ONE SOLUTION OF THE PUZZLE

properly arranged, the blocks may be transposed hundreds of different ways in a straight line, fulfilling the conditions each time.

— MOTHBALL PUZZLE AS WINDOW-ADVERTISING NOVELTY —

A druggist recently puzzled thousands with a novel window display. A small white ball displayed in a show window in a 1-in. glass tube about 10 in. long would sink to the bottom then slowly ascend, only to sink as before. A sign reading "What Makes It Move?" kept the crowd guessing. The tube was apparently filled with water. The construction is simple. The tube is about three-quarters full of carbonated soda water. The white ball is an ordinary mothball. The ball sinks, and when it becomes soaked gradually as it lowers, bubbles of gas cling to it carrying it to the top of the solution. There, the gas escapes, destroying the ball's buoyancy and causing it to sink again. This process is repeated over and over again.

— WOODEN KEY-AND-RING PUZZLE —

A puzzle that will baffle the ingenuity of many a skilled mechanic is illustrated by the drawing. The mystery of course is as to how the two blocks are put together. The small block, or key, may be made to slide very tightly into the hole in the larger one; it is thus apparent that it could not have been fitted in by any cut-

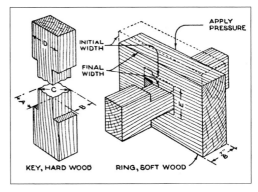

NOT ONLY THE AMATEUR BUT EVEN THE SKILLED MECHANIC MAY BE MYSTIFIED BY A PUZZLE THAT ANY BOY CAN MAKE OUT OF TWO WOODEN BLOCKS.

ting process. The frame, or ring, should be made of good straight-grained softwood, and the key of hardwood, both of about the same

VARIOUS WOODEN ANIMALS ARE SHOWN HELD IN WOODEN FRAMES, OR "TRAPS," ALL MADE ON THE SAME PRINCIPLE AS THE SIMPLE PUZZLE. IN THE CENTER IS A RATHER MORE COMPLICATED SPECIMEN, BUT ALSO MADE WITHOUT JOINTS OF ANY KIND.

thickness. The surface of both blocks may be planed smooth so that the blocks can be inspected all over for glued joints; there are no joints in either block.

The method of making the puzzle is as follows: Cut the two blocks to shape outside, and cut notches in the sides of the key so that dimension A in the drawing will be just slightly less than dimension B. Now caliper the diagonal of this smaller section, thus giving the dimension C. Cut a rectangular hole in the center of the large block of a width E, just slightly greater than this diagonal, and a length greater than the width D of the smaller block. Some notches can be made in the sides of the rectangular hole, as illustrated; these have nothing to do with the puzzle except

that they are quite likely to lead the victim astray in guessing at its solution. If the hole is made according to these directions, the small block can be thrust through it and turned upon its side so as to occupy the position it will have in the completed puzzle.

The ring block is now thoroughly steamed or boiled in water for one hour. It is then gripped in a good bench vise, with the key fitted into it, and screwed up as tightly as possible. When the wood has yielded a little the vise is screwed up again, and so on until the ring is compressed to grip the key tightly between its two sides. Then let the puzzle stand in the vise until the next day, when it will be dry and can be removed. Two stout, hard clamps can be used instead of a vise.

After one's friends have been sufficiently mystified by the question of how the two blocks were ever put together in this fashion, it is a simple matter to place the puzzle in boiling water again for about 20 minutes, when the ring block will swell to its original dimensions and the key can be taken out quite easily.

The photograph shows a number of modifications of the puzzle. All of them involve the same principle as the simple key-and-ring puzzle. Such a collection will form a curious ornament to the craftsman's shop or home.

— A PERPETUAL-MOTION PUZZLE —

The fallacy of perpetual motion is now so generally understood that the description of a new scheme for attaining it is justified only in so far as it may be instructive. The sketch illustrates such a device, apparently successful, and the discovery of the error in it is both instructive and interesting.

Mount a horseshoe magnet on a wooden base, and into the base cut a continuous groove along the three sides of a triangle opposite the poles of the magnet, N. and S. Suspend a long, narrow bar magnet on a universal joint from a standard. A pin projects into the groove from the lower end, which is its north pole, and can

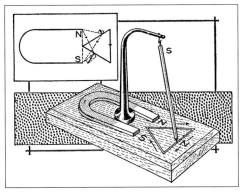

THE INTERACTION BETWEEN POLES OF THE MAGNETS CAUSES THE TRAVELER TO MOVE AROUND THE TRIANGLE.

move only along the triangular course.

Start the device with the suspended magnet in the position shown. The lower end will tend to move in the direction of the arrows, because in so doing it is getting farther away from the repelling north pole of the horseshoe magnet and nearer to the attracting south pole, which will bring it to the corner of the triangle in the foreground. It will next move down the side as indicated by the arrow, because along that line it is nearer to the attracting south than the repelling north pole. When it reaches the end of its trip, at the angle between the poles of the magnet, the attraction and repulsion will be balanced, but a slight jar will carry the traveler beyond the angle.

The third leg of the triangle will be covered similarly, the north pole repelling the traveler. On this basis the motion should continue indefinitely, but a test will show that it will not do so.

The corners of the triangle should be rounded slightly, and it would be better to use several hanging magnets, flexibly connected, so that when one is at the dead center the others will carry the traveler on.

— How to Make an Inlaid Checkerboard —

In the checkerboard design illustrated, each square is a miniature checkerboard in itself, composed of 64 light and dark squares.

For the dark squares, 16 strips each of ebony and mahogany, $3/16$ by $1/2$ by 17 in., are needed. As many strips of maple and oak of the same size will be needed for the white squares, a total of 64 strips. Using alternate strips of light and dark-colored wood, eight strips are glued together to make a laminated piece $1\frac{1}{2}$ in. wide. From this piece, after it has been glued and both faces sanded, $3/16$-in. sections are cut transversely, and eight such sections glued together to form a square of the board, using the gluing jig illus-

trated for the purpose. The sections are cut $3/16$ in. wide in a miter box. The strips are glued together so that light squares will come next to dark ones, the mahogany and ebony being used for the "black" squares, and oak and maple for the "white" ones.

All of the gluing operations should be done in a warm room and the stock should also be warmed. The wooden gluing jig should be made long enough to accommodate about eight squares at a time, each being separated from the other by a strip of paper. By rubbing the edges of the jig with paraffin, the glue will be prevented from sticking, and the blocks can easily be removed.

For a backing board use a $1/2$-in.

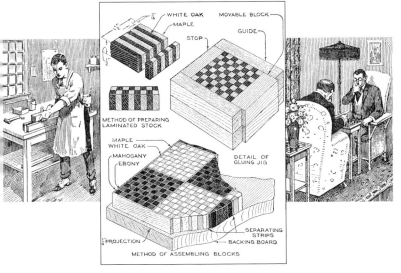

AN INLAID CHECKERBOARD, THE SQUARES OF WHICH ARE MINIATURE
CHECKERBOARDS THEMSELVES, BEING BUILT UP OF
LIGHT- AND DARK-COLORED WOODS.

pine board, 14½ in. square. Nail and glue two 1/16 by ½ in. red-oak strips near two edges, to form a right angle, and also prepare seven strips of red oak, 1/16 by ½ by 12½ in., and 56 similar strips, 1½ in. long. Paint the face of the board with glue and place in the angle formed by the strips at the edge, which should be at the lower left corner, one of the dark squares, with an ebony square in the corner, and the grain running parallel with the left edge of the board.

Glue one of the short separator strips to the upper edge, and then place a light block in position, with the grain at right angles to that of the dark, and with the light maple square in the lower left corner. When the row of eight squares has been placed against the pine strip at the left, glue one of the long separator strips to the inner edge of the row and start building up the next row. When all the blocks are assembled, enclose the two open sides with strips, and clamp them tightly until the glue sets.

When the glue has dried thoroughly, trim the ends of the separator strips flush, and glue 1/16-in. strips around the remaining two sides. Cut off the edges of the backing board to leave a 1/4-in. projection, and scrape and sand the surface smooth. Wax it or, if a higher gloss is desired, fill with a light paste filler and give three coats of varnish.

— A WIRE-WALKING TOY —

Boys can easily make a toy featuring a daring, wire-walking performer who, unmindful of the fact that a misstep may mean destruction, keeps on going, back and forth—so long as the motor runs or the crank is turned. The wire is stretched, not across Broadway, but between two 1-by 1-in. standards held upright by guy cords or fixed to a baseboard. They are fitted with forked tops, in A and B, and pulley wheels, C and D. A wire, F, is fastened to two of the prongs, in E, and a black thread, G, runs over the pulley wheels. A carriage, I, is formed from a 12-in. length of stiff wire, and weighted, in L, to balance upon the tight wire. The figure K is cut from stiff paper and made to turn upon the carriage upright J, and braced with thread, in H. Thus the figure is always drawn forward, revolving on the support J at the end of each trip. Power to turn the thread is transmitted from a hand crank or motor, M, by means of the double pulley wheel in D.

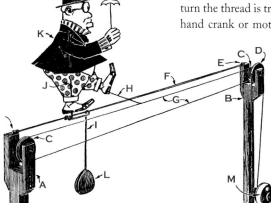

ADAPTED TO WINDOW DISPLAYS, THIS AMUSING TOY HAS AN ADVERTISING VALUE.

— AUTO HORN FOR CHILD'S PLAY VEHICLE —

A baking-powder or other tin can may be used to make the small automobile horn, shown in the illustration, for use on a child's coaster wagon. The device consists of a toothed wheel operating against several metal pawls within the can, and the warning sound is produced by

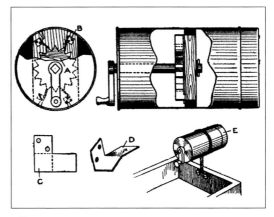

THIS SMALL AUTO HORN WAS MADE OF A TINNED CAN FITTED WITH A NOTCHED WHEEL AND PAWLS.

turning a small crank at the end of the can. The can is fixed to the side of the vehicle by means of a wire or strap-iron bracket, as shown in the sketch in E.

A piece of wood is fitted into the can to support the ratchet wheel. It is bored to carry a shaft, which bears in the end of the can, and at the exposed end of which is fixed a crank. A disk of wood, about ½ in. thick, is cut to have a notched edge as shown in A. The notched wheel is placed upon the shaft and fastened securely to it so that the ratchet

wheel revolves with the shaft when the crank on the shaft is turned. Four small pawls of sheet metal are fixed on the inner support, as shown in B. They are made by cutting pieces of metal to the shape shown in C, and folding them, as shown in D. They are fastened to the support with small screws or nails. The cover is placed on the end of the can when the device is used. The action of the ratchet wheel against the pawls produces a loud grating sound, resembling that of a horn of the siren type.

— "Moving-picture" Toy for Children —

A very interesting "moving-picture" toy for the small child can be made of cigar boxes, some wire, babbitt or lead, and a few pieces of pipe cane.

A rectangular opening is cut in the bottom of a cigar box of the size made to contain 100 cigars. A piece of window glass, cut to fit, is placed behind the opening and held in place by tacks. A frame made of cigar-box wood, shown at the upper right, fits neatly into the box. This holds the picture ribbon against the glass and carries the spools on which the ribbon is wound. A piece of pipe can is mounted at each corner of the frame to serve as a roller.

The spindles, one of which has a crank formed on one end, are made of No. 9 galvanized wire, and are provided with babbitt or lead "keys" to turn the wooden spools on which the ribbon is wound. To make these keys, a portion of the wire should be flattened as shown. A cork stopper with a groove cut in the top and a hole drilled through the center is pushed on the wire directly underneath the flattened portion. A cup is formed by wrapping heavy paper around this cork, into which the babbitt can be

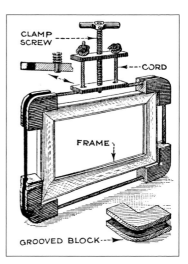

A "MOVING-PICTURE" TOY THAT IS INSTRUCTIVE AS WELL AS AMUSING CAN BE VERY EASILY MADE FROM SCRAP MATERIALS.

poured. The wooden spools upon which the ribbon is wound can be made from old film spools, cut at one end to fit the babbitt key.

Children can be amused for hours with this little toy, which can be made instructive as well as amusing. Pictures cut from the comic or rotogravure sections of newspapers and pasted to the ribbon in order make very interesting moving pictures of this kind, although, of course, any suitable pictures may be used.

— A Miniature Fighting Tank that Hurdles Trenches —

Among the engines of war in action on land, probably none has created greater interest than the now famous "fighting tank." According to reports, this machine pours out missiles of destruction on the enemy from armored turrets, and crawls over trenches, shell craters, and similar obstructions like a fabled giant creature of prehistoric ages. The tank described in this article, while not as deadly as those on the battlefields of Europe, performs remarkable feats of hurdling trenches and crawling over obstructions large in proportion to its size. The model, as shown in the heading sketches, is fully armored, and has a striking resemblance to these war monsters. The turret is mounted with a magazine gun that fires 20 projectiles automatically as the tank makes it way over the rough ground. The motive power for the tractor bands is furnished by linked rubber bands, stretched by a winding drum and ratchet device on the rear axle, as shown in *Fig. 1*. When the ratchet is released the rear axle drives the fluted wheels on it, and they in turn drive the tractor bands as shown in

the side elevation, *Fig. 6*. The wire-wrapped flywheel conserves the initial power of the rubber-band motor and makes its action more nearly uniform.

The tank will run upward of 10 ft. on the rubber-motor power, depending on the size and number of the bands used. The gun is fired by a spring hammer, activated by a rubber band. The trigger device is shown in *Fig. 1*. The pulley A is belted, with cord, to the front axle. Four pins on its inner side successively engage the wire trigger, drawing it out of the gun breech B, and permitting another shell to drop into place. As the pulley revolves, the trigger is released, firing the projectile. This process goes on until the motor runs down or the supply of shells is exhausted.

The tank is guided by the pilot wheel, shown in *Fig. 1*. The sheet-metal armor, with its turret, is fitted over the mechanism and can be removed quickly. It bears on angles bent up, as detailed in *Fig. 2,* to fit on the ends of the wooden center crosspiece of the main frame, and is held by removable pins at the ends of

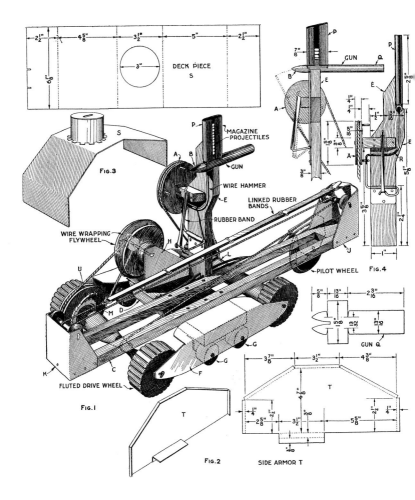

2½" 4⅝" 3½" 5" 2½"

6⅝"

3"

DECK PIECE
S

P

GUN

7⅞"

B

E

A

E

P

Q

E

2⅝"

¼" ¼"

¼" ¼"

5" 5"
16 16
16

5⅝"

A

A

E

R

3⅞"

3⅝"

2¼"

1"

FIG.4

P

MAGAZINE
PROJECTILES

A B

GUN

WIRE HAMMER

E

LINKED RUBBER
BANDS

RUBBER BAND

S

FIG.3

WIRE WRAPPING
FLYWHEEL

H

L

PILOT WHEEL

U

M D

C

K

G

G

F

FLUTED DRIVE WHEEL

FIG.I

J

5⅝" 13"
16

2 3/16"

5⅝"

13" 13"
32 16

GUN Q

3⅞" 3½" 4⅜"

7⅞"

T

¼" 2½"

2⅝" 3½" 3⅝"

5⅝" 2¼" ¼"

FIG.2

T

SIDE ARMOR T

PERSPECTIVE SKETCH, SHOWING THE ARRANGEMENT OF THE PARTS
WITH THE ARMOR AND THE TRACTOR BANDS REMOVED, AND
DETAILS OF THE GUN MECHANISM AND THE ARMOR.

this frame. Though the rubber motor is easy to make and install, the range of the tank can be increased by using a strong spring motor, the construction otherwise being similar.

The construction is best begun by making the wooden frame that supports the armor. The perspective sketch, *Fig. 1,* used in connection with the working and detailed drawings, will aid in making the latter clear. Make the frame C, as detailed in *Figs. 5* and *6,* ⅜ by 1¾ by 11 in. long, with an opening cut in the center, 1 in. wide, 1 in. from the rear, and 1¼ in. from the front end. Make the crosspiece D ⅜ by 1¾ by 5⅞ in. long; the gun support E, as detailed in *Fig. 4,* ⅜ by 1⁵/₁₆ by 6¼ in. long. Shape the support E as shown. Fasten the frame C and the crosspiece D with screws, setting the piece D 5¾ in. from the front, and its left end 3 in. from the side of the frame, as shown in *Fig. 5.* This is important, as the fitting of the other parts depends on the position of these wooden supports.

The drive-wheel axles are carried in sheet-metal hangers, F, shown in *Figs. 1* and *5,* and detailed in *Fig. 6.* These hangers also carry bearing wheels, G, *Fig. 1,* which are held between the hanger F and a metal

angle, as detailed in G, *Fig. 6.* These wheels are cut from a broomstick and mounted on nail axles. The metal for the hangers F is drilled as shown and bent double at the ends to make a strong bearing for the drive-wheel axles. The upper portion is bent at a right angle and fits over the top surface at the end of the crosspiece D, and is fastened to it with small screws or nails. Cut the stock for the hangers 2 by 6⅜ in. long.

Next make the sheet-metal support H, *Fig. 1,* for the flywheel. The rim of this is wrapped with wire to give it added weight. Cut the stock as detailed in *Fig. 6,* 1¾ by 4³/₁₆ in. long, and notch it to form the spring arrangement that holds the flywheel so that the belt will be tight. The other sheet-metal support may then be made. Cut the stock for the front support J, for the rubber motor, 4⅛ by 3¾ in. long, and shape it as shown in the detail, *Fig. 6.* Make the support K from a piece of sheet metal, in general shape similar to that used for support H, the dimensions being made as required and no spring arrangement being provided. Drill these metal fittings as indicated for the points of fastening, and mark the places for the holes in which shafts or axles run very carefully.

The driving mechanism can then be made, as shown in *Fig. 1*, and detailed in *Figs. 5* and *6*. The driving shafts and their parts, as well as the pulleys, can be turned in a lathe. Or they can be made from spools, round rods, etc. Make the front axle L and wheels, joined solidly, 5¾ in. overall. The grooved wheels are ¾ in. thick by 1 7/16 in. in diameter. Wires are used as bearings for shafts for the driving axles. If the rear axle is turned in a lathe, it is cut down to the shape indicated, thinner at the middle, to provide a place for the cord connected to the rubber motor. The grooved pulley and the fluted drive wheel at the winding-key end, shown in *Fig. 5*, are then cut loose. The drive wheel on the other end is cut loose, forming three sections mounted on the wire axle, one end of which is the winding key. Ratchet wheels, M, are fitted between the ends of the center section and adjoining pieces. The ratchet wheels are nailed to the center section and soldered to the wire axle. Pawls, U, are fitted to the inside of the two end sections as indicated in *Figs. 1* and *5*. When the rubber motor is wound up on the drum, the tractor bands are gripped until it is desired to start the tank on its trip. Then the power is communicated from the drum, or center section of the axle, to the drive wheels by means of the ratchet wheels acting on the pawls.

Mount the hangers F on the center crosspiece D, fitting the axles of the drive wheels into place. Make the weighted flywheel and mount it on its shaft, as shown, lining it up with the pulley on the rear drive shaft. Fit the supports J and K into place, setting spools for the rubber-motor cord in place on wire axles. Arrange the belt from the flywheel to the driveshaft, and connect the rubber bands for the rubber motor as shown. Fasten one end in the hook of support J, and pass the winding cord through the spools. Fix it to the driveshaft. The device can then be operated with the fluted drive wheels bearing on strips of wood for tracks.

The tractor bands N are fitted over the drive wheels, as shown in *Fig. 6*. They are built up of canvas strips on which wooden shoes are glued and sewn, as detailed in *Fig. 5*. The stitches that reinforce the gluing are taken in the order indicated by the numerals. The pilot wheel is 2 in. in diameter, and sharpened at its circumference. Make a metal shell, O, for it as detailed in *Fig. 6*. Solder the shell to the double wire, which sup-

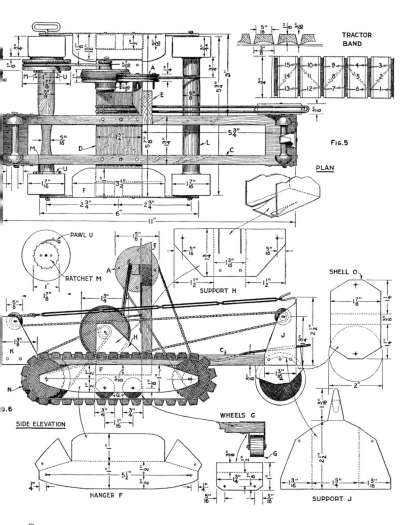

PLAN AND SIDE ELEVATION OF THE INTERIOR MECHANISM, WITH THE
ARMOR REMOVED AND DETAILS OF THE METAL FITTINGS,
THREE RATCHETS, AND THE TRACTOR BANDS.

ports the wheel and gives it a spring tension to take obstructions nicely. The wire is fastened to the crosspiece D, as shown in *Fig. 5*.

The gun and its mechanism can be made handily before the support E is fixed into place at the front of the crosspiece D. Shape the magazine P from sheet metal, making it 2⅝ in. high, as detailed in *Fig. 4*. Make the gun Q from a piece of sheet metal, as detailed, cutting the metal to the exact dimensions indicated. Mount the magazine and the gun, and arrange the wire hammer R, and the rubber band that holds it. Fix the pulley A into place on its axle, supported by a small block of wood. Belt it to the front drive-wheel axle, as shown in *Fig. 5*, after the gun support is fastened into place with screws. Make the projectiles of wood, as shown, and the fighting tank is ready to be tested before putting on the armor.

The armor is made of one deck piece, S, *Fig. 3*, into which the covered turret is set with two sidepieces

T, as detailed in *Fig. 2*. Make one left- and one right-sidepiece, allowing the flanges all around to be bent over and used for riveting or soldering the armor together. The bottom extension on the sidepieces is bent double to form an angle on which the armor is supported, where it rests on the top of the hangers F. The turret is fitted to the deck by cutting notches along its lower edge, the resulting strips being alternately turned in and out along the point of joining, as shown in *Fig. 3*. When the armor is completed, it is fitted over the main frame, the gun projecting from the turret. Small pins hold the ends of the armor solid against the ends of the main frame C, so that the armor can be lifted off readily. The various parts of the fighting tank can be painted as desired, care being taken not to injure the points of bearing on the axles and pulleys, which should be oiled. Silver bronze is a good finish for the exterior of the armor, which may be decorated with a coat of arms.

— TOY PAPER WARSHIPS —

With a pair of scissors, pins, and a newspaper or two, a fleet of warships can be made to sail the seven seas of polished floors.

Strips of paper, through which holes at opposite points have been cut and pinned together at one end as shown in *Fig. 1*, are used for the sides of the boat. Rolls of paper are slipped through the opposite holes, as shown in *Fig. 2,* and provide support for the deck. The deck is a flat piece of paper pointed at the end to fit between the sides of the craft. A second deck fit-

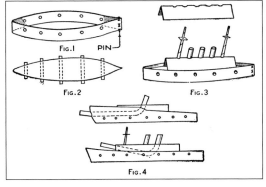

FLEETS OF BATTLESHIPS MAY BE MADE OF PAPER.

ted with funnels and masts, as shown in *Fig. 3*, is made of a folded piece of paper with holes cut through it for the masts and funnels, which are rolls of paper. If plain paper is used, the warships may be made in several colors, which adds to the effect of rivalry between the fleets. Other types of craft may eas-ily be devised, two of which are shown in *Fig. 4.* Not only the youngsters in the household, but their elders as well, may find not a little amusement and diversion in the making of a fleet of such warships, modeled after battleships, destroyers, battle cruisers, and other vessels.

— A COME-BACK ROLLING CAN —

An interesting toy may be made by fitting a rubber band into a tin can and weighting it as shown. When the can is rolled on the floor it will return to its original

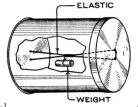

place by reason of the weight that is supported on a string at the middle of the rubber band. The latter is passed through two holes at each end of the can, and when the can is rolled along the floor the elastic is wound at the middle. The weight reverses the direction of rolling.

— MECHANICAL TOY PIGEON MADE OF WOOD —

When the head of the mechanical pigeon is lowered the tail rises, and vice versa. It is constructed as follows: Make paper patterns for the parts, which consist of two body pieces, a head, a tail, and the foot piece. The shape of the parts is shown in the sketch, the front body piece being removed to show the connections of the rubber and wire controlling the movements. The view above shows the fasten-

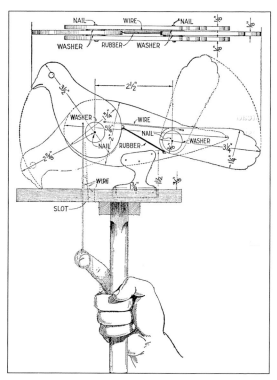

DRAW ON THE WIRE AND THE HEAD
AND TAIL BOB UP AND DOWN.

ing of the parts, which are made of ⅛ to ¼ in. softwood: head, 1¾ by 3½ in.; body, 2 by 5¼ in.; tail 1¼ by 3¼ in.; foot piece, 1⅜ by 1½ in. Mark the shapes on the wood, cut them out and mount them, with a rubber band connecting the head and tail as shown. Nail the foot piece between the body pieces and pivot the head and tail on nails. Connect the head with a wire with a loop on one end. Make the holder, and cut a slot into it for the draw wire, operated with the finger.

SLEIGHT *of* HAND

— TOSSING A CARD AT A MARK ACCURATELY —

There is an interesting old game that can be played instead of solitaire. It consists of trying to toss the greatest number of cards into a small basket or an upturned stiff hat, set at a distance. If the cards are held as shown in A, and tossed as in B, the card may be thrown with surprising accuracy after a little practice.

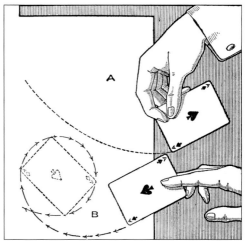

TOSSING CARDS ACCURATELY SO THAT THEY WILL FALL INTO A RECEPTACLE SET AT A DISTANCE.

— A SIMPLE CARD DECEPTION —

The effect of this trick is not new, but the method is. A card is selected by a spectator and noted, then returned to the pack, which is shuffled by the one drawing the card. Despite the thorough mixing, the correct card is located by cutting the pack. The secret is this: When the card is chosen, the chooser is allowed to remove it from the pack. The performer then takes it and holds it up and asks the audience to fix it in their minds. While doing this, allow the thumbnail of the index finger to slightly graze the edge of the card. This will not show, nor can it be detected by the holder, and he suspects nothing of the kind. When returned to the deck and shuffled, the pack is evened up for cutting. A glance at the edges will show a small white spot distinctly, as the scraped edge will contrast with the other soiled cards. It is simple to cut the pack from this key.

— A Diminishing Card Trick —

A clever diminishing card trick may be played with a piece of paper made up as shown in the illustration. Show the audience the whole card, *Fig. 1,* then fold it halfway and show again, *Fig. 2,* then again, *Fig. 3.* If this is done quickly it will not be noticed. A piece of paper is used the size of a regular playing card, and an ace is made on one side. When it is folded over, one side of the reduced size is made to show the same ace, then another fold is made and the smaller ace is made.

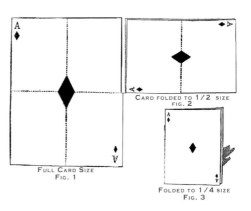

CARD FOLDED TO 1/2 SIZE
FIG. 2

FULL CARD SIZE
FIG. 1

FOLDED TO 1/4 SIZE
FIG. 3

REDUCING THE SIZE OF A PLAYING CARD WHILE HOLDING IT IN ONE HAND.

— Disappearing-coin Trick —

To make a quarter disappear from a glass of water after hearing it drop is a very puzzling trick. The articles necessary to perform this trick are a glass of water, a handkerchief, a quarter, and a piece of clear glass the exact size of a quarter. The glass can be cut and ground round on an emery wheel, and the edge polished.

To perform the trick, advance with the piece of glass hidden between the second and third fingers of the left hand and holding the quarter in plain sight between the thumb and first finger of the same hand, with the handkerchief in the right hand. Throw the handkerchief over the left hand and gather up the glass piece in the fold of the cloth, allowing the coin to drop into the palm of the left hand while covered. Remove the left hand and hold out the piece of glass with the handkerchief drawn tightly around it.

Anyone can touch the cloth-covered glass, but it cannot be distinguished from the quarter. While this is being shown, slip the quarter into a pocket. Spread the handkerchief over the glass of water and allow the glass disk to drop. A distinct click will be heard when it strikes the bottom. Raise the handkerchief and nothing will be seen, as the glass will be invisible in the water.

— TRICKS WITH KNIVES AND GLASSES —

An interesting trick may be performed with three tumblers and three table knives. Place the tumblers in an equilateral triangle on a table so that the knife ends, when the knives are laid between the glasses as shown in the plan sketch, are about 1 in. away from the tumblers. The trick is to arrange the knives so that they are supported by the tops of the three tumblers and nothing else. Most observers will say that it is impossible; some will try it and in most cases fail. It can be done, and the illustration shows how simply it may be accomplished.

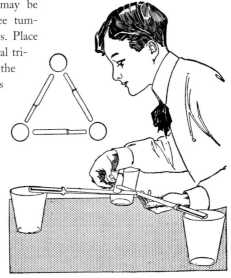

KNIVES PLACED IN SUCH A MANNER AS TO BE SUPPORTED BY THE THREE GLASSES.

— A SIMPLE GEOMETRICAL TRICK —

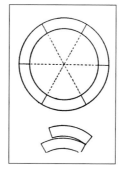

A simple geometrical trick that can be made from a piece of cardboard will provide plenty of entertainment at the efforts of others to prove that two identical circular-ring sections are of different sizes.

Two concentric circles are drawn on the cardboard with a compass, and these are carefully divided into six equal parts. Two ring sectors are cut out. Place the sectors one above the other as below, and ask someone how much longer one piece is than the other. Unless the person has seen the experiment before, he will invariably say that one is considerably longer than the other. Now reverse the pieces and repeat the question. The fact that the two pieces are the same size can be established to the satisfaction of anyone by placing one on top of the other.

— THE MAGIC PILLBOX —

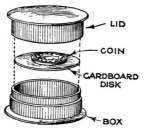

The magic pillbox makes coins disappear and return at will. The trick is very simple, and any pillbox can be fixed for performing it in a few minutes.

Cut a cardboard disk just large enough to fit into the bottom of a regulation round pillbox. Drop a coin in the box and put the lid on. Then turn it upside down and shake it, calling attention to the fact that the coin is still there by the rattling inside. Now, pull the box apart, holding the lid in the left hand so that the cardboard disk covers the coin, which has vanished. Then, still holding the lid upside down, put the box together again and reverse the operation, holding the bottom in the right hand. Upon opening the box the coin will reappear.

So That's How They Do It!

— The Magic Cabinet —

The performer calls the attention of his audience to a cabinet mounted on short legs and having doors in the front, back, and top. The back door is opened, then the top and front, and an arm is thrust through to show that the cabinet is empty and without double doors or double walls. The performer also puts his "magic" wand beneath the box to show that there is no deception there. The doors are then closed, except the top, and reaching down he takes out any number of articles, from handkerchiefs to rabbits, and then the front door is opened to show the box is empty. But upon closing the front door again, he is still able to produce articles until the supply is exhausted. Wonderful though this trick may appear, it is very simple. If a person is handy with tools, it can be made from lumber taken from a packing box.

To make the cabinet, nail together, in the shape of a rectangle, two pieces 16 in. long, 14 in. wide, and ½ in. thick, and two pieces 14 in. square by ½ in. thick. To one of the latter pieces fasten four legs, one at each corner. In the opposite piece, or the top, make an opening in the

TILTING BOX IN BACK DOOR

OPEN THE FRONT DOOR AND TOP OF THE CABINET AND IT WILL APPEAR EMPTY.

center 8 in. square. This opening is covered with a door 8½ in. square, supplied with a knob to open it easily. A piece 16 in. long by 14 in. wide, with an attached knob, is hinged to the front for a door; and another is made for the back, hinged in the same manner and with a knob. In the back there is a cutout, 9 in. long and 7 in. wide, made in the center. In this opening a swinging box is hung to hold the articles taken from the cabinet. The swinging box is made of two pieces, 9 in. long and 7 in. wide, and two pieces about ½ in. larger each way, nailed together on ends, cut triangular. This box is hinged in the opening so that it will swing in or out as desired and show a panel on either side of the door. The front door should have a panel nailed on each side of equal size to make both doors appear alike.

After loading all the things desired to be shown in the triangular box, start the trick by pushing this box into the cabinet and showing the outside. Then open the back, and in doing so, push the triangular box out as the door swings back and away from the audience. This shows that there is nothing to be seen but the panel. Open the front door and top, and the cabinet will appear empty. Close both front and back doors, and in making this change, push the triangular box in and begin to take things out through the top door.

By careful construction, the cabinet can be made so that the doors will open freely and the triangular box swing easily so that it will not be seen in operating it. With a clever performer this trick is without equal, as many variations can be made in the performance.

GO FLY *a* KITE

— HOW TO MAKE COMBINED KITES: A DRAGON KITE —

Dragon kites are made as hideous as the maker can possibly imagine them. Although the one to be considered is no beauty, it is more droll than fierce-looking. In general appearance the dragon and centipede kites are like huge caterpillars floating about in the air. The kite sometimes twists and the balancer sticks appear to be large, hairy spines. Usually the tail end swings higher than the head. It is like so many single kites, pulling hard and requiring a strong cord for the line. The individual circular sections may number 20 and if placed 30 in. apart would make a kite about 50 ft. in length, or the number of sections may be more or less to make the kite longer or shorter. The kite will fold up into a very small space, for carrying about or for storage. But care should be taken in folding not to entangle the harness.

IN GENERAL APPEARANCE THE DRAGON KITE IS LIKE A HUGE CATERPILLAR FLOATING ABOUT IN THE AIR.

The Head

The head requires much more work than any of the other sections. There are two principle rings to this section, as shown in *Fig. 1*. The inner ring is the more important, the outer one being added for the protection of the points when alighting. The construction of the framework is shown in *Fig. 2*. It is made entirely of bamboo. The bamboo is split into strips, about 3/16 in. wide, for the ring A. As the bamboo strips will be much too thick, they must be pared down to less than 1/16 in. The diameter of the ring A is 12 in., and a strip of bamboo to make this ring should be about 38 in. long, so that there will be some end for making a lap joint. The ends of the strip are held securely together by winding them with linen thread. Some boys use strips of rice paper that are about ½ in. wide and torn lengthwise. The rice-paper strips are made wet with paste before winding them on the

FIG. 1

it is useful in making all kinds of kites. Two small rings, each 3½ in. in diameter, are put in between the two parallel pieces, as shown in D and E. These are for the eyes of the dragon. The rings are lashed to the two crosspieces B and C. Because the eyes revolve in the rings, they should be made perfectly true. This can be done by shaping the bamboo about a perfectly round cylinder, 3½ in. in diameter. To stiffen the whole framework, two pieces of bamboo, 1/16 in. thick, ⅛ in. wide, and 20 in. long, are lashed to the back as shown by F and G. There is a space of 3 in. between the inner ring A and the outer ring H, giving the latter a diameter of 18 in. It is made of a bamboo strip, ⅛ in. wide, and should be less than 1/16 in. thick. It may be necessary to make this large ring from two pieces of bamboo to get the length. In such a case be careful to make a perfect ring with the ends well lashed together. Two short pieces are lashed together to the two rings, as shown in J and K.

joint. When they dry out, the shrinkage will bind the ends securely.

Two crosspieces, of the same weight as the ring stick, are placed 3½ in. apart, at equal distances from the center and parallel, as shown in B and C. The ends of these pieces are turned at a sharp angle and lashed to the inside surface of the ring A. To make these bends, heat the bamboo over a candle flame until it will give under pressure, and then bend it. The bamboo will stay in shape after it becomes cold. This method of bending should be remembered, because

The supports for the horns consist of two pieces, ⅛ in. wide and less than 1/16 in. thick, and they are lashed to the upper crosspiece and to both rings, so that the parts L and M are exactly halfway between the ends of the pieces F and G, and radiate out from the center of the ring A. The other parts, N and O, point to the center of the eye rings, respectively. The ears are unimportant and may be put on if desired. The rings on the horns and the stick ends may be from ½ to 2 in. in diameter, cut from stiff paper, but if larger, made of bamboo.

Chinese rice paper is the best material for covering, and it should be stretched tightly so that there will be no buckling or bagging places. The only part covered is that inside of the inner ring A, the horns and the ears, leaving the eye rings open. The shades are put on with a brush and watercolors, leaving the face white, or it can be tinted in brilliant colors. Leave the horns white and color the tongue red.

The Eyes

The frame for each eye is made of bamboo, pared down to 1/32 in. in thickness and formed into a perfect ring, 3¼ in. in diameter. Each ring revolves on an axle made of wire passed through the bamboo exactly on the diameter, as shown in P, *Fig. 3.* The wire should be long enough to pass through the socket ring D or E, *Fig. 2,* also, and after the eye ring is in place in the socket ring and the axle adjusted, the latter is fastened to the eye ring with a strip of paper wrapped tightly around the wire and

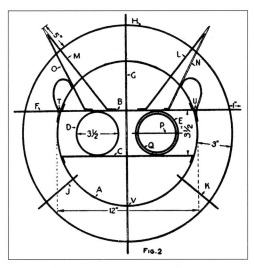

THE FRAMEWORK FOR THE HEAD SECTION
IS MADE ENTIRELY OF BAMBOO STRIPS
LASHED AT THE JOINTS.

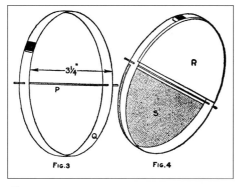

Fig.3   Fig.4

TWO BAMBOO RINGS WITH PAPER COVERINGS,
TO MAKE THEM TURN IN THE WIND,
CONSTITUTE THE EYES.

pasted to the bamboo of the ring. A glass bead, placed on the wire axle between the socket rings D or E and the eye ring Q on each side, keeps them apart and the revolving one from striking the other.

Each side of the eye ring is covered halfway with rice paper, as shown in *Fig. 4.* The part R is on the upper front half, and that shown by S is on the back lower half. Placing the two halves in this manner causes an unequal pressure of the wind on the whole eyepiece, and thus causes it to revolve on the axle. The front upper half of the eyepiece is made black, and the smaller dark portion extending below the darkened half is a round piece of paper placed just between the two halves so that half

of it will show on both front and back of the eyepiece. When the eyepiece is given a half turn in its socket, the backside will come to the front and will appear just the same as the other side. Some kite builders add pieces of mirror glass to the eyes, to reflect the light and cause flashes as the eyes revolve in their sockets.

A Section Kite

The ring for the section kite is made the same size as the inner ring of the head kite, or in this case 12 in. in diameter. The bamboo for making this ring should be ⅛ in. wide and 1/16 in. thick. The balancer stick, 36 in. long, is located about the same place as the cross stick F, as shown in *Fig. 2,* and must be made small, light, and well balanced. Small tufts of tissue paper or feathers are attached to the tip ends of the balancer sticks, as shown in *Fig. 5.* The cover for the section kite is put on tightly, the same as for the head; the builder can color them as desired. The balancer on the last section should have streamers, as shown in *Fig. 6,* for a finish. The streamers are made of light cloth.

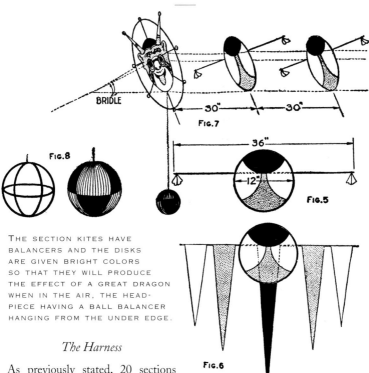

BRIDLE

FIG.7

30"   30"

FIG.8

36"

12"

FIG.5

THE SECTION KITES HAVE
BALANCERS AND THE DISKS
ARE GIVEN BRIGHT COLORS
SO THAT THEY WILL PRODUCE
THE EFFECT OF A GREAT DRAGON
WHEN IN THE AIR, THE HEAD-
PIECE HAVING A BALL BALANCER
HANGING FROM THE UNDER EDGE.

FIG.6

The Harness

As previously stated, 20 sections more or less can be used, and the number means so many separate kites which are joined together with three long cords, spacing the sections 30 in. apart. The cords should be as long as the kite from the head to the tail, allowing sufficient extra length for the knots. As such a kite will make a hard pull, the cord used should be six-ply, hard-twisted seine twine. Start by tying the three long cords to the head kite at the points T, U, and V, Fig. 2. Tie the next section at corresponding places just 30 in. from the head kite. The construction will be much easier if the head kite is fastened to a wall so that each cord may be drawn out to its proper length. Continue the tying until all sections are attached just 30 in. apart. Other spacing can be used, but the distance selected must be uniform throughout the length of the kite. The individual kites, or sections, may vary in size, or they can all be 9 in. in diameter instead of 12 in., and the balancer sticks 30 in. long instead of 36 in., but a kite of uniform sections is much better and is easier to make. The positions of the sections as they will appear in the kite are shown in *Fig. 7.*

The Bridle

The Chinese bridle is usually made of three strings, which are attached to the same points on the head kite as the harness cords, or at T, U, and V. The lower string is longer than the two upper ones so that the proper inclination will be presented to the breeze. As the head is inclined, all the section kites will also be inclined. Some makers prefer a balancer on the head kite, and in one instance such a balancer was made in the

shape of a ball. A ball made of bamboo strips is shown in *Fig. 8,* and is attached as shown in *Fig. 7.*

Flying the Kite

It will be necessary to have a helper, and perhaps two, in starting the kite up because the harness might become entangled. Quite a little run will be necessary, but when up the kite will make a steady flier and will pull very hard. If the first attempt is unsuccessful, try readjustment of the bridle or a little different position in the breeze, and see that the balancers are not tangled. Quite a number of changes may be worked out on these plans, but it is necessary to bear in mind that the distances between sections must be equal and that the general construction must be maintained.

— HOW TO MAKE COMBINED KITES: A FESTOONED KITE —

More than one kite on the same framework is known as a compound kite. The one illustrated consists of three tailless kites on one long stick, called the spine. The upper one is 3 ft., the center one, 2 ft., and the lower one, 1 ft. in width. A stick of light wood will be

needed for the construction of this kite—spruce is best, but it may be pine or bass—7 ft. long by ¼ by ½ in. If the wood breaks easily it will be better to increase the width from ½ in. to ¾ in., or the stick might be made ⅜ in. thick without increasing the width, but with a good spruce stick the dimensions first given will be sufficient. The stick should be straight grained and without a twist. If the spine is twisted, the kites will not lie flat or in a plane with each other. If one is out of true, it will cause the kite to be unsteady in the air. The bow sticks are three, the upper one being 4 ft. long by ¼ by ½ in., the center one, 2 ft. long by ¼ by ⅜ in., and the lower one, 1 ft. long by ¼ by ¼ in. About

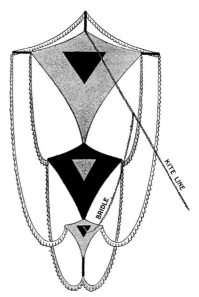

THE KITE AS IT APPEARS WITH THE FESTOONS HUNG TO THE ENDS OF THE STICKS.

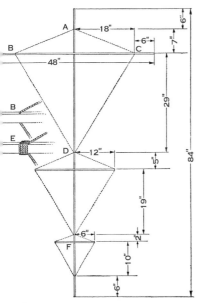

THE SPINE WITH THE BOW STICKS PROPERLY SPACED AS SHOWN BY THE DIMENSIONS.

five sheets of tissue paper will be required, but more may be needed for color combinations. The so-called French tissue paper is much better, as it comes in fine colors and is much stronger than the ordinary tissue. It costs a trifle more, but it pays in making a beautiful kite. The Chinese rice paper is the strongest, but comes only in natural colors.

It will be seen that the kites do not extend to the top and bottom of the spine stick. The first bow stick is placed 13 in. from the top end of the spine, and each of its ends extends 6 in. beyond the kite for fastening the festoons. The bow sticks should be lashed to the spine, not nailed. Wind diagonally around the two sticks, both left and right, then wind between the two, around the other windings. This draws all windings up tightly to prevent slipping.

To string up the upper kite, drill a small hole through the spine 6 in. from the top, at A. Also drill 6 in. from each end of the bow stick, at B and C. If a small drill is not available, notch the stick with a knife or saw to hold the string. Another hole is made in the spine 29 in. from the upper bow stick, or at D. Tie the outline string at A, then pass through the hole at C, then through D, up through B and back to the starting point at A. In tying the last point, draw up the string tightly, but not enough to spring the spine or bow. Measure carefully to see if the distance AC is the same as AB and if CD is equal to BD. If they are not, shift the string until they are equal and wind at all points, as shown in E, to prevent further slipping. Proceed in the same way with the center and lower kite, and it will be ready for the cover.

The cover tissue should be cut about 1 in. larger all around than the surface to be covered, but turn over about half of this allowance. This will give plenty of looseness to the cover. For the fringe festoons, cut strips of tissue paper 2½ in. wide, past ½ in. of one long edge over a string, and cut slits with scissors at intervals of 1 in. along the loose edge. After the fringe has been made, attach it as shown in the illustration. Do not stretch it tightly but give sufficient looseness to make each length form a graceful curve and keep the sides well balanced.

To bend the bows of the upper and center kites, attach a string from end to end of each bow on the back side of the kite and spring in short brace sticks.

Attach the upper end of the bridle at A. The length of the bridle string is 87 in. and the kite line is attached to it 30 in. from A, leaving the lower part from this point to F, where it is tied to the spine, 57 in. long.

The kite should fly without a tail, but if it dodges too much attach extra streamers to the ends of the bow sticks of the lower kite and to the bottom of the spine.

If good combinations of colors are used a very beautiful kite will be the result and one that will fly well.

— AN EIGHT-POINTED STAR KITE —

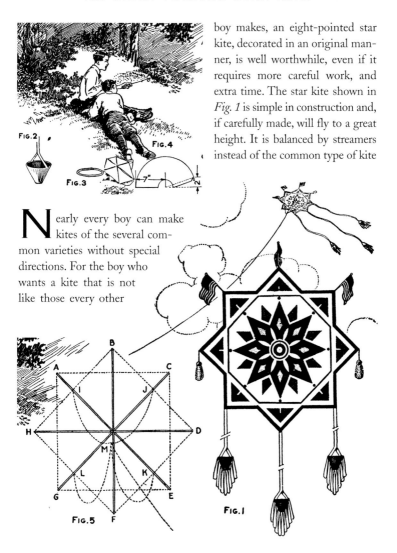

boy makes, an eight-pointed star kite, decorated in an original manner, is well worthwhile, even if it requires more careful work, and extra time. The star kite shown in *Fig. 1* is simple in construction and, if carefully made, will fly to a great height. It is balanced by streamers instead of the common type of kite

Nearly every boy can make kites of the several common varieties without special directions. For the boy who wants a kite that is not like those every other

FIG.2

FIG.4

FIG.3

FIG.5 F

FIG.I

tail. Any regular-shaped kite should be laid out accurately, as otherwise the error appears very prominent, and unbalances the poise of the kite.

The frame for this star kite is made of four sticks joined, as indicated in *Fig. 5,* with strings running from one corner to the second corner beyond, as from A to C, from C to E, etc. A little notching of each pair of sticks lessens the thickness of the sticks at the center crossing and strengthens the frame. The sticks are ¼ by ½ in. by 4 ft. long. They are set at right angles to each other in pairs and lashed together with cord. They are also held by a ¾-in. brad at the center. The strings that form the sides of the squares, A to G, and B to H, must be equal in length when tied. The points where the strings forming the squares cross each other and the sticks are also tied.

The first cover, which is put on with paste laying it out on a smooth floor or table as usual in kite making, is plain, light-colored paper. The darker decorations are pasted onto this. The outside edges of the cover are turned over the string outline and pasted down. The colors may be in many combinations, such as red and white, purple and gold, green, and white, etc. Brilliant and contrasting

colors are best. The decoration may proceed from the center out, or the reverse. The outside edge in the design shown has a 1½ in. black stripe. The figures are black. The next octagonal black line binds the design together. The points of the star are dark blue with a gilt stripe on each. The center design is done in black, dark blue, and gilt.

The flags are tied on, and the tassels are easily made of cord. The outside streamers are at least 6 ft. long and balanced carefully. Ribbons or dark-colored lining cambric are used for them. The funnel-shaped ends balance the kite. They are shown in detail in *Figs. 2, 3,* and *4,* and have 1-in. openings at the bottom, through which the air passes, causing a pull that steadies the kite. They are of dark blue, and the cloth fringe is of light blue. A thin reed or fine wire is used for the hoop that stiffens the top. Heavy wrapping or cover paper is used to cover the hoop. It is cut as shown in *Fig. 4* and rolled into shape.

A four-string bridle is fastened to the frame at I, J, K, and L, as shown. The upper strings are each 18 in., and the lower ones 32 in. long, to the point where they come together, and must be adjusted after the kite line is fastened at M.

— How to Make and Fly a Chinese Kite —

A serious kite-flying boy is not satisfied with simply holding the end of a kite string and running up and down the block or field trying to raise a heavy paper kite with a half pound of rags for a tail. He makes a kite as light as possible without any tail, which has the peculiar property of being able to move in every direction. Sometimes an expert can make one of these kites travel across the wind for several hundred feet. In fact, I have seen boys a full block apart bring their kites together and engage in a combat until one of their kites floated away with a broken string, or was punctured by the swift dives of the other and sent to earth, a wreck.

The boy makes his kite as follows: From a sheet of thin but tough tissue paper about 20 in. square, which he folds and cuts along the dotted line as shown in *Fig. 1*, he gets a perfectly square kite having all the properties of a good flyer, light and strong. He shapes two pieces of bamboo, one for the backbone and

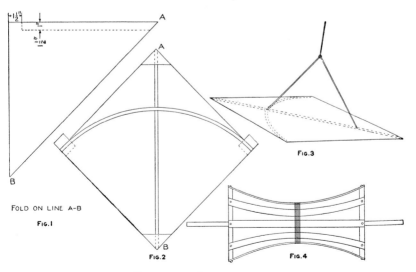

FOLD ON LINE A-B

Fig.1

Fig.2

Fig.3

Fig.4

PARTS OF A CHINESE KITE.

one for the bow. The backbone is flat, ¼ by 3/32 in. and 18 in long. This he smears along one side with common boiled rice. Boiled rice is one of the best adhesives for use on paper that can be obtained, and the Chinese have used if for centuries, while we are just waking up to the fact that it makes fine photo paste. Having placed the backbone in position, paste two triangular pieces of paper over the ends of the stick to prevent tearing. The bow is now bent and the lugs extending from the sides of the square paper are bent over the ends of the bow and pasted down. If the rice is quite dry or mealy it can be smeared on and will dry almost immediately; therefore no strings are needed to hold the bow bent while the paste dries.

After the sticks are in position, the kite will appear as shown in *Fig. 2.* The dotted lines show the lugs bent over the ends of the bow and pasted down. *Fig. 3* shows how the band is put on and how the kite is balanced. This is the most important part and cannot be explained very well. This must be done by experimenting, and it is enough to say that the kite must balance perfectly. The string is fastened by a slipknot to the band, moved back and forth until the kite

flies properly, and then it is securely fastened.

A reel is made next. Two ends—the bottoms of two small peach baskets will do—are fastened to a dowel stick or broom handle if nothing better is at hand. These ends are placed about 14 in. apart and strips nailed between them, as shown in *Fig. 4,* and the center drawn in and bound with a string. The kite string used is generally a heavy packing thread. This is run through a thin flour or rice paste until it is thoroughly coated, then it is run through a quantity of crushed glass. The glass should be beaten up fine and run through a fine sieve to make it about the same as No. 2 emery. The particles should be extremely sharp and full of splinters. These particles adhere to the pasted string and when dry are so sharp that it cannot be handled without scratching the fingers. Therefore the kite is flown entirely from the reel. To wind the string upon the reel, all that is necessary is to lay one end of the reel stick in the bend of the left arm and twirl the other end between the fingers of the right hand.

In China, a boy will be flying a gaily colored little kite from the roof of a house (if it is in one of the large cities that have flat-roofed houses) and a second boy will appear on the roof of another house perhaps 200 ft. away. Both have large reels full of string, often several hundred yards of it. The first hundred feet or so is glass-covered string, the balance common packing thread or glass-covered string. As soon as the second boy has his kite aloft, he begins maneuvering to drive it across the wind and over to the first kite. First, he pays out a large amount of string. Then, as the kite wobbles to one side with its nose pointing toward the first kite, he tightens his line and commences a steady quick pull. If properly done, his kite crosses over to the other and above it. The string is now paid out until the second kite is hanging over the first one's line. The wind now tends to take the second kite back to its parallel and in so doing makes a turn about the first kite's string. If the second kite is close enough, the first tries to spear him by swift dives. The second boy in the meantime is see-sawing his string and presently the first kite's string is cut and it drifts away.

It is not considered sport to haul the other fellow's kite down as might be done, and therefore a very interesting battle is often witnessed when the experts clash their kites.

— HOW TO MAKE A WAR KITE —

The material required is three pine sticks, each 60 in. long, one stick 54 in. long, one stick 18 in. long, all ½ in. square; 4 yards of cambric; a box of tacks; some linen thread, and 16 ft. of stout twine.

Place two 60-in. sticks parallel with each other and 18 in. apart. Then lay the 54-in. piece across at right angles to them 18 in. from the upper ends, as shown in *Fig. 1,* and fasten the joints with brads. At a point 21 in. below this crosspiece, attach the 18-in. crosspiece.

The extending ends of all three long pieces are notched, *Fig. 2,* and the line is stretched taut around them as shown by the dotted lines. If the cambric is not of sufficient size to cover the frame, two pieces must be sewn together. Then a piece is cut out to the shape of the string, allowing 1 in. to project all around for a lap. The cambric is sewn fast to the string with the linen thread. Fasten the cloth to the frame part with the tacks, spacing them 1 in. apart. The space in the center, between the sticks, is cut out. Make two pieces of the remaining goods, one 36 in. by 18 in., and the other 36 in. by 21 in. The remaining 60-in. stick is fastened to these pieces of cambric, as shown in *Fig. 3,* and the whole is fastened to the main frame so as to make a V-shaped projection. The bridle strings, for giving the proper distribution of pull on the line to the kite, are fastened one to the upper end of the long stick in the V-shaped piece attached to the kite. The other is fastened to the lower end, as shown in *Fig. 4.* The inclination can be varied to suit the builder by changing the point of attachment of the kite line to the bridle. If it is desired to fly the kite directly overhead, attach the line above the regular point. For

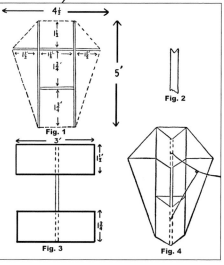

low flying make the connection below this point. The regular point is found by trial flights with the line fastened temporarily to the bridle, after which the fastening is made permanent.

THE LINE SHOULD BE A VERY STRONG ONE, THEN BANNERS CAN BE FLOWN ON IT.

Fig. 1

Fig. 2

Fig. 3

Fig. 4

— AN AEROPLANE KITE —

After building a number of kites from recent description in *Amateur Mechanics* I branched out and constructed the aeroplane kite shown in the illustration, which has excited considerable comment in the neighborhood on account of its appearance and behavior in the air.

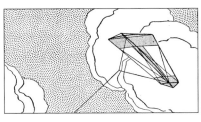

THE KITE BEING TAILLESS RIDES THE AIRWAVES LIKE AN AEROPLANE IN A STEADY BREEZE.

The main frame consists of a 31-in.-long center stick, A, and two cross sticks, of which one, B, is 31 in. long and the other, C, 15½ in. long. The location of the cross-pieces on the centerpiece A is shown in the sketch, the front piece B being 1¾ in. from the end, and the rear piece C, 2¼ in. from the other end. The ends of the sticks have small notches cut to receive a string, D, which is run around the outside to make the outline of the frame and to brace the parts. Two cross strings are placed at E and F, 7 in. from either end of the centerpiece A. Other brace strings are crossed, as shown in G, and then tied to the cross string F on both sides, as in H.

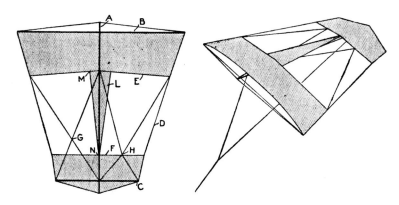

The long crosspiece B is curved upward to form a bow, the center of which should be 3¼ in. above the string by which its ends are tied together. The shorter crosspiece is bent and tied in the same manner to make the curve 2½ in, and the centerpiece to curve 1¾ in., both upward. The front and rear parts, between the end and the cross strings E and F, are covered with yellow tissue paper. This is pasted to the crosspieces and strings. The small wings L are purple tissue paper, 4 in. wide at M and tapering to a point at N.

The bridle string is attached on the centerpiece A, at the junction of the crosspieces B and C, and must be adjusted for the size and weight of the kite. The kite is tailless and requires a steady breeze to make it float in the air currents like an aeroplane.

The bridle string and the bending of the sticks must be adjusted until the desired results are obtained. The bridle string should be tied so that it will about center under the cross stick B for the best results. But a slight change from this location may be necessary to make the kite ride the air currents properly. The center of gravity will not be the same in the construction of each kite, and the string can be located only by trial, after which it is permanently fastened.

— CAMERA FOR TAKING PICTURES FROM A KITE —

When watching a kite flying at a considerable height, one frequently wonders how the landscape appears from such a viewpoint as would be possible from a kite. Few of us can have the experience of a ride in an airplane, but it is quite possible to obtain a view from the kite, by proxy as it were, through the use of a kite camera. A kite of large dimensions would be necessary to carry an ordinary camera taking pictures of fair size; hence it is necessary to devise a camera of lighter construction so that a kite of moderate size may carry it to a height of several hundred feet. Such a camera is shown in the illustration, attached to a box kite. Details of construction are shown in the smaller sketches.

A camera consists, briefly, of a lightproof box with a lens at one end and a sensitive plate of film at the other. For a kite camera, a single achromatic lens will suit the purpose. Such a lens is not expensive and may be taken from a small camera. It must be obtained before the camera is begun, because the size of the camera is dependent upon the focal length of the lens and the size of the picture to be made. A camera taking pictures 2 in. square is satisfactory for kite photography. If it is desired to enlarge the pictures, this may be done in the usual manner.

The box of the camera is made cone shaped in order to reduce the weight and air resistance. Its sides are of lightweight, stiff cardboard, reinforced at the corners to ensure that no light will enter. The back of the camera is a tight-fitting cover of cardboard having the same measurements as the picture to be taken. The lens is fitted to an intermediate partition, as shown in the sketch. It is necessary to determine the focal length of the lens and to set it at a distance from the inner side of the cardboard back of the camera—the film surface—so that it will focus properly for photographing distant objects.

The front is provided with a circular opening of a size large enough not to obstruct the view of the lens. A shutter made of thin pressboard is fitted over the opening, as shown in the sketch on the next page. A slit is cut in the shutter through which light is admitted in making the exposure as the shutter is drawn back. The size and width of the slit

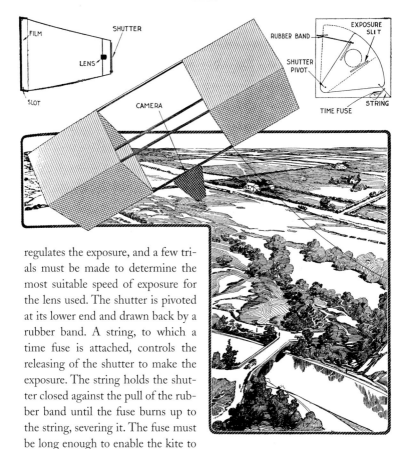

FILM SHUTTER

LENS

SLOT CAMERA

RUBBER BAND EXPOSURE SLIT

SHUTTER PIVOT

TIME FUSE STRING

regulates the exposure, and a few trials must be made to determine the most suitable speed of exposure for the lens used. The shutter is pivoted at its lower end and drawn back by a rubber band. A string, to which a time fuse is attached, controls the releasing of the shutter to make the exposure. The string holds the shutter closed against the pull of the rubber band until the fuse burns up to the string, severing it. The fuse must be long enough to enable the kite to attain a suitable height before the string is burned. When the shutter has been set and the fuse attached ready for lighting, the camera may be taken into the darkroom for loading. A piece of film, cut to the proper size, is placed carefully into the light-

THE KITE CAMERA OFFERS A DIVERSION IN PHOTOGRAPHY AND HAS PRACTICAL AND COMMERCIAL USES. THE CAMERA SHOWN IS OF LIGHTWEIGHT, SIMPLE CONSTRUCTION, AND PRODUCES FILM EXPOSURES 2 IN. SQUARE. A SECTIONAL VIEW IS GIVEN AT THE LEFT, AND THE DETAILS OF THE SHUTTER DEVICE AT THE RIGHT.

proof sliding cover, as with a film pack. The sensitive side is, of course, placed nearest the lens.

The camera is attached to the kite securely at the middle, as shown, so that when the kite is in flight a view nearly straight down will be obtained. When all is in readiness, the fuse is lighted and the kite started on its flight. By timing experimental flights, the required length of fuse may be determined in order to permit the kite to attain the desired height at the time of exposure.

The kite used for taking pictures from the air should be large enough to carry the camera easily. One of the box type illustrated is satisfactory, although other types may be used. A kite camera for the amateur has great possibilities for experimentation, but requires care in construction and a reasonable knowledge of photography. To the person willing to master the details, kite photography offers a pleasurable diversion as well as practical uses in photographing plots of ground, groups of buildings, manufacturing plants, and other subjects that cannot be photographed by other methods.

FLYBOYS

— A MODEL PAPER MONOPLANE THAT CAN BE STEERED —

An interesting bit of paper construction is a small monoplane made from a 7-in. square of paper, folded as indicated in the diagram, and provided with a paper tail. This little monoplane can be steered by adjusting the tail and can even be made to loop the loop in varying air currents. For the boy who enjoys experimenting with such a model, this little construction offers much instruction and entertainment. And the grown-up who still has an interest in such things will also find it a worthwhile job.

To make this model, fold a square of medium-weight paper on the dotted lines as indicated in *Fig. 1* in the diagram. Then unfold the sheet and refold it as in *Fig. 2*. Then bring the folded corners A and B into position as shown in A and B in *Fig. 3*. Fold

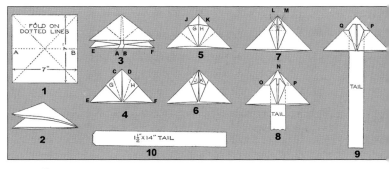

THE METHOD OF FOLDING THE PAPER IS INDICATED CLEARLY IN
THE DIAGRAMS, WHICH ARE TO BE FOLLOWED IN THE ORDER
OF THEIR NUMBERING, THE TAIL BEING INSERTED SEPARATELY.

the corners C and D upward to the position C and D in *Fig. 4*. Fold corners G and H to the corresponding letters in *Fig. 5*. Fold points J and K to the corresponding letters in *Fig. 6*. Raise the points J and K, *Fig. 6*, and fold them in so that the corners that were below them in Fig. 6 now come above them, as in L and M in *Fig. 7*. Fold the corner N back along the line OP, *Fig. 8*, so that the shape of the main portion of the model is as shown in *Fig. 9*, in OP. Make the tail 1½ by 14 in. long, as shown in *Fig. 10*, and paste it into position. This completes the model, which can be steered by bending or twisting the tail.

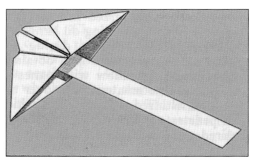

THIS MODEL MONOPLANE IS MADE OF A SHEET OF PAPER, SEVEN INCHES
SQUARE, AND CAN BE STEERED BY BENDING OR TWISTING THE TAIL.

— TOY PAPER GLIDER CAREFULLY DESIGNED —

A paper glider is an interesting and useful toy that can be made quickly. It may be used out of doors, but occasions when weather conditions make it necessary to remain indoors are especially good for this form of pastime. The glider shown in the sketch was worked out after considerable testing. With a toss, it travels 20 to 30 ft. on a level keel, with a message slipped behind a pin, as shown in the upper sketch. The inventive boy may devise many play uses for the glider, in tournaments, competitions, and for "military" flights, in which the "drivers" of the devices may "annihilate armies."

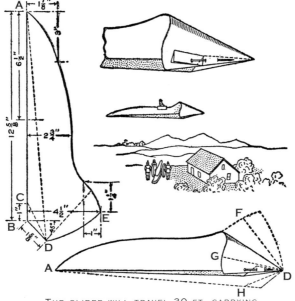

THE GLIDER WILL TRAVEL 30 FT. CARRYING
A MESSAGE IF CAREFULLY MADE.

Practical use of the toy was made in a series of air-current tests.

The glider is made as follows: Fold a piece of 10- by 15-in. paper lengthwise, and mark the outline shown at the left upon it. The dimensions should be followed carefully. Measure first from the end A to the point B, and then draw the slanting line to D, at an angle of 45 degrees. Mark the width to E, and measure the other distances from A and at the middle, to determine the curve of the edge. Mark the dotted lines extending from D, which are guides for the folding of the paper to form the glider, as shown in the lower sketch. Curl the points under the side so that the line FD comes to the position DG, and pin them to the corners H, as shown in the lower sketch. The glider is tossed by holding it between the thumb and forefinger at the middle of the fold underneath it.

— MAKING A TOY CATAPULT —

A 10-cent rat trap of the type shown in the drawing can easily be made into a marble-throwing catapult, the range of the missile being regulated by an adjustable stop. The trap is fastened to the edges of the ammunition box and the bait hook is removed. The stop is then bent from a strip of sheet metal and fastened to opposite edges of the trap as indicated. Two side arms that serve as braces for the stop are adjusted by means of a wire pin passing through holes in the stop and arms. The throwing arm should be made of ½- by ½ in. hardwood, about 10 in. long, although the length is best determined by trial. A small metal cup at the end of the arm provides a pocket for the ammunition. If desired, a trigger

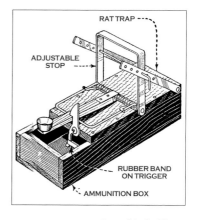

arrangement can be added. Flour tied in tissue paper may be used to make a realistic bomb because it gives off a smokelike puff when it strikes and is harmless. The longest throw the device is capable of will usually be attained when the stop is set at an angle of about 45 degrees.

— PAPER GLIDER THAT LOOPS THE LOOP —

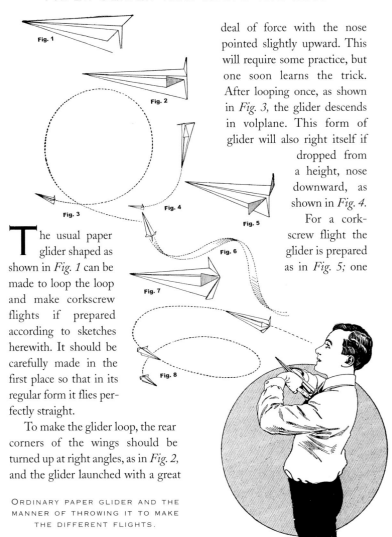

deal of force with the nose pointed slightly upward. This will require some practice, but one soon learns the trick. After looping once, as shown in *Fig. 3*, the glider descends in volplane. This form of glider will also right itself if dropped from a height, nose downward, as shown in *Fig. 4*.

For a corkscrew flight the glider is prepared as in *Fig. 5;* one

The usual paper glider shaped as shown in *Fig. 1* can be made to loop the loop and make corkscrew flights if prepared according to sketches herewith. It should be carefully made in the first place so that in its regular form it flies perfectly straight.

To make the glider loop, the rear corners of the wings should be turned up at right angles, as in *Fig. 2*, and the glider launched with a great

rear corner being bent up and the other down. In this form it flies horizontally, or downward, while rapidly rotating around its longitudinal axis, as shown in *Fig. 6.*

To make a spiral descent, the rear corners of the wings are bent up as in *Fig. 2,* and the rear corner of the keel is bent at right angles, *Fig. 7,* whereupon it is thrown in the ordinary manner. It then takes the course shown in *Fig. 8.*

— Boomerangs and How to Make Them —

A boomerang is a weapon invented and used by native Australians. The boomerang is a curved stick of hardwood, *Fig. 1,* about ⁵/₁₆ in. thick by 2 ½ in. wide by 2 ft. long, flat on one side with the ends and the other side rounding. One end of the stick is grasped in one hand with the convex edge forward and the flat side up, and thrown upward. After going some distance and ascending slowly to a great height in the air with a quick rotary motion, it suddenly returns in an elliptical orbit to a spot near the starting point. If thrown down on the ground the boomerang rebounds in a straight line, pursuing a ricochet motion until the object is struck at which it was thrown.

Two other types of boomerangs are illustrated herewith and they can be made as described. The materials necessary for the T-shaped boomerang are: one piece of hard maple

⁵/₁₆ in. thick by 2 ½ in. wide by 3 ft. long; five ½ in. flathead screws. Cut the piece of hard maple into two pieces, one 11½ in. and the other 18 in. long. The corners are cut from these pieces, as shown in *Fig. 2,* taking care to cut exactly the same amount from each corner. Bevel both sides of the pieces, making the edges very thin so they will cut the air better. Find the exact center of the long piece and make a line 1¼ in. on each side of the center, and fasten the short length between the lines with the screws, as shown in *Fig. 3.* The short piece should be fastened perfectly square and at right angles to the long one.

The materials necessary for the cross-shaped boomerang are one piece hard maple ⁵/₁₆ in. thick by 2 in. wide by 30 in. long, and five ½-in. flathead screws. Cut the maple into two 14-in. pieces and plane the edges of these pieces so

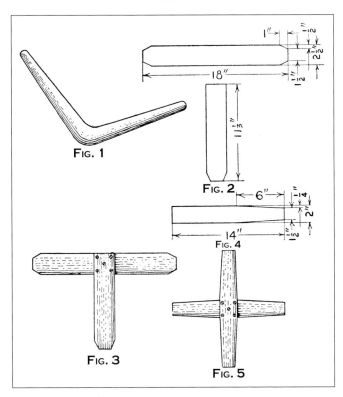

DETAILS OF THREE BOOMERANGS.

that the ends will be 1½ in. wide, as shown in *Fig. 4*. Bevel these pieces the same as the ones for the T-shaped boomerang. The two pieces are fastened together as shown in *Fig. 5*. All of the boomerangs when completed should be given several coats of linseed oil and thoroughly dried. This will keep the wood from absorbing water and becoming heavy. The last two boomerangs are thrown in a similar way to the first one, except that one of the pieces is grasped in the hand and the throw given with a quick underhand motion. A little practice is all that is necessary for one to become skillful in throwing them.

WATER (*and* FROZEN WATER) TOYS

— HOW TO MAKE A WATER TELESCOPE —

Before you decide on a place to cast your hook it is best to look into the water to see whether any fish are there. Yes, certainly, you can look into the water and see the fish that are swimming about, if you have the proper equipment. What the water telescope regularly in searching for herring shoals or cod.

All that is necessary to make a wooden water telescope is a long wooden box, a piece of glass for one end and some paint and putty for making the seams watertight. Fix the

THE WATER TELESCOPE

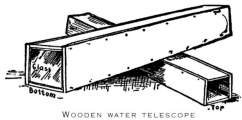

WOODEN WATER TELESCOPE

you need is a water telescope. This is a device made of wood or metal with one end of glass. When the glass end is submerged, by looking in at the open end, objects in the water are made plainly visible to a considerable depth. In Norway, the fishermen use glass in one end of the box and leave the other open to look through.

A tin water telescope is more convenient than the wooden one, but more difficult to make. The principal essential for this is a circular piece of glass for the large end. A funnel-shaped tin horn will do for the rest. Solder in the glass at the large end, and the telescope is made. Sinkers consisting of strips of lead should be soldered on or near the bottom to counteract the buoyancy of the air contained in the watertight funnel and also to help submerge the big end. The inside of the funnel should be painted black to prevent the light from being reflected on the bright surface of the tin. If difficulty is found in obtaining a circular piece of glass, the bottom may be made square and square glass used. Use plain, clear glass, not magnifying class. To picnic parties the water telescope is of great amusement, revealing numerous odd sights in the water which may never have been seen before.

— A SIMPLE DIVING RAFT —

Campers on the shores of a lake or river frequently discover to their dismay that the water near the shore is too shallow to permit diving. The answer to this is a floating springboard, such as shown in the

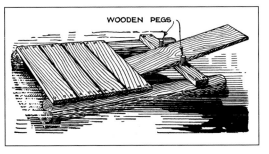

SPRINGBOARD MOUNTED ON A HEAVY RAFT MAKES DIVING POSSIBLE WHEN THE WATER OFF SHORE IS SHALLOW.

drawing. Two logs, about 20 ft. long and 18 in. in diameter, are fastened, about 5 ft. apart, with heavy planks that form the platform. The springboard rests on a heavy wooden crosspiece, and the end underneath is attached to a similar crosspiece. To prevent the springboard from shifting its position, a wooden pin is driven into the front crosspiece on each side of the board. Instead of using one heavy plank for the diving board, two comparatively thin planks may be arranged like the leaves of an elliptic spring, the longer board being on top. A stone anchor prevents the raft from drifting too far from shore.

— A Homemade Punt —

A flat-bottom boat is easy to make and is one of the safest boats, as it is not readily overturned. It has the advantage of being rowed from either end, and has plenty of good seating capacity.

This punt, as shown in *Fig. 1*, is built 15 ft. long, about 20 in. deep, and 4 ft. wide. The ends are cut sloping for about 20 in. back and under. The sides are each made up from boards held together with battens on the inside of the boat near the ends and in the middle. One wide board should be used for the bottom piece. Two pins are driven in the top board of each side to serve as oarlocks.

The bottom is covered with matched boards not more than 5 in. wide. These pieces are placed together as closely as possible, using caulk between the joints and nailing them to the edges of the sideboards and to a keel strip that runs the length of the punt, as shown in *Fig. 2*. Before nailing the boards place lamp wicking between them and the edges of the sideboards. Only galvanized nails should be used. In order to make the punt perfectly watertight, it is best to use the driest lumber obtainable. At one end of the punt a skeg and a rudder can be attached as shown in *Fig. 3*.

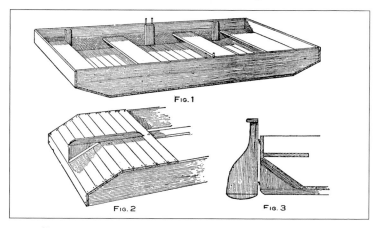

Fig. 1

Fig. 2

Fig. 3

FLAT-BOTTOM BOATS ARE EASY TO BUILD AND SAFE TO USE.

— How to build a "Pushboat" —

Much fun can be had during the swimming season with a "pushboat" of the type illustrated, which operates on the same principle as a variety of popular small-wheeled vehicles.

The hull—for lack of a better name—is made from a single thick plank, the bow end of which is pointed. After smoothing off the surface of the board, it is given at least two coats of good paint. A piece of 10-in. plank, 3 ft. long, is spiked to the deck and in the center of the hull as shown. Then a seat, made from a 10- by 18-in. board, is nailed to the stern end of the upright. Round off the edges so that they won't cut the

A HAND-PROPELLED PADDLE-WHEEL WATERCRAFT OF THE CATAMARAN TYPE; THE BACK-AND-FORTH MOVEMENT OF THE HAND LEVERS DRIVES THE PADDLES THROUGH CONNECTING RODS AND A CRANKSHAFT. A CURVED OUTRIGGER SUPPORTS WOODEN AND PNEUMATIC FLOATS ON EITHER SIDE.

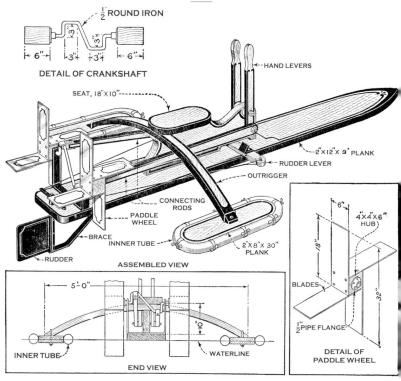

DETAIL OF CRANKSHAFT

½ ROUND IRON

6" — 3" — 3" — 6"

HAND LEVERS

SEAT, 18"×10"

2"×12"× 9' PLANK

RUDDER LEVER

OUTRIGGER

CONNECTING RODS

PADDLE WHEEL

BRACE

INNER TUBE

2"×8"× 30" PLANK

RUDDER

ASSEMBLED VIEW

5'-0"

10"

INNER TUBE

WATERLINE

END VIEW

6"

4"×4"×6" HUB

18"

BLADES

32"

½" PIPE FLANGE

DETAIL OF PADDLE WHEEL

DETAIL DRAWINGS OF THE "PUSHBOAT" THAT CLEARLY SHOW HOW THE CRAFT IS ASSEMBLED. SUCH A BOAT IS INEXPENSIVE TO BUILD AND CAN BE MADE EASILY WITH FEW TOOLS. THE OUTRIGGER FLOATS MAKE CAPSIZING OR SINKING DIFFICULT IF NOT IMPOSSIBLE, AND IT CAN BE DRIVEN AT GOOD SPEED IN QUIET WATERS.

legs. A mortise is cut into the upper edge of the upright under the stern end of the seat, to receive the outrigger, and a recess under the forward end, to clear the rudder lever. A curved piece of timber 5 ft. long is used for the outrigger, and two round-end planks are fastened to its ends, as in the drawing. These outboard planks should be slightly lower than the hull. The outrigger is then spiked to its mortise in the upright so that the planks will be at the same distance away from the hull and parallel to it. The planks are given buoyancy by tying an inflated inner tube around the edge of each; they can be protected with a wrapping of canvas or burlap.

Movement—forward or backward—of the craft is made by paddle wheels, operated by a pair of levers mounted in front of the seat. The paddle wheels are made by screwing four sheet-metal blades to the sides of an oak hub, as indicated in the detail drawing. Two such paddle wheels are required, and they are attached to the ends of a crankshaft, as detailed. Each end of the shaft is threaded to screw into the pipe flanges fastened to the paddle wheels. The crankshaft is supported on a U-shaped piece of heavy iron, the bearing holes being drilled 10 in. above the deck. In screwing the paddle wheels onto the crankshaft, the flange threads should be coated with white lead and screwed as tightly as possible to prevent them from turning loose by the action of the wheels in motion.

Then bolt a pair of levers, about 30 in. long, one on each side of the bow end of the upright in front of the seat. The pivot bolt goes through the top corner of the upright and should be provided with washers. Form smooth handles at the top of

the levers and drill holes about 6 in. below the pivot bolt, for the connecting-rod bolts. The levers must work back and forth freely. Motion from the levers is communicated to the paddle wheels by means of connecting rods, which are made of oak or ash. These rods are loosely bolted to the levers in front, while the rear ends are round-notched and fitted with flat-iron bearing straps that fit around the crankshaft. By moving the levers back and forth, the paddle wheels are revolved.

Any sort of rudder can be hung from the stern and fitted with a tiller as in the drawing, so that the hands are not required to guide the craft. After completion, the whole craft is given several coats of paint to protect it from the water.

With the operator aboard, the hull will be nearly submerged, but the two inner-tube floats at the ends of the outrigger will keep it afloat and steady so that there will be no possibility of its capsizing or sinking in smooth water.

Sit facing the bow, grasping a lever in each hand and the feet on the steering lever, and then commence to pump the hand levers back and forth at the same time steadying the rudder.

— A PORTABLE FOLDING BOAT —

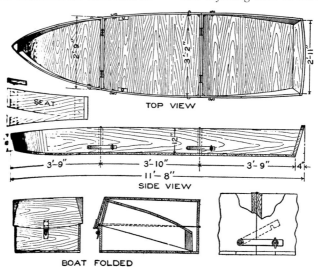

A boat that is inexpensive, easily made, and readily transported is shown in the illustration. Because the bow section folds inside of the stern portion, it is important that the dimensions be followed closely. The material used is ⅞-in. throughout.

Make a full-size diagram of the plan to determine the exact sizes of the pieces. Brass screws are best for fastening this type of work, but copperplated nails may be used. Tongue-and-groove stock is best for the bottom. The joints should not be driven together too firmly, to allow for expansion, and all joints in the boat should be packed with pitch.

The adjoining ends of the sec-

THE CONSTRUCTION OF THE PORTABLE BOAT IS SIMPLE. WHEN FOLDED IT MAY BE TRANSPORTED READILY AND MAY EVEN BE CARRIED IN THREE PARTS. IT IS INEXPENSIVE AND SHOULD PROVE A VALUABLE ADDITION TO THE CAMPING OUTFIT.

tions should be made at the same time to ensure a satisfactory fit when joined. Braces are fixed into corners.

Metal straps hold the sections together at the bottom of the hinged joints. These should be fitted so that there is little possibility of their becoming loosened accidentally. The front end of each strip is pivoted in a hole and the other end is slotted ver-tically on the lower edge. Their bolts are set firmly into the side of the boat, being held with nuts on both sides of the wood. A wing nut, prevented from coming off by riveting the end of the bolt, holds the slotted end. Sockets for the oars may be cut into hardwood pieces fastened to the gun-wales. The construction of the seats is shown in the small sketch at the left.

— A Snowball Maker —

Snowball making is slow when carried on by hand. Where a thrower is employed in a snow fort it becomes necessary to have a number of assistants in making the snow-balls. The time of making these balls can be greatly reduced by the use of the snowball maker shown in the illustration.

The base consists of a board, 24 in. long by 6½ in. wide by 1 in. thick. A block of wood, A, is hol-lowed out in the center to make a depression in the shape of a hemi-sphere, 2 1/12 in. in diam-eter by 1¼ in. deep. This block is nailed to the base about 1 in. from one end. To make the dimensions come out right, fasten a block, B, 6 in. high—made of one or more pieces—at the other end of the base with its back edge 14½ in. from the center of the hemispherical depression. On top of this block a 20-in.-long lever, C, is hinged. Another block, D, is made with a

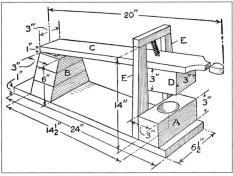

A DEVICE FOR MAKING SNOWBALLS QUICKLY AND PERFECTLY SPHERICAL IN SHAPE.

hemispherical depression like the block A, and fastened to the underside of the lever so that the depressions in both blocks will coincide. The lever end is shaped into a handle.

Two uprights, E, are fastened to the backside of the block A as guides for the lever C. A piece is fastened across their tops and a spring is attached between it and the lever. A curtain-roller spring will be suitable.

In making the balls a bunch of snow is thrown into the lower depression and the lever brought down with considerable force.

— An Inexpensive Bobsled —

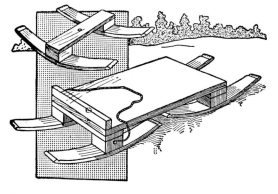

Any boy who can drive a nail and bore a hole can make a bobsled on short notice. The materials necessary are four good, solid barrel staves; four blocks of wood 4 in. long, 4 in. wide, and 2 in. thick; two pieces 12 in. long, 4 in. wide, and 1 in. thick; one piece 12 in. long, 2 in. wide, and 1¾ in. thick; and a good board, 4 ft. long, 12 in. wide, and 1 in. thick.

A BOBSLED OF SIMPLE CONSTRUCTION USING ORDINARY BARREL STAVES FOR THE RUNNERS.

The crosspieces and knees are made with the blocks and the 1-in. pieces, 12 in. long, as shown, to which the staves are nailed for runners. One of these pieces with the runners is fastened to one end of the board, the other is attached with a bolt in the center. The 1¾-by 2-in. piece, 12 in. long, is fastened across the top of the board at the front end. A rope fastened to the knees of the front runners provides a means of steering the sled.

The sled can be quickly made, and it will serve the purpose well when an expensive one cannot be had.

— A Homemade Yankee Bobsled —

A good coasting sled, which I call a Yankee bob, can be made from two hardwood barrel staves, two pieces of 2- by 6-in. pine, a piece of hardwood for the rudder, and few pieces of boards. The 2- by 6-in. pieces should be a little longer than one-third the length of the staves, and each piece cut tapering from the widest part, 6 in., down to 2 in., and then fastened to the staves with large wood screws as shown in *Fig. 1.* Boards 1 in. thick are nailed on top of the pieces for a seat and to hold the runner together. The boards should be of such a length as to make the runners about 18 in. apart.

A 2-in. shaft of wood, *Fig. 2,* is turned down to 1 in. on the ends and put through holes that must be bored in the front ends of the 2- by 6-in. pieces. A small pin is put through each end of the shaft to keep it in place. The rudder is a 1½ in. hardwood piece that should be tapered to ½ in. at the bottom and shod with a thin piece of iron. A ½ in. hole is bored through the center of the shaft

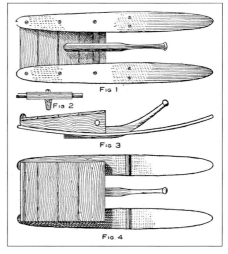

RUNNERS MADE OF BARREL STAVES.

and a lag screw put through and turned in the rudder piece, making it so the rudder will turn right and left and up and down. Two cleats are nailed to the upper sides of the runner and in the middle lengthways for the person's heels to rest against.

Any child can guide this bob. All he has to do is to guide the rudder right and left to go in the direction named. If he wants to stop, he pulls up on the handle and the heel of the rudder will dig into the snow, causing too much friction for the sled to go any farther.

— MAKING A COASTING TOBOGGAN —

Essentials of good toboggan, whether for coasting or use in transportation, are strength and lightness. And when it is to be made in the home shop, the construction must be simple. That shown in the illustration and detailed in the working sketches was designed to meet these requirements. The materials for the toboggan proper and the forms over which it is bent may be obtained at small expense.

Smoothness of finished surface, freedom from tendency to splinter, and ability to stand up under abuse being requisite qualities in the wood used to make a toboggan, three varieties may be mentioned in their order of merit: hickory, birch, and oak. Birch is softer than hickory and easily splintered

but acquires an excellent polish on the bottom. Oak stands bending well but does not become as smooth on the running surface as close-grained woods. Do not use quarter-sawn oak because of the cross-grain flakes in its structure.

THIS TOBOGGAN WILL AFFORD THE MAKER MUCH PLEASURE. IT MAY BE MADE AS AN INDIVIDUAL PROJECT OR AS A JOINT UNDERTAKING BY SEVERAL BOYS.

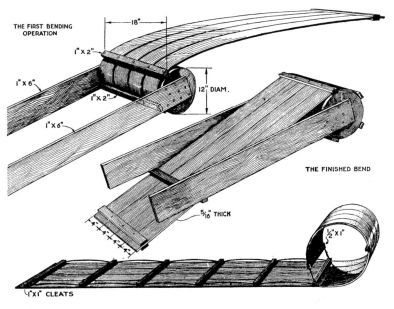

THE FIRST BENDING OPERATION

1" X 2"

1" X 6"

1" X 2"

1" X 6"

18"

12" DIAM.

THE FINISHED BEND

5/16" THICK

1/2" X 1"

4"
4"
4"

1"X1" CLEATS

THE BOARDS FOR THE BOTTOM ARE STEAMED OR BOILED AT THE BOW ENDS AND BENT OVER THE FORM. AS THE BENDING OPERATION PROGRESSES, THE BOARDS ARE NAILED TO THE FORM WITH CLEATS AND PERMITTED TO DRY IN THIS POSITION.

Though the best toboggan is made of a single board, both the securing of material and its construction are rather difficult. Narrow strips are easily bent to shape but do not make a durable article. A toboggan made of four boards is practical. The mill bill for one 7 ½ ft. long by 16 in. wide and for the bending frame is as follows: 4 pieces, 5/16 by 4 in. by 10 ft., hardwood; 7 pieces, 1 by 1 in. by 16 in., hardwood; 2 pieces, ½ by 1 in. by 16 in., hardwood; 2 pieces 1 by 6 in. by 6 ft., common boards; 6 pieces 1 by 2 in. by 18 in., common boards; 1 cylindrical block, 12 in. diameter by 18 in. long.

The form for the bending of the pieces if made of the common boards and the block. A block sawn from the end of a dry log is excellent. Heat it, if convenient, just before bending the strips. The boards for the bottom should be selected for straightness or grain and freedom from knots and burls. Carefully plane the side intended for the wearing surface, and bevel the edges so that, when placed together, they form a wide "V" joint half the depth of the boards. The 1- by 1-in. pieces are for cross cleats and should be notched on one side, 1 in. from each end, to receive the side ropes. The two ½- by 1-in. pieces are to be placed one at each side of the extreme end of the bent portion, to reinforce it.

Bore a gimlet hole through the centers of the 1- by 2- by 18-in. pieces, and 4¼ in. each side of this hole, bore two others. Nail the end of one of the 6-ft. boards to each end of the block so that their extended ends are parallel. With 3-in. nails, fasten one of the bored pieces to the block between the boards, temporarily inserting a ½-in. piece to hold it out that distance from the block.

Steam about 3-ft. of the ends of the boards, or boil them in a tank. Clamp or nail the boards together at the dry ends, edge to edge, between two of the 1- by 2-in. pieces. Leave about ¼-in. opening between boards. Thrust the steamed ends under the cleat nailed on the block, the nails

that hold it slipping up between the boards. Bear down on the toboggan carefully, nailing on another of the bored cleats when the toboggan boards have been curved around the block as far as he floor will permit. The nails, of course, go between the boards.

Now turn the construction over and bend up the toboggan, following the boards around the block with more of the nailed cleats, until the clamped end is down between the two 6-ft. boards where it can be held by a piece nailed across. More of the cleats may be nailed on if desired. In fact, the closer together the cleats are the less danger there is of splintering the boards, and the more perfect the conformity of the boards to the mold.

Allow at least four days for drying before removing the boards from the form. Clamp the ½- by 1-in. pieces on each side of the extreme ends of the bent bows, drill holes through, and rivet them. A 1- by 1-in. crossbar is riveted to the inside of the bow at the extreme front and another directly under the extremity of the curved end. These cleats are wired together to hold the bend of the bow. The tail-end crossbar should be placed not nearer than 2 ½ in. from the end of the boards, while the remainder of the crossbars are evenly spaced between the front and back pieces, taking care that the notched side is always placed down. Trim off uneven ends, scrape and sand the bottom well, and finish the toboggan with oil. Run a ⅜-in. rope through the notches under the ends of the crosspieces and the toboggan is completed.

Screws are satisfactory substitutes for rivets in fastening together the parts; and wire nails, of a length to allow for about ¼ in. clinch, give a fair job.

In *the* Playground

— A Ferris Wheel —

The whole wheel is carried on two uprights, each 3 by 4 in., by 10 ft. long. In the upper ends of these pieces, A, a half circle is cut out to receive the main shaft B. The end of the uprights are sunk 3 ft. into the earth and about 4 ft. apart, then braced as shown. They are further braced by wires attached to rings that are secured with staples near the top. The bearings should each have a cap to keep the shaft in place. These

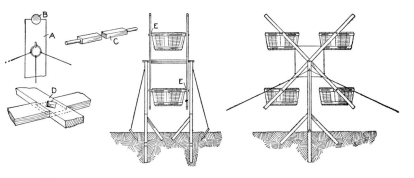

DETAIL OF THE UPRIGHTS, AXLE, AND SPOKES, AND THE END
AND SIDE ELEVATIONS OF THE COMPLETED WHEEL,
SHOWING BRACES AND CARS ATTACHED.

can be made of blocks of wood with a semicircle cut out, the blocks being nailed over the shaft, while it is in place, the nails entering the ends of the uprights.

The main shaft C is made of a 2½ in. square piece of good material, 4 ft. long. The ends are made round to serve as bearings, and the square part is fitted with the spokes or car carriers. These consist of 4 pieces, each 1 in. thick by 4 in. wide by 13 ft. long. In the center of each piece cut a notch one-half the thickness, so that when each pair of pieces is crossed they will fit together with the surfaces smooth, as shown in D. A square hole is cut through the pieces as shown to fit on the square part of the main axle. Though it is not shown in the illustration, it is best to strengthen this joint with another piece of wood, cut to fit on the axle and securely attached to the spokes.

The cars or carriers are made of two sugar barrels cut in half. The hoops are then securely nailed inside and outside. A block of wood, E, is securely attached to the half barrels on the outside, and another block on the inside opposite the outside block. Holes are bored 2½ ft. from the ends of the spokes and a bolt run through them and through the blocks on the edges of the half barrels. The extending ends of the spokes are used to propel the wheel. Four children can ride in the wheel at one time.

— A TWISTY THRILLER MERRY-GO-ROUND —

"Step right up! Three twisting thrillers for a penny— a tenth of a dime!" was the familiar invitation that attracted customers to the delights of a homemade merry-go-round of novel design. The patrons were not disappointed but came back for more. The power for the whirling thriller is produced by the heavy, twisted rope suspended from the limb of a tree or other suitable support. The rope is cranked up by means off a notched disk, A, grasped at the handle B, the car being lifted off. The thriller is stopped when the brake plate I, rests on the weighted box L.

Manila rope, ¾ in. or more in diameter, is used for the support. It is rigged with a spreader about 2 ft. long, at the top, as shown. The disk is built up of wood as detailed, and notches, C, provided for the ropes. The rope is wound up and the car is suspended from it by the hook, which should be strong and deep enough so that the rope cannot slip out, as indicated at H.

The car is made of a section of 2- by 4-in. lumber, D. The lumber should be 10 ft. long, to which braces, E, of 1- by 4-in. lumber are fastened with nails or screws. The upper ends of the pieces E are blocked up with the centerpiece F, nailed securely, and the wire link G is fastened through the joint.

The seats, J, are suspended at the ends of the 2- by 3-in. bar, with their inner ends lower, as shown. This provides better seating when the thriller is in action. The seats are supported by rope or strap-iron brackets, K, set 15 in. apart. The box should be high enough so that the seats do not strike the ground.

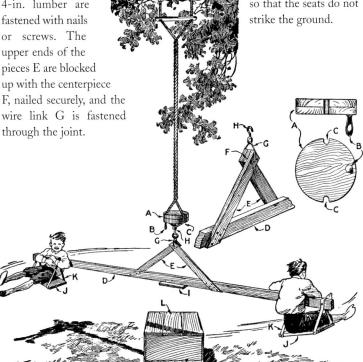

THE SUPPORTING ROPES ARE WOUND UP AT THE DISK A. THE CAR IS HOOKED INTO PLACE AND THE PASSENGERS TAKE THEIR SEATS FOR A THRILLING RIDE, UNTIL THE BRAKE PLATE I RESTS ON THE BOX.

— CHILD'S SWING BUILT OF PIPES IN A NARROW SPACE —

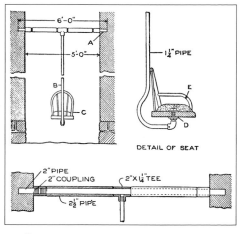

A narrow space between two city houses was used to erect a swing as detailed in the illustration. A piece of 2-in. iron pipe, A, was cut 1 ft. longer than the space between the walls. Two pieces of 2½ in. pipe and a 2½- by 2½- by 1¼-in. tee, as shown in the detail, was slipped over the 2-in. pipe, which was built into the walls. A 1¼-in. pipe, B, 20 ft. long, bent as shown, was joined to the tee. And a seat, C, was attached. The construction of the seat is shown in detail, being fixed to the wooden part with washers, nuts, and a threaded nipple,

THIS SUBSTANTIAL SWING GUARDS THE YOUNGSTERS FROM INJURY BRUSHING AGAINST THE BRICK WALLS.

D. A cushion and a removable safety bar, E, were also features. This swing is safer than one of rope, and will stand much greater wear.

— ADJUSTABLE STILTS —

T he beginner with stilts always selects short sticks so that he will not be very far from the ground. But as he becomes more experienced, the longer the sticks the better. Then, too, the small boy and the large boy require different lengths of sticks.

The device shown makes a pair of sticks universal for the use of beginners or a boy of any age or height.

To make the stilts, procure two long hardwood sticks of even length, and smooth up the edges; then begin at a point 1 ft. from one end and bore 12 holes, ⅜ in. in diameter and 2 in. apart from center to center. If there is no diestock at hand, have a blacksmith or mechanic make a thread on both ends of a ⅜-in. rod, 12 in. long. Bend the rod in the shape shown, so that the two threaded ends will be just 2 in. apart from center to center. The thread on the straight horizontal end should be so long that a nut can be placed on both sides of the stick. A piece of garden hose or small rubber hose, slipped on the rod, will keep the shoe sole from slipping.

STILTS HAVING STIRRUPS THAT CAN BE SET AT ANY DESIRED HEIGHT.

The steps can be set in any two adjacent holes to give the desired height.

— BEGINNER'S HELPER FOR ROLLER SKATING —

One of the most amusing as well as useful devices for a beginner on roller skates is shown in the sketch. The device is made of ¾-in. pipe and pipe fittings, with a strip of sheet metal 1 in. wide fastened about halfway down on the legs. On the bottom of each leg is fastened one ordinary furniture caster that allows the machine to roll easily on the floor. The rear is left open to allow the beginner to enter, then by grasping the top rail he is able to move about the floor at ease, without fear of falling.

BEGINNER CANNOT FALL.

— A MERRY-GO-ROUND POLE —

An inexpensive merry-go-round can be made of a single pole set in the ground where there is sufficient vacant space for the turning of the ropes. The pole may be of gas pipe or wood, long enough to extend about 12 ft. above the ground. An iron wheel is attached on the upper end so that it will revolve easily on an axle, which may be an

THE ROPES TIED TO THE WHEEL RIM WILL EASILY TURN AROUND THE POLE.

iron pin driven into the post. A few iron washers placed on the pin under the wheel will reduce the friction.

Ropes of varying lengths are tied to the rim of the wheel. The rider takes hold of a rope and runs around the pole to start the wheel in motion. He then swings clear of the ground. Streamers of different colors, and flowers for special occasions, may be attached to make a pretty display.

— SEESAW BUILT FOR ONE —

A single child, seeking means of entertaining herself, has a hard time in getting any pleasure out of the ordinary seesaw.

The drawing shows a combination of seesaw and rocking horse that can be used by one child. The construction is quite simple, the dimensions and weight of the counterweight being varied to meet different requirements. The seat is supported on an iron axle by a pair of strap hinges, one end of each hinge being bent to fit around the axle. The counterweight, which may be an iron casting or a block of cement, is attached to a curved iron bined weight of child and board, and a little experimenting will be necessary to strike the correct balance. The exact mass of weight can be found by first attaching a bucket

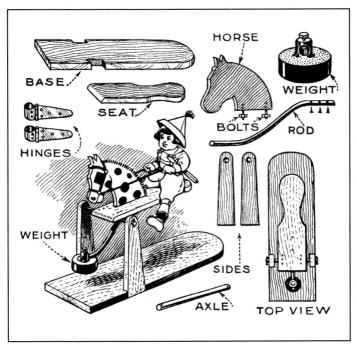

A COMBINATION OF ROCKING HORSE AND SEESAW THAT MAKES IT POSSIBLE FOR A LONE YOUNGSTER TO ENTERTAIN HERSELF. A COUNTERWEIGHT IS PROVIDED FOR BALANCING THE WEIGHT OF THE CHILD AND SEAT.

rod fastened under the front end of the seat. The counterweight should be a trifle heavier than the com- or bag of sand to the end of the rod, and adding or removing sand until the proper weight has been found.